America and the Le

Socialist History 16

Rivers Oram Press
London, Sydney and New York

Published in 2000
by Rivers Oram Press, an imprint of Rivers Oram Publishers Ltd
144 Hemingford Road, London N1 1DE

Distributed in the USA by
New York University Press
838 Broadway
New York, NY 10003–482

Distributed in Australia and New Zealand by
UNIReps
University of New South Wales
Sydney, NSW 2052

Set in Garamond by
NJ Design Associates, Romsey, Hants
and printed in Great Britain by
TJ International Ltd, Padstow, Cornwall

British Library Cataloguing in Publication Data
A catalogue record for this publication is available from the British Library
ISBN 1 85489 116 2 (hb)
ISBN 1 85489 117 0 (pb)
ISSN 0969 4331

Contents

Editorial

Un-American or anti-American, the left has not had the easiest of relationships with the American dream. Long before the contingencies of cold war politics, America was taken as a byword for unrestrained capitalism, its claims of opportunity, initiative and popular freedoms confronted with its other face of violence, racism, commercial hegemony and cultural impoverishment. Above all, America stood for the rule and values of capital, whose dissemination across the globe seemed inseparable from its own geopolitical interests. If this ends up looking something like an 'American century', no wonder that the left is prone to moods of pessimism.

One response, recently proposed by Tony Blair but, as usual, of only superficial newness, is that the European left should accept the century's verdict and find its exemplar across the Atlantic. To that, many of us will reply, as Steve Platt did in his *Tribune* column: *Pur-lease!* Blair's embrace of a transatlantic model appears but another symptom of his innocence of either radical or social-democratic instincts, and his enthusiasm instead for a world remade in the image of middle (or is it corporate?) America. With Wal-Mart, Monsanto, and Nato air chiefs incredibly presented as its acceptable face, no wonder that old left-wing prejudices die hard. Even on its own terms—forgetting, that is, the un-American losers in the new world order—America, like 'England', is far more than just its middle. As Platt reminds us, 'Among the nineteen most prosperous industrialised nations, the US is first, per capita, in both the number of billionaires and of children living in poverty; total health spending and the percentage of the population not covered by any health insurance; the number of lawyers and the number of prisoners; defence spending and infant mortality; military aid to developing countries and debt repayments from them; second homes and homelessness; food consumption and malnutrition—and so the list goes on'. (*Tribune*, 12 March 1999.) The polarities are old ones, and as long as they remain, so will old responses retain validity.

Nonetheless, America has always demanded other responses too. Even in its dominant version, Americanism has posed the left significant challenges to do with mass consumption and the nature of industrial society, and the doggedness and discomfort of the left's response has often made it seem ill-at-ease with its own ostensible constituency. The story, in that regard, is the familiar one of the left's strained and sometimes patronising relationship with the popular, but also of a rich vein of cultural criticism reaching beyond the mores and power relationships of a class-ridden society. The difficulty has always been to extricate the two.

Nor were these complexities less evident in America than anywhere else. On the contrary, the dominant version of Americanism was always contested from within, sometimes running explicitly 'against the American grain' but often, perhaps more productively, cast as a radical reworking of American identities. 'Communism is twentieth-century Americanism' said communist leader Earl Browder; which certainly had more pazazz than the British variant once proposed of 'Communism is twentieth-century puritanism'. Whatever we think of Browder and the American popular front, the audacity of such a claim—and it is echoed in other periods, by other traditions on the left—is a reminder that a minoritarian left need not be an irrelevant or lachrymose one. That reminder seems especially relevant to our present predicament, and the resilience of the 'other America' is in many ways more sustaining than the familiar triumphalist narratives we have presently lost hope of recreating. Here is an America that can be set against Blair's.

From widely differing perspectives, the contributors to the present all touch upon some or other of these issues. Both Neville Kirk and David Howell throw into question the notion of America as somehow *sui generis*. 'Why is there no socialism in the United States?', Werner Sombart famously asked, but perhaps the very terms of the question were too loaded and prescriptive. Certainly, in David Howell's review of syndicalism, as it ranges widely across national boundaries, a vivid sense is given of the cross-fertilisation of movements and ideas to which the United States was central. Home to one of the most vibrant syndicalist movements in the shape of the Wobblies, its interconnections with European militants were personified in the migrations described here of the Irish socialists Larkin and Connolly. Behind the detail of circumstance and locality, Howell argues that syndicalism raised enduring issues of democratic theory and practice which were too easily forgotten with its displacement by purportedly higher forms of socialism.

Samuel Gompers, by most accepted definitions, was not a socialist. Nevertheless, Neville Kirk in his contribution shows that even Gompers, the epitome of what is supposed to have been 'different' about American labour, appears on closer examination to have been a far more complex and radical figure than exceptionalist paradigms will allow. Both class rhetoric and anti-imperialist sentiments are clearly documented, brought together in a form of working-class Americanism whose reconstruction in Gramscian or Thompsonian terms the American Marxist Brian Lloyd has recently criticised. Certainly, the Gompers presented here may seem obliquely reminiscent of Thompson's Free Born Englishman. Whether Thompsonian or Gramscian are really such damning epithets, on the other hand, will no doubt be questioned by many readers of this journal.

The ambiguous meanings of Americanism also link the following two contributions. Rosalyn Baxandall and Elizabeth Ewen show how the American suburb, heartland of the American dream, could nevertheless be imagined in innovative ways, as part of a 'social and aesthetic agenda for the machine age'. Though this never became the major dynamic behind American housing provision, the early settlements which were built provided a source of inspiration for both New Deal America and the world beyond. Part of their appeal lay in their efficiency in the satisfaction of housing needs, and yet Kevin Morgan's contribution suggests that in Britain the costs of such efficiency, and indded the whole American social equation of the 1920s, aroused intense suspicion and antagonism on the left. However, this was by no means the universal response of European labour movements, nor ever a wholly dominant one in Britain itself. These divergent constructions of America may provide some stimulating comparative perspectives on the evolution and distinctive characteristics of European labour movements.

Finally, where the other contributions fall within the period from the 1880s to the 1920s, Alan Hooper and Michael Williams provide a longer historical perspective with their comparative treatment of the revolutions of 1848 and 1968. In focusing on the responses of four major thinkers—Marx, de Tocqueville, Dwight MacDonald and C.L.R. James—they explore the apparent symbiosis of America and modernity, and show how various were the responses this called forth. An irony that may be thought symbolic is that of the American social critic MacDonald being lambasted at a forum of the British new left for his undemocratic attacks on Hollywood and 'masscult'. As Alan Hooper and Michael Williams point out, the issues were—and remain —as much cultural and political as geographical, and it is not just a question of running 'against the American grain', but of which American grain we want to run against.

The current issue began life as a guest-edited issue, but during its gestation the guest editor has become the regular editor. This therefore seems an appropriate moment to pay tribute again to Willie Thompson's tremendous achievement in establishing the journal on its present basis, supported by the rest of the editors and especially the reviews editor, Mike Waite. the truncated reviews section in this issue does not represent a change in policy, and full coverage will be resumed in our next issue. The new reviews editor, Stephen Woodhams, is currently compiling a list of prospective reviewers: if you would like to be added to the list, please write to Steve at 103 Coopers Lane, London E10 5DG, indicating areas of interest.

Offers of longer contributions are always welcome. However, do please try to contact the editors beforehand: each issue of the journal is organised around a particular theme, and the earlier we know of possible contributions, the easier it is to plan future themes and provide contributors with specific deadlines. The theme of the next issue is 'international and comparative labour history', with issues on radical sub-cultures and life histories planned to follow. For the life histories issue we would be particularly interested in possible articles or reports arising from oral history projects. In the next issue we will also be carrying a report of a recent event on the origins of the Garden City movement organised at Letchworth by the Socialist History Society.

Socialist History Journal

The *Socialist History Journal* explores and assesses the past of the socialist movement and broader processes in relation to it, not only for the sake of historical understanding, but as an input and contribution to the movement's future development. The journal is not exclusive and welcomes argument and debate from all viewpoints.

Other *Socialist History* titles:

A Bourgeois Revolution?
Socialist History 1 · 1993
0 7453 08058

What Was Communism? Pt 1
Socialist History 2 · 1993
0 7453 08066

What Was Communism? Pt 2
Socialist History 3 · 1993
0 7453 08074

The Labour Party Since 1945
Socialist History 4 · 1994
0 7453 08082

The Left and Culture
Socialist History 5 · 1994
0 7453 08090

The Personal and the Political
Socialist History 6 · 1994
0 7453 08104

Fighting the Good Fight?
Socialist History 7 · 1995
0 7453 10613

Historiography and the British
Marxist Historians
Socialist History 8 · 1995
0 7453 08120

Labour Movements
Socialist History 9 · 1996
0 7453 08139

Revisions?
Socialist History 10 · 1996
0 7453 08147

The Cold War
Socialist History 11 · 1997
0 7453 12411

Nationalism and Communist
Party History
Socialist History 12 · 1997
0 7453 12675

Imperialism and Internationalism
Socialist History 13 · 1998
1 85489 1073

The Future of History
Socialist History 14 · 1998
1 85489 109X

Visions of the Future
Socialist History 15 · 1999
1 85489 1154

America and the Left
Socialist History 16 · 1999
1 85489 1170

American 'Exceptionalism' Revisited
The case of Samuel Gompers

Neville Kirk

During recent years the notion of US labour's 'exceptionalism', as manifested in a general absence of 'class consciousness' and lack of commitment to European—and British-style socialist and labour-party politics, has come under sustained historical attack. Not only have US workers been shown to have exhibited, at various points in time, militant and class-conscious actions and values—both within and beyond the workplace—and serious, if often shortlived, commitments to socialist, labour and other radical third-party political movements, but their British and European counterparts have also been shown to have been generally less class conscious, at least in Marxian and socialist ways, than the traditional wisdom of exceptionalism would have us believe. In addition to these serious substantive objections, the very assumptions, procedures and conclusions of the mode of argument of exceptionalism—revolving around the core belief in a 'normal' pattern of labour-movement and working-class development, moving towards a common 'end'—have invited well-founded charges of linearity and teleology. Above all, perhaps, the model of exceptionalism has been insensitive to the complexity, diversity and contingency of labour-movement and working-class development on both sides of the Atlantic. As a result of these convincing substantive and methodological criticisms, the crude and static paradigm of 'exceptionalism' is increasingly being superseded by more historically nuanced explorations of common, similar, different and unique issues in terms of workers' and organised labour's structured conditions of experience, actions and beliefs both across and within nations.[1]

A 'man of extraordinary parts'

The main purpose of the present article is further to question the continued utility of the notion of US exceptionalism, with reference to the particular case of Samuel Gompers. Born in London in 1850, the son of poor Jewish parents who emigrated to New York City in 1863, Gompers became, in the words of David Brody, 'a man of extraordinary parts'.[2] The latter embraced, *inter alia*, cigarmaker (also the occupation of his father); 1870s associate of Marxian socialists; longserving president of the American Federation of Labour (AF of L) from its formal establishment in 1886 to his death in 1924 (with the sole exception of 1895, following his defeated candidature at the AF of L's 1894 convention); and class-conscious labour leader with deep, and arguably enduring, philosophical commitments to republicanism and militant and inclusive trade unionism, fundamental social change, and, at least from the late nineteenth century to the eve of the First World War, trade-union internationalism and peace and opposition to war and the 'formal' imperialism of force and conquest. Yet Gompers was also president of an AF of L increasingly associated with conservative, defensive and 'class-collaborationist' 'craft' unionism and sectionalism, with the marginalisation or exclusion of many women, African-Americans, 'new' immigrants (mainly from southern and eastern Europe) and non-skilled from its ranks, and with immigration restriction and, at least in the cases of all 'Orientals' and some African-Americans, outright racism.[3] In addition, Gompers and the mainstream AF of L vigorously opposed 'radicals' and 'subversives', whether of the syndicalist, socialist or Bolshevik type, and, especially during the First World War and its immediate aftermath, loudly trumpeted the virtues of 'patriotic' loyalty to the state, commitment to the war effort and the superiority of 'democratic American' over 'alien'/'autocratic' values, and the necessary 'Americanisation' of recent and new immigrants.[4] The attempts of socialist and other advocates of a labour party to commit the AF of L to the creation of a such a party along British lines were likewise opposed and defeated. And sustained opposition to formal imperialism and support for AF of L-style trade unionism in Mexico and elsewhere, were combined with condemnation of more radical trade-union influences and models (such as that offered by the Industrial Workers of the World, or 'Wobblies') and endorsement of the notions of 'informal' imperialism (by means of the peaceful methods of trade, commerce and the demonstrable superiority of US Equal Rights republicanism over 'European' attachments to the 'privileges and inequalities' of 'monarchy' and 'aristocracy') and, in conscious references to the Monroe Doctrine, the hegemony of the United States over the entire American continent.[5]

On balance, and notwithstanding the recognition of radicalism as one of Gompers' 'extraordinary parts', it has indeed been the conservative and 'exceptional' elements within his own character, and of the federation over which he presided, which have been dominant in the historiography. For example, due note has has been registered of Stuart Kaufman's strong case in favour of the persistence of Gompers' radicalism and class-consciousness up to the mid 1890s.[6] However, the predominant view is that a 'transition to conservatism' took place—in some accounts by the mid 1890s, in others certainly by the early 1900s.

The notion of a mid-1890s transition[7] is often explained in terms of two key factors. First, Gompers' defeat of the considerable forces of the socialist/labour party left at the AF of L's 1894 convention and the consolidation of his power within the federation, from his re-election as president in 1895 onwards, meant that the security of his continued leadership was dependent neither upon the support of the left nor upon a resort to radical, class-based language.[8] Secondly, the serious defeats suffered by workers in the mass conflicts at Homestead (1892), Pullman (1894) and elsewhere, effectively led the AF of L president and the mainstream federation more profoundly and consistently to adopt a position of, at best, 'incremental gradualism' or, at worst, defensive conservatism; of 'digging in', based upon an increasingly narrowed version of craft unionism and hardened commitments to 'pure-and-simple' trade unionism and the eschewal of party-political partisanship.[9]

The second version of 'transition', associated most closely with Philip Foner,[10] further takes into account Gompers' and the AF of L's late 1890s anti-imperialism and anti-militarism, as seen in support for Cuban independence and opposition to the 1898 war with Spain and US annexation of Hawaii, Puerto Rico and the Philippines. However, it is claimed that after 1901, 'when imperialist annexation was no longer the major aspect of American imperialism', the AF of L 'ceased to condemn the acquisition of Hawaii, Puerto Rico and the Phillipines', and that within the labour movement 'anti-imperialist activity gradually receded'. Notwithstanding his prominent role in the Anti-Imperialist League, Gompers is seen by Foner and others as increasingly less opposed to the actual practice of US imperialism, than with more narrowly spreading abroad the virtues of AF of L-style trade unionism in order to avoid 'competition from labor in the colonial possessions'. Furthermore, both Gompers and the AF of L are believed to have become, in effect, instruments of US foreign policy and capital—working closely during the 1900s with pro-union and pro-imperialist employers and financiers in the National Civic Federation; and supporting a form of US hegemony in Cuba based upon the latter's 'independence' subject to the former's 'intervention and control'. This, observes Foner, was to become the model for much of American foreign policy in Latin America during the twentieth century.

In sum, according to this second version of transition, Gompers' anti-imperialism rapidly gave way to pragmatic and opportunist concerns with narrow, self-interested trade unionism, with class collaboration and with accommodation to the corporate foreign-policy interests of the state and big business.[11] A final conclusion to be drawn from both versions is that Gompers and the AF of L were effectively retreating from the wide-ranging, transforming vision of 'artisan republicanism' held by the 'producerist' Knights of Labour into a narrow, 'wage-earning' concern with the achievement of 'the American standard'—in Gompers' famous definition, '*more*'—within the confines of a seemingly permanent capitalist system. In effecting this closure, Gompers is seen to epitomise the 'business-unionist' exceptionalism of US labour.[12]

Any attempt to make convincing statements about the defining characteristics of individuals such as Gompers, of fundamental changes, transitions or watersheds in their thoughts and actions, and 'truthfully' or 'objectively' to read their spoken and written statements and non-verbal means of communication is, of course, fraught with all manner of difficulties. In making such an attempt one must be careful to balance actions and effects against stated intentions, deeds against words and self-perceptions against the ways in which historical subjects are viewed by others. The sources must be scoured for elements of continuity as well as discontinuity and a balanced assessment made as to the relative weight and influence of these elements. And, as postmodernists have usefully reminded us, language conveys many meanings which are often contested, elusive and which can change over time. As such it does not lend itself to a single, incontrovertible reading or truth. More generally, historians have long been trained to display a healthy scepticism towards their sources, to ask troublesome questions, to cross-check statements and references, to explore unexpected, unintended and often awkward issues and sources, to avoid taking statements at face value, to 'read against the grain' and so on. This checklist of historical rules of method must accordingly be constantly be borne in mind when attempting convincingly to characterise Gompers.

So forearmed, we wish to suggest, on the basis of a study of the pages of the *American Federationist* (the official organ of the AF of L from March 1894 onwards), the annual proceedings of the federation, Gompers' autobiography and other writings and speeches, and the views of contemporaries and historians, that the thoughts and actions of the AF of L president, at least during the late-nineteenth and early-twentieth centuries, were consistently more radical and simultaneously far less closed than historical orthodoxy would have us believe. As such, we are in agreement with Brody's view, also found in the work of Kaufman, Lawrence Glickman and Gregg

Andrews,[13] that Gompers was a far more complex, interesting and multi-faceted character than conveyed by the limited and somewhat flat descriptions of him as conservative, class-collaborationist, opportunist and pragmatist.[14] Finally, attention should be drawn to the fact that while references are made to preceding and subsequent periods, the main focus here is on the decades of the 1890s and 1900s. These constituted crucial decades in the history of the federation which, as we will see below, combined great 'official' hostility to the labour movement with the rise of Gompers' AF of L to a position of unprecedented strength and importance as the 'House of Labor'.[15]

Gompers and class

As the first point in our case, we may refer to Gompers' sharp and predominantly class-based critique of American society during the 1890s. This critique was rooted in a number of interrelated developments within the political economy of capitalism.[16] As was the case in many other countries, the late nineteenth century in the US witnessed a crisis of small-scale 'competitive' or 'individualistic' capitalism, as manifested in price deflation; increased business competition (both domestically and internationally); downward pressure on profit margins and money wages and declining and erratic rates of growth in key sectors of the economy; seemingly more frequent and threatening periods of recession and depression; and mounting unease, anger and assertiveness on the part of growing numbers of workers and small producers, both urban and rural, and on the part of increasingly mass labour movements.

Among the various responses made to ease or resolve these problems, attention should be drawn to two in particular. The first was a resort to the 'new imperialism', an international development, underpinned by political, cultural and ideological as well as economic factors, in which the United States nevertheless joined Britain, Germany and other western countries in the scramble for new spheres of influence and markets in order to 'keep the wheels of the factories turning', find profitable new sources of investment, divert the 'masses' from their domestic ills and radical solutions, and promote the cause of, predominantly white, national greatness.[17] The second resided in the formation and consolidation of larger units of production seeking more effective regulation and control over their various spheres of activity. Generally speaking, the dominance of the family firm gave way to that of the factory. There occurred within the US a marked growth of trusts, corporations and other forms of oligopoly and monopoly. Characterised by mass production techniques, an increased division of labour and the growth of the semi-skilled component of the workforce, and 'modern' methods of management, especially scientific management or 'Taylorism', these corporations sought more thoroughly to achieve both formal and informal control over the labour process. And this search increasingly involved opposition to the control over the labour process exercised by craftsmen, along with trade unionism and other collective means of working-class defence and advancement.

In terms of the international economy, the transition from 'competitive' to 'monopoly' or 'corporate' capitalism was a very chequered process. However, in the United States the transition took place rapidly, and often with considerable violence and lack of respect for tradition. Most significantly in the present context, there developed the widespread belief among labour activists that many employers and their powerful allies in the judiciary and other organs of the state machinery and within the mainstream political parties were intent upon resolving the crisis of competitive capitalism and effecting the transition to corporate capitalism largely at the expense of the worker. This general feeling was given harsh concrete expression by the specific events and developments of the early and mid 1890s: mass, set-piece battles such as Homestead and Pullman, violent conflicts in coalmining and the widespread introduction of 'scab' labour; the march of Jacob Coxey's 'Commonweal Army' of the poor on Washington DC; extensive employer 'driving' within the workplace and attacks upon craft control and trade unionism; the increasing resort to injunctions and other anti-labour legal devices; the use of troops and private detectives to break strikes; and the seeming inability or unwillingness of the political parties and the government to alleviate or end the mass unemployment and suffering attendant upon the worst depression of the century between 1893 and 1896.

It was within this context that Gompers repeatedly argued that politicians and the main political parties, and large sections of the press, the courts, indeed the state as a whole, were becoming the instruments of 'plutocrats', such as Carnegie and Rockefeller, who sought to undermine the rights of 'the people', the 'toiling masses', the 'working class' in the interests of the 'selfish' and 'monopolistic' 'capitalist class', lacking 'human sympathy', and schooled in unbridled 'self-interest' and 'avaricious tyranny'. Republican America, rooted in a society of small independent producers, Equal Rights and ample opportunities for social mobility, was now in grave danger of passing into 'un-American' 'plutocratic power' and 'corporation (sic) rule', and a Europeanised system of 'class oppression', permanent 'wage-slavery' and 'economic thraldom'. As he declared in July 1894:

On every hand we see the capitalist class, the corporate and moneyed interests concentrating their efforts for the purposes of despoiling the people of their rights, encroaching upon our liberties and endeavoring to force the workers down in the social, economic and political scale. Allied with them are the governmental powers, national, state and municipal. Their efforts are concentrated, their actions united. Nothing is allowed to interfere with the full development of the protection and advancement of their interests.[18]

And in 1896:

The founders of the republic and their immediate successors did not anticipate an era of money power, with giant corporations in control of the production of the earth and transportation...They did not contemplate that it would become necessary for American citizens to unite in order to protect themselves and oppose attempted control and regulation of skilled and unskilled labor by centralized wealth...They did not intend that the regular army should be massed and state troops mobilized at industrial centers wherever and whenever a corporation suggested that 'life' and 'property' were in danger...They spurned aristocracy, classes and military rule when independence was achieved, and they legislated for a republican form of government in accord with the definition of democracy.[19]

While especially marked during the turbulent and hostile decade of the 1890s, Gomper's radical-republican *and* class-based critique of corporate power and the state was not confined, in either expression or application, to that decade. Elements of the critique were consistent with his earlier political ideas, dating back to his contact with Marxian socialists during the 1870s, and, as we will see below, were carried forward, contrary to the conventional wisdom of conservatism and closure, into the twentieth century. The state, according to Gompers, had 'always been the representative of the wealth possessors', and legislation designed to regulate trusts had 'simply proved incentives to more subtly and surely lubricate the wheels of capital's accumulation'.[20] Furthermore, Gompers was articulating a set of ideas which were widely shared by labour activists, both inside and outside the AF of L, in late nineteenth-century America.[21]

Gompers' attack upon corporate subversion of the democratic republic was part of a wider critique in which the experiential facts of class conflict, struggle and consciousness co-existed with, and in many instances took precedence over, the Knights of Labour's 'producer-based' form of 'artisan radicalism'. For example, the preamble to the AF of L's constitution referred to:

> ...A struggle...going on in all nations of the civilized world, between the oppressors and the oppressed, a struggle between the Capitalist and the Laborer, which grows in intensity from year to year...[22]

Class conflict was attributed, by Gompers and many other labour activists, not just to the actions of a few capitalist 'bad apples'—'dishonourable' employers who refused to abide by union recognition and the 'American standard' of remuneration—but, more fundamentally, to the very nature of the productive system itself. For the latter was characterised by necessary competition between labour and capital for their relative shares of the social product; and capital 'purchasing labor as cheaply as it can', 'selling in the dearest market' and stimulating competition among workers 'so that wages shall go down and the condition of the laborer become deteriorated'.[23]

It was beholden upon workers to offer resistance to their position of structured inequality and exploitation under a dependent system of wage labour and in the face of an aggressive capitalist drive for total mastery in the workplace. And while labour leaders set great store by the virtues of personal independence and initiative, it was the common perception that self-help and organisation of a *collective* kind mattered most to labour's successful organisation and eventual emancipation. As Gompers wrote in 1902:

> where economic and social conditions admit of individual action, that is the ideal situation. But when we find on the one hand a great concentration of wealth and power, accompanied by a marked concentration of industry, with the direction of the great industrial and distributing forces placed in the hands of a few, it is as idle for the individual worker to attempt to obtain redress for bad conditions as it is for a vessel to survive a hurricane without rudder or seamen to guide her.[24]

The collective labour movement, 'in its essence *a class struggle in the interests of humanity*'[25] (emphasis added), was seen to constitute the bedrock of labour's defence and advancement, the solution to labour's many ills under capitalism. In turn, the activities of the labour movement should, in Gompers' opinion, assume two main forms, trade unionist and political, with the former taking 'natural' precedence over the latter. Indeed, it is to a brief examination of Gompers' belief in 'the primacy of trade unionism' that we now turn in order to make the second point in our case for his continuing class-based radicalism.

Gompers stated in the *American Federationist* in 1897 that the AF of L trade unions were 'organizing the wage earners in the class conscious struggle against all profit mongers under whatever shape they may appear or form they may assume'. To the AF of L president, trade unions had not only 'always possessed the exclusive character of a class organization of the wage earners', but had also, 'exercised and demonstrated their unqualified class consciousness'. The latter quality signified to Gompers that, 'those who belong to that class are conscious of that fact, and are conscious too, that their interests are separate and distinct from any other class'.[26] Such statements, repeated on several occasions, lead us to question not only the accuracy of Marc Karson's widely accepted claim that Gompers saw 'class consciousness' as 'a Socialist myth that would never become a reality in the minds of the mass of American workers',[27] but also the view that both Gompers and the AF of L were simply or solely narrow and exclusive in their trade unionism and conservative and 'limited' in their aims and outlook on the world.

We have noted earlier in this article that many AF of L 'craft' unionists did increasingly, and especially in practice, erect substantial barriers against the full entry of women, African-Americans, 'new' immigrants and many unskilled workers into their unions. Similarly, in articles in the *American Federationist* and elsewhere, Gompers could be found bemoaning the supposedly 'limited' capacity of Afro-Americans (due to the 'deferential' and 'dependent' legacy of slavery and their continued employment as strike-breakers), women (as bearers of the ideal of 'true womanhood' and their 'limited' and 'recent' entry into the world of social production), and some recent and prospective immigrants (unschooled in their native lands in the ways of trade unionism and 'the American standard') for the cultivation of that *independence*, of mind and action, and especially that '*manly*' independence, believed to be vital to the successful establishment and development of trade unionism.[28] But while fully appreciating the importance of detailed attention to the gendered, racialised and 'skilled' exclusions and limitations of the thoughts and actions of Gompers, the AF of L and its constituent unions, we must also remember not to blank out class from a historical record of which it was undoubtedly an important part.

The validity of the latter claim may be demonstrated with reference to an 'alternative' reading of some of Gompers' utterances. The starting point of Gompers' philosophy was the belief that, thus rooted in the mass fact of wage-earning in modern capitalist society, trade unionism constituted the 'natural' or 'organic', form of working-class organisation. As he declared in 1898:

> The trade unions are the legitimate outgrowth of modern societary (sic) and industrial conditions. They are not the creation of any man's brain. They are organizations of necessity. They were born of the necessity of the workers to protect and defend themselves from encroachment, injustice and wrong. They are the organizations of the working class, for the working class, by the working class...[29]

As such, trade unionism, unlike religious and party-political movements with their divisive and weakening effects upon labour movements, was seen to constitute *the* unifying force among workers in production. In principle, therefore, and notwithstanding the gendered, racialised and skilled dimensions of union practice, Gompers' brand of trade unionism aimed to be all inclusive, to embrace all those who were wage earners. For example, in the first volume of his autobiography he denied the primacy of gender to trade unionism in the following way:

> ...the labor movement, like all primary human movements, is neither male nor female—it is the instrumentality of unity. So I have never felt that there was properly a sex (sic) phase to the fundamentals of trade unionism.

Setting out to 'protect all who work for wages, whether male or female', trade unionism further led 'to an interest in movements for freedom in all walks of life'. 'Consequently', declared Gompers, 'I was early interested in the movement for equal suffrage. Equal rights for all brought me logically to endorse the women's struggle for equal political and legal rights'.[30] Furthermore, it is very important to remember that, notwithstanding limited practical results, Gompers was consistent, throughout the period in question and beyond, in his strong advocacy of the necessity of union organisation among women, African-Americans and many European immigrants, both 'old' and 'new'. The *American Federationist* charted progress among these groups, praised their achievements—Gompers paying, for example, full tribute to women organisers within the AF and the work of the Women's Trade Union League—and articulated Gompers' view that unity and organisation must proceed 'irrespective of creed, color, sex, nationality or politics'.[31] And it is equally important to remember that Gompers believed that the attainment of trade-union 'independence' and 'manliness' (the latter often being a code for the former) was within the capacity of all, men and women, white and black, immigrant and native born, who had spent a sufficient learning period of time within the world of social production. As such, the attainment of trade union consciousness was historically rather than biologically grounded.[32]

The 'primacy of trade unionism'

Intent upon improving immediate conditions of work, the unions were nevertheless accredited by Gompers with 'nobler' and more ambitious aims than the dominant historiographical emphases upon pragmatic self-interest and immediate material gain or 'more' would suggest. The unions' far-reaching agenda thus included the attainment of continuous gains in both the quantity and quality of life and 'complete social justice', as manifested in the workers' realisation of 'the full product of their labor'; the more widespread cultivation of 'manly independence'; helping the 'lower depths' to organise; and forging links, by means of the fraternal delegate system, conferences and correspondence, with their trade-union brothers and sisters in Britain and elsewhere overseas in support of the causes of internationalism and peace, and in opposition to war and imperialist conquest and annexation. In addition the AF of L sought to bring 'order'—by means of the more widespread introduction of standard rules governing workplace relations and labour market regulation more generally—out of capitalist 'disorder' and 'anarchy', and to 'civilize' the 'brutal' and 'inhuman' marketplace by means of the cultivation and spread of the 'moral-economic' values and practices of mutuality, co-operation, 'fairness' and 'common humanity'.[33]

In these various ways the AF of L unions would continue to embody the 'moral universality', the 'moral brotherhood of man', which had underscored many nineteenth-century labour movements. However, this 'moral universality' would henceforward assume the form less of 'producerism' than a radical, indeed transforming, 'wage-earning consciousness'. The latter was hardly in accord with the supposedly hegemonic influence of narrow 'business unionism' conventionally bestowed by historians upon the AF of L. Indeed, at times Gompers anticipated the abolition of class society by trade-union means. For example, in 1897 he wrote in the *American Federationist*:

The wage earning class of the world occupies the lowest rung in the ladder of economic life. With its emancipation comes the abolition of classes based upon possession of wealth and power; with its dis-enthralment comes the abolition of all profit or interest in any form...the freedom of labor must be accomplished by the workers themselves. Therefore, they organize in the trade unions—the class conscious organizations of labor—for the gradual and natural elimination of all classes and the emancipation of man.[34]

Notwithstanding his growing opposition to socialist 'wreckers' and 'splitters', he also retained a good deal of respect for, and at times worked with, those socialists whom he considered to be committed, above all, to the establishment, development and *unity* of a mass labour movement.[35] And he displayed far more ambivalence, indeed at times open-minded pragmatism, towards various socialist ideas than we have commonly been led to believe. In 1894, while opposed to Thomas Morgan's 'Plank 10' proposal, calling upon the AF of L to commit itself to 'the collective ownership by the people of all means of production and distribution', Gompers nevertheless did imagine that 'more than likely it will be necessary for our people to go through that phase' of state socialism, or 'at least a portion of it', and expressed his support for 'Government ownership of the railroads and of all means of transportation and communication and all other productive forces which are in those monopolies'.[36] As late as 1918 he was still judging the strengths and weaknesses of public and private ownership primarily in terms of the needs of the workers involved:

> Whether either system has advantages over the other depends entirely upon the principles upon which operation is based. Either system may provide democratic conditions under which workers have an opportunity to present and to maintain their rights and best interests.[37]

Gompers remained, furthermore, strenuous in his opposition to socialist claims that his 'primacy of trade unionism' approach—with non-partisan independent politics as an auxiliary to trade unionism—was inherently limited, conservative and class collaborationist. As against the largely empty, 'pie in the sky', political promises of socialism, it was claimed that the 'primacy of trade unionism' approach had resulted, by the late 1900s, not only in the survival but in the impressive growth of the AF of L and the attainment of the 'American standard' by increased numbers of its members.[38] In 1912, in a remarkable piece in the *American Federationist*, Gompers declared that within trade unionism:

> there is positively no 'Gomperism', no fatuous conservatism that refuses

consideration to radical ideas, no entangling alliance with capitalism, no respect for the unearned wealth of the plutocracy, no thought of putting on the brakes against progressive thought, no compromise with the spirit that is blind to the advances of the times toward economic justice, no 'chloroforming' of any thought or sentiment that points to a speedy evolution of society—aye, even on upward to the millenium.

'Never in the history of the American Federation of Labor', continued Gompers,' have I ever said or hinted that there was or could be "harmony between labor and capital"'. And he continued:

No man who pretends to be a leader of public opinion today advocates harmony between privilege and privation, legalized robbery and honest citizenship, swollen fortunes and scant wages. No trade union leader finds fault with just social discontent. The scheme of 'industrial peace' which has its advocates signifies no more than the fact that it is better for employer and employed to confer and deal under conditions of the least friction in the labor market and in the field of immediately practical betterment for the industrial wage-earners. In that pursuit no union man need give up the least of his radical sentiments, or the highest aspiration for industrial disenthralment and social justice.[39]

Strong, vigilant and voluntary trade unionism, on occasion necessarily militant and prepared to resort to the strike weapon—the 'spark of their manhood and their honor'—constituted the very bedrock and safeguard of labor's independence, high level of ambition and freedom from governmental and employer domination.[40]

To be sure, the passage of time and varied experience induced modifications and changes to Gomper's class-based radicalism and militant trade unionism. There were also, at times, tensions and contradictions between radical rhetoric and concrete practice. For example, the major improvements in workers' living standards and the fortunes of the AF of L between 1897 and 1904 lent themselves to the adoption of a more moderate and accommodating position.[41] These were the years when severe economic depression gave way to boom and when the federation impressively increased it membership, albeit unevenly, from approximately 272,000 to 1,682,000, and truly became the 'House of Labor'. Success led many AF of L unions to become more circumspect in their attitudes towards strikes and militancy and more exclusively white and male in their composition. In conjunction with those employers organised in the National Civic Federation, Gompers emphasised the new-found ability of capital and labour to reason together and their mutual commitment to 'binding contracts, industrial peace and social harmony and progress'.

Even during this period of relative calm, however, Gompers continued to see 'militant trade unionism' as a necessary factor in inducing a more widespread acceptance of the legitimacy of organised labour among employers. Furthermore, the 'inevitable' conflict among 'the social elements' had only been 'raised to humane plane' rather than eradicated. Furthermore, between 1904 and 1908 many employers turned against the conciliatory approach of the National Civic Federation to adopt, often as members of the National Association of Manufacturers, a very aggressive 'open-shop' policy towards labour. In addition, rampant judicial anti-unionism was perceived by Gompers to have resulted in 'the most grave and momentous situation which has ever confronted the working people of this country'. The situation was reflected most notoriously in three particular judgements: the damages awarded against the Danbury Hatters' Union for 'restraint of trade' in 1903–8; the injunction obtained by the Buck's Stove and Range company against the AF of L's attempted boycott of its products in 1907–8; and the subsequent prison sentence passed, but never actually imposed, upon Gompers and other AF of L leaders in 1909 for being in contempt of the Buck's Stove injunction.

Given this extremely hostile context, radical language once again came to the fore at AF of L conventions and in the pages of the *American Federationist*. For example, at the AF of L's 1907 convention, Gompers' report made reference to 'the continuous struggle of labor against tyranny, brutality and injustice', the 'shortsightedness and greed of industrial captains', the 'machinations of financiers', and 'the cupidity of the worst elements of the capitalist class'.[42] And as a result of successful judicial anti-unionism, workers were, by 1908, liable for financial damages and unable to advocate in print the boycott of products of anti-union employers (a reference to the Buck's Stove case). In addition, workers now 'enjoyed' the 'rights' to be 'maimed and killed without liability to the employer', to 'be discharged for belonging to a union' and to 'work as many hours as employers please'.[43]

Gompers' philosophy of 'the primacy of trade unionism' was applied not only to the domestic scene but also to international affairs. In terms of the latter, it had important radical implications for the issues of labour internationalism, peace and war, and imperialism. It is to an examination of these issues that we now turn in order to make the third and final point in our case.

International solidarity

Throughout the 1890s and 1900s Gompers actively promoted the cause of international trade-union solidarity. He corresponded with a wide range of foreign labour leaders, including socialists, and invited them to contribute to the *American Federationist*.[44] He was keen to develop 'fraternal links' with 'the wage earners of all countries' in order 'to aid and encourage every movement calculated to materially, morally and socially improve the conditions of the workers, no matter where they may be located'. Towards this end, he played a key role in setting up the fraternal delegate system with the British and Canadian trade union movements.[45] The international exchange of fraternal delegates would, in Gompers' opinion:

> soon lead to a general holding of international trade union congresses, wherein the brotherhood of man will not only be dreamed of and advocated, but will contribute largely to its full realization.[46]

In 1896 Gompers proposed the 'holding of bona fide International Trade Congresses every few years', but this was rejected by the AF of L Executive Council.[47] In 1909 he was the unofficial delegate from the AF of L to the International Secretariat, a periodic conference of trade unionists in Europe, and in the following year the AF of L voted to affiliate with the secretariat. While critical of the socialism and revolutionary syndicalism to be found among some of the affiliates, the AF of L remained loyal to the secretariat, supporting better labour legislation and housing, international cooperation and national trade-union autonomy, and opposing 'the movement of strike-breakers between countries when strikes existed or were contemplated', and the inducement of trans-national migration during periods of industrial depression. In Amsterdam in 1919 the AF of L was represented at the meeting to form a new, post-war trade-union international, the International Federation of Trade Unions [IFTU]. But in the wake of the international's call for socialism, and against Gompers' wishes, in 1921 the AF of L's Executive Council rejected affiliation with the IFTU. Gompers' post-war internationalism was increasingly channelled into the creation of the Pan-American Federation of Labor, formed in 1918 to promote 'the improvement in the working conditions of the workers of the United States and Latin America, and the promotion of better understanding between the peoples of the Western hemisphere'; into involvement in the Commission on International Labor Legislation, whose recommendations paved the way for the formation of the International Labor Organization; and into support for the infant League of Nations, having, as Gompers believed, the potential to develop into 'an international parliament, that shall maintain justice in the world'. 'Gompers always dreamed of the A.F. of L', concludes Philip Taft, 'as a member of a democratic trade union international devoted to advancing the causes of peace, freedom and the security and welfare of the workers of the world'.[48]

To return to our specific focus upon the 1890s and 1900s, Gompers' internationalism during these two decades was characterised by important anti-war and anti-imperialist emphases. In striving to attain 'the brotherhood of man', trade unionists would be making a strong case in favour of 'international amity and universal peace', the 'elimination of the cruel barbarism of war' and the settlement of international disputes by conciliation and arbitration, in opposition to jingoism and the imperialist rivalries—'the mad struggle of the world for the acquisition of territory'—which threatened world peace.[49] Throughout these two decades the AF of L remained loud and consistent in its view that war was brutal, unnecessary and a means of class-based domination. War, generally pursued for 'monarchical' and 'capitalist' gain, profit and power, was perceived to stimulate the development of 'tyranny' by means of the creation of 'unrepublican' standing armies, the bloated state machinery and the silencing or stifling of dissent.[50] It imposed its greatest human and financial burden upon 'the working class'. It diverted 'the attention of the people from redress of domestic grievances'; and 'when the smoke of war has cleared away...it will be the same old story of hunger, poverty and misery for the masses'.[51] Gompers and the AF of L did applaud the 'heroism and loyalty' of those 'patriots' who were prepared 'honorably' to fight for 'peace with justice'. But in most cases war was 'barbarous', 'hellish' and 'inhuman'.[52] Workers of all nations, with 'primarily identical' interests, were accordingly exhorted to organise for international peace and arbitration. 'May we not look forward to the time', asked Gompers in his report to the 1905 AF of L convention, when:

> the wage-earners of the world will be so thoroughly organized, and will understand their interests and their rights so well, that they will refuse to permit themselves to be arrayed against their brother workmen of another country for the purpose of serving the machinations of tyrants, whether political or commercial? Organized labor stands for peace...[53]

The next annual convention, held at Minneapolis, adopted a resolution which claimed that 'action which makes for the peace of nations is intimately bound up with the welfare of the workers of all nations'. And as late as 1913, Gompers, while counselling against the renunciation of 'all means of self-defense', had no hesitation in confidently stating that the AF of L 'in its first convention, held in Pittsburgh in 1881, declared for international peace, and has consistently and insistently maintained that position'.[54] In support of the latter, Gompers was a regular attender and speaker at peace conferences between the 1890s and the outbreak of the First World War.[55]

The issues of peace and war were closely linked to opposition to the 'new imperialism' of 'formal conquest, annexation and administration'.[56] During the 1890s Gompers was increasingly alarmed by the growing strength of pro-imperialist sentiments within the US, as manifested in the 1898 war with Spain and his country's designs on Hawaii, Cuba, the Philippines and Puerto Rico. Once in progress, war against the 'barbarism and cruelty' of monarchical and imperialist Spain was seen to be justified. Gompers, however, was anxious to ensure that the Cubans, and those other peoples formerly subjected to Spanish 'tyranny', now be afforded the opportunity genuinely to determine their own futures rather than become the 'slaves' or subject people of a newly imperialistic US. It was, for example, within this context that the AF of L opposed the American annexation of Hawaii and extended important organisational and ideological support to those workers in Cuba and Puerto Rico attempting to set up and gain recognition for trade unions and develop civil and formal political rights and freedoms. By way of interest, the leading trade unionist and close and lasting ally of Gompers in Puerto Rico was to be Santiago Iglesias, formerly a carpenter in Brooklyn, who had become leader of the Socialist Party in Puerto Rico.[57]

At the 1899 AF of L convention Gompers portrayed the new imperialism as being fundamentally at odds with the self-determining tradition of American republicanism:

A marked change within the recent past has overcome the policy and trend of our country...A humane war, undertaken for the independence of Cuba from Spanish domination and misrule...has been taken advantage of to ruthlessly trample underfoot every principle upon which our Republic was founded...Hawaii is annexed in spite of the protests of her people. Slave-like conditions of labor obtain there...Porto Rico has by armed force been conquered and annexed; Cuba, promised her freedom and independence, is held by the armed military forces of our country...the principle of self-government is being denied the Filippines (sic).[58]

Furthermore, having deprived the Cubans, Philippinos and Puerto Ricans of 'the right of self-government', the American 'ruling class' was in a position to place 'our political rights...in jeopardy'. Thus:

> When the military arm of the government unduly enlarged is permitted to exhibit its inherent tendency, whether such be in Cuba, in Idaho, or in the Philippines, then freedom is in the gravest danger. Absolutism, protected and stimulated by a large standing army...crushes all opposition.[59]

Gompers' opposition to imperialism was informed not only by democratic, but also by material concerns. In keeping with his 'classed' outlook on the world, the 'bondholders and speculators', 'the money power', the 'capitalists' and the 'ruling class' were perceived to be the main forces driving his country to compete internationally for new markets and power bases, and new sources of investment, raw materials and cheap labour. For example:

> the money-makers—whose god is the almighty dollar—came to the conclusion that if poor, suffering Cuba can be handed over to their tender mercies, their diety (sic) and their deviltry can hold full sway. These gentry, when there is a question between liberty and profit, present or prospective liberty is thrown to the dogs as a wornout and threadbare thing of the past.[60]

As in the case of politics, the imperialist economic experiment was seen to pose a serious threat to the rights of workers and 'the people' at home. Thus, in searching out and fully exploiting 'cheap', 'servile' and even 'semi-barbaric' labour in the Philippines, Hawaii and elsewhere, American capitalists would be sorely tempted to import such 'slavery' into the United States itself in order to undermine the 'American standard', the AF of L and the 'independence', 'freedom' and 'manhood' of the worker.[61] The annexation of Hawaii 'would be the admission of a slave state side by side with the free States of America'. And if the Sandwich Islands were permitted 'to continue a species of labor repugnant to the free institutions of our country', then there would be 'no safeguard against the extension of the same species of contract slave labor to the sugar industry of Louisiana and the cotton fields of the Southern States'.[62]

To be sure, as in the case of Gompers' class-based critique of domestic affairs, so also his labour internationalism, support for peace and opposition to imperialism were, at various points, subjected to the forces of qualification and change. For example, as noted previously, once annexation had become a generally accepted fact of life, so Gompers and the 1900s AF of L were far less concerned with the very fundamentals of imperialism than with its most vexing symptoms, and especially the threat to American workers of cheap labour competition from within the imperial system. Similarly, Gompers accepted the 'informal' or 'open door' imperialism of 'industry, commerce and superior mentality and civilization'.[63] And spreading the AF of L version of the trade union word in Mexico and other countries of Central and Latin America went hand-in-hand with opposition to 'IWWism', 'Bolshevism', the containment of revolutionary nationalism and subscription to the Monroe Doctrine and 'Americanisation'. As Gompers observed of Puerto Rico, 'there is no influence so potent for the Americanization of the people of the island as our labor movement there'.[64]

Yet to assume, as do a number of critics, that the 'anti-imperialism' of the post-1900 AF of L amounted to little, if anything, more than a concern with competition from cheap labour, and that both the federation and Gompers became, in reality, simple instruments of corporate US foreign policy, is greatly to oversimplify a more complex picture.[65] For example, Gompers continued to offer the genuine hand of friendship to AF of L-style trade unionism in Puerto Rico, Cuba and Mexico. It is true that in so doing, he was aware not only of the interests of the AF of L but also the wider and larger geo-political interests of the USA. And, given the threat of 'undue' European and British influence in the American continent, he was not averse on occasion to recommend armed US intervention.[66] But in supporting trade unionism in Mexico and elsewhere, he also came into frequent conflict with the anti-union and pro-interventionist sentiments of sections of US big business and their allies in the state machinery and government.[67] Furthermore, he encountered similar conflicts as a result of his continued defence of the political rights and ambitions of the people of Puerto Rico.[68] In sum, there continued to operate a 'classed' 'dialectic of conflict and consensus' within Gompers' attitude to US foreign policy and imperialism.[69]

Support for the war effort, accommodation to, and unprecedented participation in, the state machinery and opposition to 'alien subversion' undoubtedly revealed the full limitations of Gomper's pacifism and internationalism during the First World War. Opposition to the 'open door' policy of immigration and, especially, vitriolic anti-'Orientalism' and support for Asian exclusion, similarly exposed the contradictions of his 'inclusive' trade unionism.[70] But in the war and post-war years the AF of L president did continue to demonstrate, in the Pan-American Federation of Labor, in his efforts on behalf of post-war European reconstruction and world peace, and in his continued defence of 'democracy' versus 'autocracy', his internationalist faith. In sum, while most pronounced in the 1890s and 1900s, Gompers' internationalism, support for peace and anti-imperialism did survive, albeit in attentuated form, the traumas of the First World War and the years of revolution in Europe and Mexico.

A revisionist perspective

In 1925 C.T. Cramp, chairman of the British Labour Party, and fraternal delegate to the AF of L's 1924 convention, offered the following verdict on Gompers:

> It has been our fashion in this country to regard the late Samuel Gompers as being a great reactionary, who was responsible for the backward attitude of the American Trade Unionists towards political problems. My experience, both in conference and in private conversation with Gompers, totally discredits this belief. True, Gompers held strong views which he never hesitated to express...but it is the opinion of everyone who has been in contact with the American movement, including those people in unions which are outside of the American Federation of Labour, and who regard themselves as advanced in their outlook, that Gompers was far ahead of many of his supporters, and had, indeed, in his nature a strong element of idealism which is notably absent from the great body of Trade Unionists composing the Federation.[71]

Notwithstanding its idealisations and exaggerations, Cramp's 'revisionist' perspective has much in common with the view expressed in this article. We have attempted to demonstrate that the ideas and actions of Samuel Gompers, especially during the years of the 1890s and 1900s, were both more consistent and radical than the conventional picture of US 'exceptionalism', as reflected in Gompers' 'transition to conservatism', 'opportunism' and 'closure', would suggest. While Gompers' ideas and actions were influenced and modified by the continuing play of tension and contradiction, conservatism and radicalism, self-interest, pragmatism and the historically contingent factors of time and place, nevertheless they displayed a high degree of radical consistency and continuity, as manifested centrally in domestic and international applications of the principle of the 'primacy of trade unionism'. Furthermore, Gompers' radical language cannot convincingly be portrayed primarily either as 'mere rhetoric', devoid of 'real' substance, or as an opportunist or strategic device to secure and consolidate his position within the AF of L. As demonstrated in his battles at the AF of L in 1893 and 1894, and in his continuing conflicts with socialists inside the federation into the 1900s and beyond, Gompers was, of course, acutely aware of the tactical, strategic and power-based dimensions and uses of language and ideas. But the very longevity and continuity of his radical language, including periods both preceding and subsequent to his 'rise to power', suggest that something more fundamental was at work. It is our claim that 'that something more' resided in his 'trade unionism first' philosophy which he attempted, however imperfectly and subject to historical constraints, consistently and continuously to put into practice.

These conclusions are, of course, based upon a limited amount of source material and refer to a limited period of time in Gompers' careeer in the labour movement. As such, they are highly tentative and provisional. However, they will hopefully act as a spur to further revisionist research in order to allow us to make a more detailed and complete reassessment of one of the most important figures in US labour history.

Acknowledgements

I would like to thank Leon Fink and David Montgomery for their helpful comments on this article. I am extremely grateful for the assistance provided by the Inter-Library Loans librarians at Manchester Metropolitan University and Grace Palladino and Peter Albert at the Gompers Papers, University of Maryland, USA. This article could not have been written without their assistance and generosity.

Notes

1. For debates about 'exceptionalism' see, for example, Sean Wilentz, 'Against exceptionalism: class consciousness and the American labor movement', *International Labor and Working-Class History*, 26 (1984); Neville Kirk, *Labour and Society in Britain and the USA*, 2 vols. (Aldershot, 1994); Seymour M. Lipset, *American Exceptionalism: A Double Edged Sword* (New York, 1996); Rick Halpern and Jonathan Morris (Eds), *American Exceptionalism? US Working Class Formation in an International Context* (London, 1997); Larry G. Gerber, 'Shifting perspectives on American exceptionalism: recent literature on American labor relations', *Journal of American Studies*, vol.31, no.2 (1997).

2. David Brody, *Workers in Industrial America: Essays on the 20th Century Struggle* (Oxford, 1993), p.23. For studies of Gompers' career in the labour movement see Samuel Gompers, *Seventy Years of Life and Labour: An Autobiography*, 2 vols. (New York, 1967 edn); Nick Salvatore, 'Introduction' to *Seventy Years of Life and Labor* (Ithaca, 1984); Bernard Mandel, *Samuel Gompers: A Biography* (Yellow Springs, Ohio, 1963); Philip Taft, *The AF of L. in the Time of Gompers* (New York, 1957); *Stuart B. Kaufman, Samuel Gompers and the Origins of the American Federation*

of Labor 1848–1896 (Westport, Connecticut, 1973); Kaufman, ed. *The Samuel Gompers Papers. Volume 1: The Making of a Union Leader 1850–86* (Urbana, 1986); John H.M. Laslett, 'Samuel Gompers and the Rise of American Business Unionism', in Melvyn Dubofsky and Warren van Tine, eds., *Labor Leaders in America* (Urbana, 1987); Bruce Laurie, *Artisans into Workers: Labor in Nineteenth Century America* (New York, 1989); Julia Greene, *Pure and Simple Politics:The American Federation of Labor and Political Activism 1881–1917* (Cambridge, 1998).

3. For the gendered nature of AF of L unionism see Ileen A. Devault, '"To Sit Among Men": Skill, Gender and Craft Unionism in the Early American Federation of Labor', in Eric Arnesen, Julie Greene and Bruce Laurie, eds., *Labor Histories: Class Politics and the Working-Class Experience* (Urbana, 1998), pp.159–83; Elizabeth Faue, *Community of Suffering and Struggle: Women Men and the Labor Movement in Minneapolis 1915–1945* (Chapel Hill, 1991), pp.9–10. For the AF of L and the issue of racism see Philip S. Foner, *Organized Labor and the Black Worker 1619–1981* (New York, 1982), chs. 5–6, 10–12; Eric Arnesen, *Waterfront Workers of New Orleans: Race Class and Politics 1863–1923* (Urbana, 1991). Andrew Gyory, *Closing the Gate: Race Politics and the Chinese Exclusion Act* (Chapel Hill, 1998) deals with anti-Chinese attitudes up to 1882. For Gompers' and the AF of L's virulent and persistent anti-'Orientalism' see, for example, *American Federationist*, February 1906, pp.98–9; AF of L, *Proceedings*, 1906, p.179. See also Lawrence Glickman, 'Inventing "the American standard of living"; gender, race and working-class identity 1880–1925', *Labor History*, vol.34, nos 2–3 (1993), pp.221–35.

4. For the AF of L's role during the First World War see Joseph A. McCartin, *Labor's Great War: The Struggle for Industrial Democracy and the Origins of Modern American Labor Relations 1912–1921* (Chapel Hill, 1997).

5. See the illuminating study by Gregg Andrews, *Shoulder to Shoulder? The American Federation of Labor The United States and the Mexican Revolution 1910–1924* (Berkeley, 1991). For Gompers' contrast of 'American' with 'European' values see *American Federationist*, December 1909, p.1086 and January 1910, pp.55–61.

6. Kaufman, *Samuel Gompers and the Origins*, pp.xiii–xiv, ch. 11; Laslett, 'Samuel Gompers', pp.67–72.

7. See Laslett, 'Samuel Gompers', p.23.

8. A predominantly instrumental and opportunist view of Gompers—of self-interest and power as his prime motivations, and appropriate linguistic and rhetorical tactics and strategies being employed to suit these purposes—has figured strongly in much of the dominant historiographical tradition. See, for example, Mandel, *Samuel Gompers*, pp.202–6, 213–14; Simeon Larson, *Labor and Foreign Policy: Gompers the AFL and the First World War 1914–1918* (London, 1975), p.14.

9. For such developments see Kirk, *Labour and Society. Volume 2: Challenge and Accommodation 1850–1939*, pp.124, 134–40.

10. Philip S. Foner, *History of the Labor Movement. Volume 2: From the Founding of the American Federation of Labor to the Emergence of American Imperialism* (New York,

1975), chs. 26–7, especially pp.426–9, 437–9; Foner, *The Spanish-Cuban-American War and the Birth of American Imperialism 1895–1902*, (New York, 1972), 2 vols., vol.1, p.ix, vol.2, p.509. See also, Mandel, *Samuel Gompers*, pp.202–6, 213–14; Simeon Larson, *Labor and Foreign Policy*, p.14; the socialist organ, *Appeal to Reason*, June 17, 1905, for a view of Gompers as the 'agent of the capitalists to fool the working class'.

11. For the notion of 'corporatism' as a major shaping factor in twentieth-century US foreign policy see Thomas J. McCormick, 'Drift or mastery?: A corporatist synthesis for American diplomatic history', *Reviews in American History*, 10 December 1982, pp.318–30. For a balanced assessment see Andrews, *Shoulder*, pp.4–9.

12. Kirk, *Challenge*, pp.59, 124, 136–40; Kaufman ed., *Gompers Papers*, vol.1, xv.

13. Brody, *Workers*, p.23; Kaufman ed., *Gompers Papers*, p.xv; Andrews, *Shoulder*, introduction; Lawrence B. Glickman, 'The Religion of Trade Unionism', *Documentary Editing* (December, 1994). I am grateful to Larry Glickman for a copy of his insightful review article.

14. For an international point of comparison see the interesting reassessment of Robert Knight, leading British craft unionist and anti-socialist, offered by Alastair J. Reid, 'Old Unionism Reconsidered: The Radicalism of Robert Knight, 1870–1900', in Eugenio F. Biagini and Alastair J. Reid eds., *Currents of Radicalism: Popular Radicalism, Organised Labour and Party Politics in Britain 1850–1914* (Cambridge, 1991).

15. David Montgomery, *The Fall of The House of Labor: The Workplace, the State and American Labor Activism 1865–1925* (Cambridge, 1987), pp.5–6

16. The following section is heavily indebted to Kirk, *Challenge*, ch.1.

17. For the 'new imperialism' and labour see, for example, John C. Appel, 'The Relationship of American Labor to United States Imperialism 1895–1905', University of Wisconsin PhD, 1950; Michael Hunt, *Ideology and US Foreign Policy* (New Haven, 1987); Eric J. Hobsbawm, *The Age of Empire 1875–1914* (London, 1995), ch.3.

18. This section on Gompers' critique of 'un-republican' America is heavily indebted to Kirk, 'Transatlantic Connections and American "Peculiarities": The Shaping of Labour Politics in the United States and Britain, 1893–1908', paper presented to the 113th Annual Meeting of the American Historical Association, Washington DC, January 1999; Stuart B. Kaufman and Peter J. Albert eds., *The Samuel Gompers Papers. Volume 3, Unrest and Depression 1891–94* (Urbana, 1989), pp.514–15, 518. For the expression of similar sentiments see AF of L, *Proceedings*, 1893, pp.11, 14–15; 1895, pp.17, 59; 1899, p.15; 1906, p.32; *American Federationist*, August 1894, pp.120–5 and December 1894, p.228.

19. AF of L, *Proceedings*, 1896, pp.86–7.

20. AF of L, *Proceedings*, 1899, pp.15, 148.

21. Leon Fink, 'The new labor history and the powers of historical pessimism: consensus, hegemony and the case of the Knights of Labor', *The Journal of American History*, vol.75, no. 1 (1988), pp.115–36; David Montgomery, 'Labor

and the republic in industrial America, 1860–1920', *Le Mouvement Social*, April-June 1980, pp.201–15; Kirk, *Challenge*, pp.122–4, 131–44.

22. See, for example, AF of L, *Proceedings*, 1893, for the full preamble.

23. 'Excerpts from Samuel Gompers' Testimony Before the US Strike Commission', in Kaufman and Albert, *Gompers Papers*, pp.569–74. In 1914 Gompers declared that: 'From my earliest understanding of conditions that prevail in the industrial world I have been convinced and I have asserted that the economic interests of the employing class and those of the working class are not harmonious. *That has been my position ever since—never changed in the slightest.* There are times when, for temporary purposes, interests are reconcilable; but *they are temporary only*', *American Federationist*, August 1914, p.624; and in the same issue, pp.623–4, 'Employers, capitalists, stockholders, bondholders—the capitalist class generally—oppose the efforts of the workers in the AF of L and in other organizations to obtain a larger share of the product'.

24. *American Federationist*, February 1902, p.55.

25. AF of L, *Proceedings*, 1895, p.59.

26. *American Federationist*, August 1897, pp.115–16.

27. Marc Karson, *American Labor Unions and Politics 1900–1918* (Carbondale, Illinois, 1958), pp.38–9.

28. See, for example, *American Federationist*, February 1896, pp.221–3; April 1901, pp.118–20; October 1903, pp.1052–3; February 1906, p.97; November 1909, pp.969–70; January 1911, pp.34–5; for the 'difficulties of organizing the negro labor of the South', AF of L, *Proceedings*,1898, p.49.

29. *American Federationist*, March and May 1898; AF of L, *Proceedings*, 1898, pp.5–6.

30. Gompers, *Seventy Years*, vol.1, pp.479–82

31. Ibid., pp.479–91. For trade union progress and developments among these groups see, for example, *American Federationist*, June 1899 for Gompers' letter to Lady Dilke; September 1898, p.138; April 1901, pp.118–20; August 1905, pp.507–10; January 1906, pp.19–21, 36; February 1906, pp.85–6, December 1906, pp.963–7 for the AF of L as 'the only force in society which has concerned itself to any great extent with active and practical work for the advancement of wage-earning women'; April 1910, pp.314–15; August 1910, p.691; January 1911, p.35 for Gompers' continued commitment to the organization of African-Americans; AF of L, *Proceedings*, 1900, pp.12–13, 92; 1905, pp.148, 154, 172; 1906, pp.161–73; 1907, pp.207–8.

32. See, for example, *American Federationist*, February 1896, pp.221–3; October 1897, p.186; June 1911, p.483 for 'working women's' increased 'self-reliance'; August 1913, pp.624–6 for similar comments; April 1912, pp.294–5 for the ability of immigrants to acquire 'American' (ie trade-union) habits; and January 1911, p.36 for more ambiguous attitudes towards the trade-union capacities of African-American workers.

33. See, for example, *American Federationist*, July 1896, pp.90–1; February 1897, p.257; August 1914, pp.621–35; AF of L, *Proceedings*, 1905, p.22; 1907, pp.21–3; 'Excerpts from Samuel Gompers' Testimony', p.579; Montgomery, 'Labor and

the Republic'.

34. *American Federationist*, August 1897, p.116.

35. Gompers, *Seventy Years*, vol.1, pp.381–4, vol.2, pp.33–8; Kaufman and Albert, *Gompers Papers*, pp.516, 588; *American Federationist*, April 1896, p.33; May 1896, p.52; June 1896, p.71; April 1898, p.38; November 1898, pp.175–7; September 1909, p.784; January 1911, p.37; Kirk, 'Transatlantic Connections'; Andrews, *Shoulder*, pp.59–60.

36. Kaufman and Albert, *Gompers Papers*, pp.574, 617, 627–58; Joseph Finn, 'The Great Debate, 1893–1894: A Study of the Controversy on Independent Political Action in the American Federation of Labor in the first half of the 1890s', University of Warwick MA (1969).

37. Samuel Gompers Papers, University of Maryland, reel 231, letterbooks 1883–1924: Gompers to H.C. Frank, 6 February 1918.

38. *American Federationist*, August 1909, p.661; December 1909, pp.1077, 1086; February 1910, p.151; March 1910, pp.225, 243.

39. *American Federationist*, February 1912, pp.135–41.

40. James Gray Pope, 'Labor's constitution of freedom', *The Yale Law Review* 106 (1997) esp. pp.987–90, 1000–2

41. The following section borrows freely from Kirk, 'Transatlantic Connections'.

42. AF of L, *Proceedings*, 1907, pp.17, 21–3.

43. *American Federationist*, April 1908, pp.261–2.

44. See, for example, Kaufman and Albert, *Gompers Papers*, pp.504–5 (letter to Tom Mann); *American Federationist*, November 1895, pp.159–60 (Keir Hardie), and July 1901 (Pete Curran).

45. Kaufman and Albert, *Gompers Papers*, pp.517, 587; AF of L, *Proceedings*, 1896, p.18; 1898, pp.9, 11, 101.

46. *American Federationist*, January 1897, p.237.

47. The following section relies heavily upon Philip Taft, *The AF of L in the Time of Gompers* (New York, 1970), chs 26–7. See also, Gompers, *Seventy Years*, vol. II, chs. 27, 37 and 46; *American Federationist*, November 1909, p.977; December 1909, pp.1076–7.

48. Taft, *The AF of L.*, p.438.

49. *American Federationist*, February 1897, p.259; November 1897, p.215; AF of L, *Proceedings*, 1906, p.178.

50. *American Federationist*, February 1897, pp.259–60.

51. *American Federationist*, February 1897, p.260; August 1898, p.107.

52. *American Federationist*, May 1907, pp.321–30; July, 1913, pp.539–42.

53. AF of L, *Proceedings*, 1905, pp.20–1.

54. *American Federationist*, May 1907, pp.321–30; January 1913, p.42; July 1913, pp.539–42.

55. Delber Lee McKee, 'The American Federation of Labor and American Foreign Policy, 1886–1912', Stanford University PhD, 1952, pp.207 ff., 258; *American Federationist*, May 1907 for a report of Gompers' address to the International Peace Congress, held in New York City; July 1913, p.539.

56. Hobsbawm, *Age of Empire*, p.57.

57. *American Federationist*, March 1900, pp.56–62 for a very interesting account of Gompers' trip to Cuba. See also AF of L, *Proceedings*, 1900, p.21 for the eight-hour strike of Havana workers being broken 'through the arbitrary action' of General Ludlow, the US Governor-General of Havana. For a useful account of the history of Gompers' and the AF of L's assistance to Iglesias and the Puerto Rican labour movement see *American Federationist*, May 1914, pp.320, 325, and Gompers' article in the same issue, 'Porto Rico: Her Present Condition and Fears for the Future', esp.377–88; Gompers, *Seventy Years*, vol. 2, pp.69–74.

58. AF of L, *Proceedings*, 1899, p.16.

59. Ibid., p.148.

60. *American Federationist*, November 1898, p.180. For similar references to the capitalist motive force underlying the new imperialism see the issues of May 1898, p.53; July 1898, p.93 and December 1898, p.203.

61. See, for example, *American Federationist*, November 1897, pp.215–17, July 1898, p.93; Stuart Kaufman, Peter J. Albert and Grace Palladino eds, *The Samuel Gompers Papers*, vol. 5, *An Expanding Movement at the Turn of the Century 1898–1902* (Urbana, 1996), pp.xv–xvi.

62. *American Federationist*, May 1898, p.53; July1898, p.93; AF of L, *Proceedings*, 1899, p.148.

63. AF of L, *Proceedings*, 1898, p.20.

64. McKee, 'The American Federation of Labor', p.229; *American Federationist*, April 1913, p.315; Andrews, *Shoulder*, pp.105, 111, 177.

65. See the references to Foner, Mandel and Larson in note 10 above. For a similar view see Appel, 'The Relationship', p.352.

66. See, for example, *American Federationist*, March 1900, pp.56–62; May 1914, pp.377–88; McKee, 'The American Federation of Labor', ch.3; Andrews, *Shoulder*, p.41, ch.7.

67. Andrews, *Shoulder*, ch.1.

68. *American Federationist*, May 1914, pp.377–88.

69. Andrews, *Shoulder*, p.8, ch.7.

70. Whereas Gompers expressed 'reluctant' support for immigration restriction in relation to European immigrants (on the grounds of 'ruinous' wage and job competition and 'the self-preservation of the American working classes'), he saw Asian workers as 'cheap', 'degraded', and as unable to 'assimilate with our race'. See *American Federationist*, February 1906, p.98; August 1910, p.691; January 1911, pp.17–20; AF of L, *Proceedings*, 1904, pp.170, 240; 1905, pp.29–31; 1906, p.24; 1907, pp.207–8, 315. I am currently undertaking a comparative study of the attitudes of US, British and Australian labour towards 'Orientals' during the late-nineteenth and early-twentieth centuries.

71. C.T.Cramp, 'Impressions of America', *The Labour Magazine*, February 1925, pp.435–7. I am indebted to Kevin Morgan for this reference.

Taking Syndicalism Seriously
David Howell

It is not the Sorels...and such figures who count the most—it is the obscure Bill Jones on the firing line, with stink in his clothes, rebellion in his brain, hope in his heart, determination in his eye, and direct action in his gnarled fist.

Industrial Worker, *8 May 1913*

they burned his big broken bulk of a body and buried the ashes under the Kremlin wall.

John Dos Passos on Big Bill Haywood in The 42nd Parallel *(1930)*

Interpretations of the labour unrest which affected many capitalist societies from the 1900s through to the early 1920s have differed widely and have illuminated the methodological and ideological dispositions of individual historians. There are those who seek to reduce revolts to basic economic concerns: workers act collectively to improve working conditions when labour market conditions favour such activities. In such accounts actors are reduced to the fundamental economic priorities favoured by many economists; wider social agendas are simply ruled out. In contrast, some scholars would argue that such reductionism offers inadequate explanation and social conservatism. Workers' revolts must be understood within the values and standards of their communities; programmes for social change, however fragmentary, should be taken seriously. Once this perspective is applied, then these mobilisations offer a rich reservoir of options on labour movement strategy and democratic alternatives.

One key problem concerns the relevance or irrelevance of syndicalist ideas for these events.[1] Obviously, it would be difficult to argue that vast numbers of workers were inspired to mass action by syndicalist literature. Yet two countervailing points can be made. At a more popular level, amongst some sections of the working class in a range of societies, Direct Action sentiments were powerful. And the debates engendered by these struggles left a significant legacy that included critiques of established forms of democratic politics. This inheritance has often been obscured and deserves to be reassessed—for both its strengths and its weaknesses.

An international movement

Critical assessment can begin with radical images which recover something of the quality of these movements. Some of the most evocative are provided by the Industrial Workers of the World, or 'Wobblies', founded in Chicago in 1905—the songs, the martyrs, the free-speech fights, the strikes against despotic employers. If the resonance of these images has been international, their roots were specifically American. Some lay in the frontier conditions that produced the radical Western Federation of Miners (WFM), others in the craft and ethnic exclusions that characterised the American Federation of Labor. The Wobblies organised amongst the miners and lumber men of the far West, and amongst Eastern factory workers drawn often from ethnic groups excluded by older unions.[2] Few American trade union leaders could have been more expressive of a radical variant on national identity than 'Big Bill' Haywood, miner and WFM organiser, who became perhaps the Wobblies' most symbolic figure.[3] The IWW achieved a brief early flowering in the newly established Nevada mining town of Goldfield, where Wobblies organised not just in the mines but also in the service sector, the bars, the restaurants. The zenith came in January 1907 with a mass parade to commemorate the massacre of St. Petersburg demonstrators in 1905, and to support Haywood and two colleagues awaiting trial in Idaho on a murder charge. 'Down with capitalism! long live the International working class republic', was the theme. But this was a climax, not a prelude.[4]

The radical moment in the malleable conditions of a boom town where the class structure had not solidified was shattered as mineowners allied with the local middle class, with the state government, and through deceit with the federal administration. Yet the IWW, despite internal schisms, continued to have moments of achievement, not least on the East Coast, in the Lowell and Paterson textile strikes. The latter produced a pageant in Madison Square Gardens, a brief alliance between Wobbly activists and New York City's radical intelligentsia.[5]

The influence of the Wobblies soon spread beyond the United States, most predictably perhaps to Western Canada where railroad construction workers in British Columbia and miners on Vancouver Island were influenced by radical union sentiments from across the 49th Parallel.[6] Similar sentiments affected sections of the Australian labour movement. In the summer of 1909, men at the Broken Hill lead mines in western New South Wales fought a long and ultimately unsuccessful strike over wage reductions. Their mistrust of labour politicians and of the conciliation and arbitration system deepened. One of their leaders was Tom Mann, a time-served craftsman and parliamentary socialist. He had left Britain for Australasia in 1902; shortly after the Broken Hill dispute, he returned to Britain via South Africa with a strong commitment to syndicalism.[7] Sentiments supportive of Direct Action were also strong amongst the coalminers of New South Wales. The union president on the state's northern coalfield had been in contact with the Western Federation of Miners.[8] The miners embarked on a long and ultimately failed strike late in 1909. The state government's response was coercive and effective; the setback hindered the development of radical industrial sentiment. There were promising electoral prospects for the Labour Party at both federal and state levels; but as radicals began to indict Labour administrations for non-delivery, so the plausibility of Direct Action revived.

When Tom Mann returned to Britain he rapidly found himself in an industrial situation marked by widespread strikes of both organised and unorganised workers, by violence on picket lines and against individuals seen as transgressing appropriate codes of conduct.[9] 1911 saw the first British railway strike that transcended company identities. If not a thorough national stoppage, the action was highly effective in the industrial areas of northern England, the Midlands, and South Wales. The mobilisation was the achievement of activists who pressurised cautious leaders. 1912 witnessed the first national coal stoppage. Across many industries union membership rocketed. Much more was at stake than attempts to restore real wage levels in conditions of relatively high employment. Workers opposed new managerial practices, criticised the caution of their own officials and attempted to redefine their own communities as places run by workers for workers. When South Wales miners employed in the Cambrian Combine entered a year long and ultimately abortive strike over price lists, one of their guest speakers was 'Big Bill' Haywood.[10]

Perhaps the most dramatic episode within the British Isles occurred in Ireland. Outside the industrial economy of the North East, trade unionism developed slowly and was limited largely to small craft societies. But in 1908, a Liverpudlian Irishman, James Larkin, founded the Irish Transport and General Workers Union (ITGWU).[11] This sought to organise the so-called 'unskilled' and the casually employed, seeking to construct an effective solidarity through the doctrine of 'tainted goods'. In August 1913, there began that great set-piece battle, the Dublin Lockout, as employers combined to combat Larkin's union. The conflict ended over five months later in defeat for the workers. Larkin's attempts to secure sympathetic action by British unions had failed, collapsing into bitter recriminations as he attacked British leaders for their caution.[12]

Larkin was an Irish counterpart to Haywood. A contemporary portrait by a sympathiser can stand as a representation of the movement's style:

> He is one of those born revolutionaries who know not diplomacy, but who believe that the kingdom of Heaven must be taken by violence to-day and tomorrow and the day after...His utopia...would be a world where a general strike was going on all the time. Big and black and fierce, he is a Syndicalist of the street corners...He calls to the surface the very depth of unrest. His theory seems to be that a city should never be allowed a moment's peace so long as there remains a single poor man whose wrongs have not been righted. His genius...is inflammatory. He preaches turmoil.[13]

His second in command, James Connolly, was no gifted platform orator, but a thoughtful exponent of this new trade unionism, and of much else besides. His years in the United States had included involvement with the Wobblies; and he had begun to reason through the promise and problems of the organisation as an instrument for Socialism.[14] In the aftermath of the lockout, Larkin left Ireland for an American lecture tour. His planned brief visit which lasted over eight and a half years and ended with incarceration in Sing-Sing as a casualty of the post-war purge of radicals. Prior to this devastating onslaught, one moment captured the style and the internationalism of this radical movement. In November 1915 the funeral of the executed 'Wobbly' Joe Hill was held in Chicago. Larkin and Haywood spoke from the same platform. The tragedy brought Larkin closer to the IWW, which he eulogised as displaying 'more real revolutionary spirit, greater self-sacrifice, than any other movement the world of labour has produced'.[15]

Beyond the imagery, the romance, the myths, here was a significant radical movement which has been buried under subsequent defeats and political orthodoxies. It was not of course restricted to English-speaking labour movements, although the network that emerges from these examples is a significant one. Syndicalist sentiments were strong in southern Europe and developed a significant presence on the left of established parties such as the German Social Democrats. The radicals expressed in their varied contexts a deep antipathy not just to capitalism but to all forms of bureaucratic elitism, not least to that represented by trade union officialdom. The resource that mattered was neither ballot nor parliament, but the power of the workers at the point of production. As one Welsh syndicalist put it: 'Why cross the river to fill the pail?'[16]

Such sentiments appealed to diverse groups. One early and sympathetic Australian critic noted the similarities between the workers attracted to the IWW in the American West and migrant Australian workers—cane cutters, the casual workers in the shearing sheds and slaughterhouses.[17] They had no network of institutions binding them to the established order, they knew all too well the vagaries of casual employment; their lifestyle could incorporate a rampant individualism but it could equally produce an appreciation of the benefits of solidarity. Yet this radicalism appealed also to those excluded from ethnically privileged and craft based unions and to workers who felt threatened by new techniques of managerial control which imposed onerous new hierarchies and challenged old customs.[18] Railway workers, often accustomed to some autonomy at work, felt oppressed by new supervisory methods; the appeal of Direct Action linked readily to an agenda for 'Worker's Control'. There was also the pressure from an increasingly interventionist state which offered short-term advantages to some workers but set these in the context of a modernising drive towards a rationalised capitalism. Exemplars could be found in Britain's Edwardian Liberalism, in United States' Progressivism, and perhaps above all in Australian 'New Protectionism'. This extended to Labour administrations and the domination of industrial relations by conciliation and arbitration procedures. Whether this framework counted as a relative empowerment of the labour movement has been keenly debated; what is clear is that pre-1914 Australian radicals could see the arbitration system as a powerful mechanism for integrating and disabling the trade union movement.

Syndicalism and socialism

Syndicalism and Direct Action became the spectre haunting polite bourgeois society. During the British coal strike of 1912 a bishop condemned the doctrine as 'wicked, cruel, criminal'.[19] For many Second International socialists, syndicalism and Direct Action were tainted with anarchism, the anathema of the 1890s. Self-consciously ethical socialists such as Ramsay MacDonald and Philip Snowden argued that syndicalism was the antithesis of the constructive community-based socialist project of their rhetorical dreams.[20] Similarly, in the United States Haywood's alleged position on violence led to a critical onslaught within the Socialist Party.[21]

Whatever the credibility of such critics, obviously the syndicalist agenda had clear limitations. An emphasis on workplace struggle meant that radical hopes could collapse into or indeed never transcend militant sectionalism. Indeed, the focus on workplace issues and struggles represents a privileging that has distorted both labour movement strategies and historical explanations. The politics of production has often dominated the politics of consumption; attention has been placed on one public sphere to the detriment of others. Some actors have been placed centre stage; others have been relegated to walk-on parts or to the audience. Syndicalism and Direct Action in this respect shared certain preconceptions with the conventional trade union strategies and labour and social-democratic politics that they so vigorously denounced. Their core constituency was unionised or about to be unionised workers, usually male. The rhetoric of struggle in the workplace and on the picket line celebrated (allegedly) male (supposed) virtues. Many Direct Actionists were not anti-women in an overt sense. No doubt many shared the conventional prejudices of their time; predictably so in an economy like the South Wales coalfield where paid women's work was scarce, and most women carried out intensive unpaid labour to service successive shifts of male family members. Some syndicalists had a credible record in the organisation of women workers; for examples the Wobblies in textile disputes in the eastern United States. But they shared the viewpoint of most progressive contemporaries. The exploitation of women could be ended only through class-based action. For working-class women that meant entry into the paid workforce, trade union experience and political mobilisation.[22] That these supposed instruments of emancipation might themselves be sexually inegalitarian in their internal practices seems to have been rarely discussed.

Despite such limitations, there are two basic reasons why this tradition should be re-examined. One centres around the expression—or non-expression—of working-class interests within capitalist societies. These radicals firmly rejected collaboration and integration; their experiences allow some assessment of the feasibility and value of such a response. Secondly, significant issues are raised about democratic theory and practice, about the openness of allegedly democratic societies and about the democratic credentials of supposedly emancipatory institutions. These issues can be approached through the location of syndicalism and Direct Action within a broader socialist controversy, and through the analysis of an example.

Syndicalism can be situated within the context of Second International socialism, its adherents' assumptions and expectations and their dilemmas. At the end of his life in 1895 Frederich Engels wrote a new introduction to *The Class Struggles in France*. He acknowledged that, in the optimism of 1848, he and Marx had been wrong about the imminence of proletarian revolution and had been influenced excessively by an image of revolution that owed much to perceptions of late 18th century France. Indeed, Engels emphasised that a revolution to end capitalism could not resemble earlier revolutions. In part this was because changes in military technology, communications and city street patterns had meant an end to the era of the barricade. More fundamentally Engels believed that the anticipated socialist revolution could not be an action by a minority:

> The time of surprise attacks, of revolutions carried through by small conscious minorities at the head of unconscious masses is past. When it is a question of a complete transformation of the social organisation, the masses themselves must also be in it, must themselves already have grasped what is at stake...[23]

Engels believed that there existed already a potentially powerful instrument for such a transformation—the Social Democratic Party (SPD). In Germany it had already survived attempts to cripple it by legislation; its encouraging growth showed how socialists could utilise the space provided even by a relatively illiberal state to propagandise, to widen support, to strengthen confidence. But Engels' optimism in 1895 went further. Existing political institutions could be employed to pose a real alternative to the established order:

> And so it happened that the bourgeoisie and the government came to be much more afraid of the legal than of the illegal action of the workers' party, of the results of elections rather than of those of rebellion.[24]

In the last months of his life Engels saw the SPD's progress as inexorable. Its electoral support would expand beyond the industrial working class, a prospect that should not be put at hazard in quixotic demonstrations. Engels believed that the Social Democrats would remain a revolutionary party, but this need not entail a commitment to early confrontation:

> To keep this growth going without interruption until it of itself gets beyond the control of the prevailing governmental system, not to fritter away the daily increasing shock force in unguarded skirmishes, but to keep intact until the decisive day, this is our main task.[25]

The Wilhelmine state continued to subject socialists to a variety of harassments and penalties, but to a considerable degree Engels' expectations about party growth were fulfilled.

In the early 1890s the SPD vote was approaching 1,500,000 and by 1912 it had topped four million; the SPD had become the largest party group in the Reichstag. Party organisation flourished—the celebrated State within a State. The SPD provided an exemplar for similar developments across much of Europe. Yet the forward march of social democracy had its limitations. Even in 1914, only a minority of industrial workers backed the Party; electoral growth had not been a smooth upward progression. The irresponsible character of the German political system meant that progress brought the SPD no nearer to effective power.[26]

Most fundamentally socialist and labour parties had become increasingly fractious forums. The SPD had its celebrated battles between Bernstein, Luxemburg and Kautsky; French Socialists split over the propriety of joining a coalition; for a while many Italian Socialists seemed bewitched by the great liberal conjuror Giolitti, a liaison which provoked thorough criticism from the party's left-wing, including Benito Mussolini.[27]

The tactic of building the party, pursuing electoral success, awaiting the decisive day seemed to some to mean the suffocation of radicalism. The process was portrayed sardonically by Max Weber in 1906:

> Among the masses, the 'respectable' Social Democrats drill the spiritual parade...They accustom their pupils to a submissive attitude towards dogmas and party authorities, or to indulgence in the fruitless play acting of mass strikes or the idle enjoyment of the enervating howls of their hired journalists which are as harmless as they are in the end, laughable in the eyes of their enemies. In short, they accustom them to an 'hysterical wallowing in emotion' which replaces and inhibits economic and political thought and action.[28]

The topic under discussion was Russian socialism, but the target was clearly a broader one. Weber, a liberal in a society where liberalism was at a discount, understood better than many of his contemporaries, the limited character of the SPD's challenge. The decisive day was not that anticipated by Engels, but the party vote in August 1914 for the war credits.

Those socialists who perceived a problem of deradicalisation began within their theoretical assumptions to search for answers. One avenue for investigation was clearly economic. One classic and early instance had been Engels' thesis in the 1880s that the weakness of British socialism could be explained by reference to early industrialisation and consequential monopoly. But by 1886 Engels acknowledged that the monopoly was ending, and it was broadly agreed amongst pre-1914 Socialists that the British case was unique.[29] It needed the trauma of 1914 for Lenin to develop an explanation of socialist degeneration that depended on a conception of monopoly capitalism; in contrast before the War, Kautsky and Hilferding had suggested that the development of monopoly capitalism could advantage social democracy.[30]

In contrast, the syndicalists offered a powerful pre-1914 response. Their diagnoses and strategies raised fundamental questions of socialist and democratic politics. The indictment was thorough—the root of the malaise lay in the agenda of constructing mass socialist parties. Such bodies had to triumph on terrain that worked against them. The quest for votes inevitably meant the dilution of principled class-conscious arguments; parliamentarianism meant acquiescence in bourgeois conventions and thereby a deeper consent to bourgeois ideology. Such priorities distorted the procedure of socialist parties. Not least, a bourgeois intelligentsia came to play a preponderant and conservative role within socialist organisations. After all they had the techniques and self-confidence needed for effective parliamentary performances, often complemented by the crafts of the journalist.[31] Thus syndicalists saw the hierarchy of the wider society replicated within socialist parties; as these parties attempted to succeed under conditions which favoured their opponents.

Some syndicalists acknowledged that the role of bourgeois socialists could not be so straightforward and negative. Thus Robert Michels—a syndicalist before his encounter with and acceptance of elite theory—suggested that deradicalisation was not just a consequence of middle-class contamination.[32] Socialist and trade union organisations offered full-time and relatively well-paid posts to individual workers who were unlikely to put their new-found security and status at risk in any quixotic venture. Such functionaries would see the preservation of party organisation as their objective; any concern with social transformation would become merely a rhetorical means to the organisational goal.

Beatrice and Sidney Webb—intellectually and emotionally antipathetic to syndicalism—had recognised in the 1890s that trade union imperatives generated a leadership stratum with its own interests. As the extent of collective bargaining grew, so trade union officials required not just negotiating skills, but technical knowledge. British cotton textile unions appointed officials only after formal examination which included complex arithmetical calculations.[33] Such divisions based on attributions of expertise weakened any control exercised over officials by members. The Webbs viewed this as a tendency central to the growth of a stable and effective trade unionism; any element of democratic practice had to be accommodated within the rule of the expert.

In contrast, a thorough syndicalist agenda involved the development of organisations that were democratic in structure and practice, and radical in policy. They should be industrial in character, thereby avoiding the corrupting compromises of electoral and parliamentary politics, and also perhaps the isolation of some socialist groups. Moreover, such organisations would be thoroughly proletarian in character. Yet the broad agenda raised one obvious difficulty. The actually existing trade unions that syndicalists were familiar with hardly seemed potential vehicles for radical change. Within the SPD trade unionists typically adopted cautious positions that were the despair of the left. The American Federation of Labor (AF of L) under Samuel Gompers was the despair of socialists and radicals of diverse persuasions. By 1910 the character of the Australian labour movement had been significantly influenced by the arbitration system.

The critics' responses varied. In the United States syndicalists went it alone through the Industrial Workers of the World and ignored the affiliates of the AF of L. The strategy was plausible given the class and ethnic exclusivities practised by many AF of L unions. British syndicalists usually rejected dual unionism and argued for the radical reform of existing organisations. With the formation and wartime expansion of the Irish Transport and General Workers' Union, the labour movement in nationalist Ireland became heavily influenced by ideas of direct action and the One Big Union. Whatever choice radicals made on the question of dual unionism they faced the major problem of devising democratic structures for their organisations.

The Miners' Next Step

The central themes and problems emerge with particular force in a vibrant piece of applied political theory written in 1911–12, not by a great name but by a group of young talented South Wales miners—the pamphlet entitled *The Miners' Next Step*.[34] It was produced within an environment which might have been deliberately designed to radicalise. The South Wales coalfield had continued to expand its output, basically through increasing the workforce, a strategy which meant declining productivity. With many firms dependent on export markets this meant that employers became increasingly concerned to cut wage costs; they attacked the problem through the erosion of customs and the holding down of piece rates. One storm centre developed over the custom of compensation for work in 'abnormal places' where geological problems made it difficult to earn an adequate wage. The issue was a window on a question of principle—should wage levels be determined by profitability or by notions of justice and of need? Some capitalists responded to the changing world by amalgamations linked to new systems of managerial control. It was perhaps significant that a year-long stoppage in 1910–11 involved the miners of the Cambrian Combine, one of the largest amalgamations.[35] The search for additional labour led to massive immigration into South Wales from rural southern England; demographic change sapped the consensual power of pre-existing cultural institutions such as the nonconformist chapels. Instead of community identities founded on shared interests and values expressed perhaps through the Welsh language, a class identity was heightened, a development facilitated by the region's dominance by one industry. Superficially the coalfield could be portrayed as buoyant down to 1914—its boosters spoke of 'American Wales'—but from 1910 onwards the tensions within the coalfield were expressed in stoppages, in increasingly radical rhetoric and by the emergence of a significant left within the South Wales Miners' Federation.

Within this turbulent world the conciliatory policies and style of established miners' leaders were subject to increasing criticism. The industry's conciliation system worked ponderously and only produced meagre economic gains. This is the starting point of *The Miners' Next Step*; it leads directly to a critique not of specific leaders, but of a particular tradition of leadership. One aspect of leaders' deradicalisation links with the contention that such positions serve as means of individual social mobility: 'They, the leaders, become "gentlemen", they become MPs and have considerable social prestige because of this power'. But beneath the social ethos, there is the logic of the system of wage bargaining:

> The policy of conciliation gives the real power of the men into the hands of a few leaders...The conference or ballot is only a referee...The workmen for a time look up to these men and when things are going well they idolise them. The employers respect them. Why? Because they have the men, the real power in the hollow of their hands.

For the critics the policy and the leadership strategy are linked:

> What is really blameworthy is the conciliation policy which demands leaders of this description...they are 'trade unionists by trade' and their profession demands certain privileges. The greatest of all these are plenary powers...every inroad the rank and file makes on this privilege lessens the power and prestige of the leader...The leader then has an

interest—a vested interest—in stopping progress. They have...in some things an antagonism of interests with the rank and file.[36]

There follows a balance-sheet on the qualities of trade-union leadership. On the positive side of the ledger, leadership has a potential for efficiency and system, and for responsibility; but against this, leadership implies an unequal power relationship which corrupts the leaders and degrades the led. The leader protects himself by bestowing patronage on the pliable; the autonomy and creativity of the membership are frustrated. 'Sheep cannot be said to have solidarity.'[37] The animosity between officials and rank and file achieved sharp expression after four months of the Cambrian Combine Strike. Two officials sent to South Wales by the Miners' Federation of Great Britain were met at the strike storm-centre of Tonypandy by a hostile crowd suggesting that they 'go back to England'. One of the officials saw the breakdown of ordered trade unionism: 'Anything is better than the state of anarchy and red riot such as prevails at Tonypandy today.'[38]

Oligarchy and democracy

The negative portrait has similarities with Weber's dismissal of the socialist pretensions. Positive alternatives can be found in socialist literature; for instance in Marx's insistence that working-class emancipation must be the achievement of the workers; there are also images within John Stuart Mills' discussion of decentralised socialism, and his insistence that such a reformed society requires agents technically and morally capable of its achievement.[39]

Such images were rejected not just by Weber, but also by his one-time syndicalist correspondent Michels, once the latter had imbibed elite theory. For such sceptics, domination by the few was inevitable; all that could be debated was the identity of the few and the very limited checks upon them. The authors of *The Miners' Next Step*, in denying such pessimism, contributed not just to debates about trade union democracy, but also to a much broader pre-1914 argument about oligarchy and democracy.

Thus the pamphlet's proposals commence with the aspiration: 'Workmen the "Bosses", "Leaders" the Servants'.[40] The proposed constitution is constructed around two principles. The priority given to rank-and-file democracy requires decentralisation and incentives for mass participation. Power must be taken from the full-time officials and given to the membership. They should determine policy through lodge and ballot votes, the union executive should be composed of lay members and would be responsible to a delegate conference. Officials should be subject to the control of this democratised structure. The authors were optimistic that the reforms would facilitate increased and more informed participation. This would result from a growing awareness that 'the lodge meetings are the place where things are really done'. The scenario has a resemblance to Mill's developmental view of democracy.

> *It will raise the Status of the Workers.* By giving them *real* powers in the lodge room. It will stimulate every available ounce of intellect to work full pressure. There the workers will learn to legislate for themselves on matters which touch them most closely.[41]

This decentralised participatory vision has to confront the problem of effectiveness. If there is to be 'decentralisation for negotiating', there must be 'Centralisation for Fighting'. If local negotiations produce no solution, then the decision on whether to widen the issue would be taken by the executive in consultation with a delegate conference. The decisive criterion for widening a dispute is that of principle as opposed to sectionalism:

> The effect of the constitution would abolish sectional strikes. All questions become, under this system, either questions of principle which we are prepared to fight with the whole strength of our organisation, or questions which should be fought locally...Grievances are not questions with us so much of *numbers* as of *principles*. It might, and probably would be, deemed advisable to have a strike of the whole organisation to defend one man from victimisation...[42]

The constitutional agenda is linked thoroughly to the espousal of a militant industrial policy. Conciliation is rejected in favour of a bald assertion of conflicting interests: 'The old policy of identity of interest between employers and ourselves be abolished, and a policy of open hostility installed.'[43]

Informed by this antagonism, the tactic is to gain as many benefits as possible within the existing order:

> a continual agitation be carried in favour of increasing the minimum wage, and shortening the hours of work, until we have extracted the whole of the employers' profits.[44]

This strategy has as its ultimate objective the construction of an organisation that would take over the coal industry and administer it in the interest of the workers. Such a vision involves a rejection of state ownership—'a

National Trust with all the force of the Government behind it'. Instead there must be workplace democracy. Instead of private capitalists controlling the coal industry, decisions should be taken by those most affected:

> To have a vote in determining who shall be your fireman, manager, inspector, etc is to have a vote in determining the conditions which rule your working life.[45]

The ultimate vision is of industries organised around a principle of workers' control responding in ways determined by workforces to the requirements of a co-ordinator—a Central Production Board. The authors declare: 'Any other form of democracy is a delusion and a snare'. Yet they acknowledge the vision can be realised only slowly. It can occur only on an economy wide basis. All industries have to be organised in the same fashion. 'Their rate of progress conditions ours, all we can do is to set an example and the pace'.[46]

The strategic conception is influenced heavily by syndicalism. Yet the pamphleteers also envisage a limited place for political action. Parliamentarians would be subject to control by the delegate conference; they should express members' views on legislation relevant to working conditions, and they can oppose governmental tendencies to act on behalf of employers.[47] Nevertheless, the authors clearly felt that the industrial struggle was decisive and that it was there that questions of procedure, institutions and strategy must be conclusively settled.

Scepticism about the blueprint is all too easy. Whatever the formal constitution, full-time officials would retain distinctive and significant resources—knowledge, presentational skills and time for example. Accordingly 'control' by the membership would be a matter more of form than of substance. When some British railway unions amalgamated in 1913 to form the National Union of Railwaymen (NUR), the new organisation's structure was influenced by contemporary debates about trade union democracy.[48] The NUR Executive was composed of lay members and subject to the authority of the annual general meeting, yet the principal full-time officers generally dominated policy-making. Such a pattern of decision-making cannot be separated from the content of policy debates, yet the expertise and status of the full-time officials was clearly important. Moreover, even an 'unofficial' executive set up to control the officials could develop distinctive interests and resources; not least that some Executive members hoped to become full-time officers. Most fundamentally, the achieved levels of participation and of competence by members would perhaps be insufficient to achieve a significant rank and file control. In the South Wales coalfield where many miners lived in a pit village next to their workplace, there was at least the credible prospect of significant levels of participation at least on issues of fundamental concern. Amongst workers in many other industries—and indeed amongst miners in some other coalfields—the same umbilical link between workplace and residence did not exist. Accordingly the prospects of effective control through high levels of participation could seem implausible.

The criticisms are familiar and are so perhaps because experience suggests that they have some validity. Yet two responses to the sceptic are significant. One is provoked by Michels' rejection of his earlier syndicalism, in *Political Parties*, with its uneasy synthesis of elite theory and Marxist vocabulary, its fidgety oscillations between an insistence on an iron law of oligarchy, and the noting of widespread oligarchic tendencies. Amidst so much uncertainty of discourse and conclusion, Michels is adamant about one thing; the details of formal institutions are irrelevant. Any syndicalist who honestly applies his analysis to his own organisation becomes on this argument an elite theorist. Yet Michels' brief chapter on the syndicalist alternative is notably weak and lacks any proper consideration of syndicalist proposals for constitutional reform.[49] From Michels' standpoint their content is irrelevant. All socialist and syndicalist cats are grey. Yet arguably any organisation where full-time officials are banned from the executive and where ballots are frequent has the potential to operate in a fashion different from one where full-time—and perhaps permanent—officers dominate discussion and references to the membership are rare. The outcome may not be the mass participatory organisation desired by the syndicalists let alone the Rousseauesque democracy sometime used by Michels as a misleading measuring stick. But if divergent union constitutions can be assessed for their capacity to engender more mass involvement and influence, then the Michels of *Political Parties* was thoroughly mistaken whilst these South Wales miners at least were posing a meaningful question. If the sceptic's admonitions are taken too far, then they threaten not simply traditions of socialist democracy, but also that developmental liberal tradition associated with Mill which claimed that with appropriate resources and incentives individuals would expand their political capacities through action, most notably through decentralised structures. For the pamphleteers, consideration of organisational structures and practices cannot be divorced from policy:

> no constitution, however admirable in its structure, can be of any avail
> unless the whole is quickened and animated by that which will give it the

breath of life—a militant, aggressive policy.[50]

The feasibility of this prospect links back to the hope that some issues can be generalised across the whole workforce and generate a united response. This expectation arguably made more sense in the South Wales coalfield than it could amongst many other groups of workers. In 1912 close to 200,000 men worked in the South Wales mines offering a density and a regional homogeneity of occupation that had few parallels. But amongst South Wales miners there were diverse interests. There were divisions produced by skill and by working conditions; the physical structure of the coalfield with its deep valleys produced a sense of place that could lead to both immediate solidarity and parochialism. If shared perceptions and commitment were needed to produce an effective radical union then arguably even in South Wales, the obstacles loomed larger than the syndicalists implied.

The pamphlet's longer-term vision of a flowering of equivalent radical and democratic unions in other industries raises another fundamental question. What would be the character of the consciousness generated within such organisations, especially given the authors' insistence that one core element in any democratic society must be the democratisation of the work place? Perhaps the outcome would be a strong occupational consciousness, with miners keenly aware of miners' interests, and other workers of their own occupational priorities. Indeed far beyond the problematic of syndicalism, arguably historians and activists have all too often read occupational solidarities in class terms.

The connection within the pamphlet between internal democracy and radical policies is paralleled by a continuing concern of Michels in both his syndicalist and elite theory phases. Yet why should the linkage be readily assumed? There have been trade unions where the leadership have been more radical on policy than many of their members. The British National Union of Mineworkers after 1982 is an obvious case. The syndicalist assumption surely has apparent validity only if there is a definitional sleight of hand, whereby the characterisation of policy as radical is restricted to organisations with genuinely democratic procedures.

Beyond these problems lies the core of the syndicalist critique. Workers' interests can be advanced only by a militant policy aimed at the abolition of capitalism and incorporating transitional policies that provide both immediate benefits and a contribution to that fundamental objective. Syndicalist writings resonate with a passionate belief in the potential power of the working class, a potential whose realisation is thwarted by a range of factors including the structures and procedures of existing trade unions. Scepticism about such a class capacity must affect any appraisal. If syndicalist optimism about such collective self-emancipation is assessed as unrealistic, then the limiting compromises made by parliamentarians and trade union leaders may be more in the interests of those they represent.

A syndicalist moment?

Here is the complex but necessary problem of counterfactuals. Historians have debated how far by 1914, the appeal of Direct Action was on the wane. Auguries were mixed; what is clear is that within the changed context of societies at war, industrial radicals were able to draw on sentiments that resulted from shortages, inflation and the growth of state authoritarianism. In Australia, such radicalisation was influenced by the perceived failures of labour administrations and by the increasingly bitter debate over conscription, a furore which provoked sentiments of anti-militarism, the threat of industrial regimentation and hysteria that conscription would produce a White Australia defenceless against the 'Asiatic hordes'.[51] The integration of British trade unions into the wartime state produced space for effective shop stewards committees especially in sections of the engineering industry which resisted attempts to dilute the craftsmen's preserve through the employment of workers—both men and women—who had not served their time.[52] Within some of the mining unions Miners' Reform Committees emerged which criticised entrenched leaderships in the radical terms of *The Miners' Next Step*.[53] The Wobblies expanded significantly within the United States in the period between the start of the European War and American entry in April 1917. The IWW organised effectively amongst the harvest workers, 'timber beasts' and miners of the West; in his office in Chicago Haywood could claim to be the leader of a radical union with an exciting future.[54] Ireland after the Easter Rising of 1916 was not just a society where the old Nationalist Party gave way to Sinn Fein. The spiral of misunderstanding, repression and alienation that produced the War of Independence was intertwined with the advent of a radical labour movement. From 1917, the ITGWU achieved major breakthroughs in small town and rural Ireland: this, more than 1913, was arguably Ireland's syndicalist moment.[55]

Yet these advances were sharply repelled, highlighting what many critics have viewed as the fundamental flaw in the syndicalist position. The early months of the war in the United States saw an onslaught on the IWW despite the concern within the organisation that the issue of American intervention should not be seen as a matter of principle. Both the state and vigilantes combined with employers to attack the IWW's organisation. In July 1917 combination produced the forcible deportation of striking miners from Bisbee, Arizona. They were taken by train to the middle of the Arizona desert where a mass tragedy was averted by the intervention of the army. Instead of a return to Bisbee, the strikers were kept in a military camp for three months. Strike actions in Butte, Montana were destroyed through intimidation and the lynching of a Wobbly leader, Frank Little. Most decisively, in September 1917 Wobbly halls were raided by federal agents and 166 Wobblies were indicted on conspiracy charges. The outcome was a mass trial in Chicago with the predictable consequence of sentences of up to twenty years.[56] This was an harbinger of the extensive repression against the American left after the Armistice.

The Australian counterpart was a Sydney trial of Wobblies on charges of seditious conspiracy and incendiarism. Conviction was based on flimsy evidence by informers; a threadbare justification that precipitated a campaign for the prisoners' release.[57] Yet the trial and accompanying harassment weakened the power of Australian Direct Action as did the failure of the New South Wales General Strike of 1917.[58] In Britain repression was used less often, but the leaders of the Clyde Workers Committee, opponents of dilution and of conscription, were arrested and deported from Glasgow. Socialists who backed the committee but lacked an industrial base were jailed.[59]

These harsh experiences indicated that the Direct Action perspective had been thoroughly naive about state power. The idea that somehow power in the workplace could undercut or circumvent the state was exposed as a dangerous illusion. This was demonstrated forcefully after the war as established rulers, already neurotic in the light of the Russian experience, confronted radical industrial challenges. The United States left was battered into submission through the repression symbolised by the Palmer Raids.[60] British radical trade unionists found themselves ensnared in the critical year of 1919 with a state that offered a powerful blend of inducement, conciliation and coercion.[61] The ITGWU had a complex relationship with Sinn Fein during the War of Independence. As the Republicans set up a system of dual power, so the trade unions used the incapacity of the British state as the opportunity to seek wage increases through Direct Action. When workers in nationalist Ireland struck for two days in support of political hunger strikers, several trades councils labelled themselves Soviets to administer services. Yet with the establishment of the Free State, the national revolution was openly revealed as socially conservative. In the context of spiralling economic depression, employers sought to roll back the unions' post-1917 gains. With the murderous civil war settled, the state threw its weight behind the employers. Eventually in the autumn of 1923 a trade union movement whose radical identity was already eroded was defeated heavily on several fronts. The national revolution had happened; the radical trade union movement had been destroyed.[62]

The collapse of Direct Action agendas in Britain also indicated the brittleness of the claim that power lay in the workshop or the mine. Radical self-confidence, high in 1919 during the brief post-war boom, collapsed as boom turned into recession in some well unionised sectors, and strategy was undercut by the capacity of employers to victimise activists. In Glasgow during the 1920s, it was commented bitterly but accurately that yesterday's shop steward is today's leader of the unemployed. One symbolic moment in this collapse—perhaps symptomatic rather than causal—came on 15 April 1921, the 'Black Friday' of the British labour movement when the Triple Alliance of Miners, Railwaymen and Transport Workers collapsed as the two latter groups called off their imminent sympathetic action in support of locked-out miners. An academic close to events wrote of the panic that struck delegates faced with the need to put theory and rhetoric into practice—a panic on which cautious union leaders could capitalise readily. Such capitalisation involved appeals to sectionalism as Jimmy Thomas the Railwaymen's leader—the very model of a business unionist—emphasised the security and value of members' conditions which should not be hazarded in support of intemperate miners' leaders.[63] This victory for sectionalism arguably highlighted and facilitated the post-war stabilisation. For radical trade unionists, it was the ultimate sell-out which significantly they were powerless to prevent.

The defeat of syndicalism was not simply at the hands of states and employers. This radicalism was also a victim of the Bolshevik revolution—or at least of what became the orthodox interpretation of that event. Many syndicalists became communists, many were zealously orthodox, a few carried the stigmata of their former allegiance. The suppression of Anarcho-Syndicalists in the Spanish Civil War was a brutal finale. As the One Way to Revolution crystallised through canonical texts, so this older tradition of revolutionary socialism and democracy was patronisingly dismissed. Robin Page Arnot pronounced many years later an epitaph for *The Miners' Next Step*. Lenin 'mercilessly' exposed syndicalism's 'theoretical pretensions'. Yet as Page Arnot acknowledged, 'it was not until the artillery of Lenin was brought to bear on it in 1920 that the Syndicalist doctrines were overcome.'[64]

The tone, the imagery, the sense of dismissal and closure are familiar. The rupture on the revolutionary left is captured in the last years of Bill

Haywood. He jumped bail in the United States and took refuge in the Soviet Union, submerging his radicalism in vodka, communicating in sign language with his Russian wife, a tragic testimony to syndicalism's defeat. And yet the collapse of old certainties about socialism suggests the need to abandon a teleological vision in which primitive strategies give way to more scientific ones. Arguably the problems of socialism and democracy have been viewed through a limited—and limiting—range of lenses for too long. The historical context of the syndicalist moment should be re-examined; with all its strategic and political limitations; its arguments about democracy, its critiques of instruments and strategies deserve to be taken seriously.

Notes

1. For recent analyses Marcel van der Linden 'Second Thoughts on Revolutionary Syndicalism', *Labour History Review*, vol. 63 no. 2 (1998), pp.182–96; Richard Price, 'Contextualising British Sydicalism c1907-c1920', *Labour History Review*, vol. 63 no. 3 (1998), pp.261–76
2. For an account of the IWW see Melvyn Dubofsky *We Shall Be All* (Chicago, 1969); also Stewart Bird, Dan Georgakas and Deborah Shaffer, *Solidarity Forever. An Oral History of the IWW* (Chicago, 1985).
3. For Haywood see Melvyn Dubofsky, *Big Bill Haywood* (Manchester, 1987).
4. Sally Zanjani *Goldfield, The Last Gold Rush on Western Frontier* (Athens, Ohio 1992); Sally Zanjani and Guy Louis Rocha, *The Ignoble Conspiracy: Radicalism on Trial in Nevada* (Reno, 1986); *60th Congress 1st Session House of Representatives*, Document No. 607: Papers Relative to Labour Troubles at Goldfield, Nevada; J. Anthony Lukas, *Big Trouble* (New York, 1987).
5. Robert A Rosenstone, *Romantic Revolutionary: A Biography of John Reed* (Harmondsworth, 1982), ch. 8; Eric Homberger, *John Reed* (Manchester, 1990), pp.46–51.
6. Mark Leler, *Where the Fraser River Flows* (Vancouver, 1990).
7. Joseph White, *Tom Mann* (Manchester, 1991), ch. 5.
8. Robin Gollan, *The Coalminers of New South Wales* (Melbourne, 1963) ch. 6.
9. Bob Holton, *British Syndicalism* (London, 1976).
10. Ibid., ch. 5.
11. Emmet Larkin, *James Larkin* (London, 1965).
12. Ibid., chs 6–7; Bill Moran, '1913, Jim Larkin and the British labour movement', *Saothar 4* (1978), pp.35–49.
13. 'Anarchism in Dublin', *New Statesman*, 6 September 1913.
14. David Howell, *A Lost Left: Three studies in socialism and nationalism* (Manchester, 1986), esp. ch.4.
15. See Larkin, *James Larkin*, pp.208–10 for this episode.
16. The statement is attributed to the miners' leader Noah Ablett; for a study of

his politics see David Egan 'Noah Ablett, 1883–1935', *Llafur* (1986), pp.19–30.

17. Vere Gordon Childe, *How Labour Governs: A study of workers' representation in Australia* (Melbourne, 1964 edn; first published 1923 by the Labour Publishing Co Ltd, London); see esp. pp.132–4 for a discussion of the similarities—and differences—between the United States and Australia.

18. For discussion of the United States see David Montgomery, *The Fall of the House of Labor* (Cambridge Mass., 1989), esp. ch.5 for changing managerial techniques.

19. The Bishop of Southwell cited J.E. Williams, *The Derbyshire Miners* (London, 1962) p.424.

20. J. Ramsay MacDonald, *Syndicalism. A critical examination* (London, 1912); Phillip Snowden, *Socialism and Syndicalism* (London, n.d.).

21. See Nick Selvatore, *Eugene V. Debs: Citizen and Socialist* (Urbana, Illinois, 1982) pp.242–58; Sally M. Miller, *Victor Berger and the Promise of Constructive Socialism 1910–20.* (Westport, Conn., 1973) chs 3 and 6; Ira Kipnis, *The American Socialist Movement: 1897–1912* (New York, 1968) chs. 7 and 18.

22. For a classic statement of this position see Clara Zetkin, 'Proletarian Women and Socialist Revolution' in R. Miliband and J. Saville, eds, *The Socialist Register 1976* (London, 1976) pp.192–201.

23. In Karl Marx, *Selected Works Volume 2* (London, 1942), p.187.

24. Ibid., p.183.

25. Ibid., p.189.

26. The classic analysis remains Carl Schorske, *German Social Democracy 1905–1917. The Origins of the Great Schism* (Cambridge Mass., 1955).

27. Gwyn Williams, *Proletarian Order* (London, 1975), chs. 1–2.

28. Max Weber, 'The prospects for liberal democracy in Tsarist Russia' (1906) in W. G. Runciman, ed., *Weber Selections in Translation* (London, 1978) p.283.

29. See Engels, 'England in 1845 and In 1885', originally in *Commonweal* 1 March 1885, then utilised in his preface to the English edition of *The Condition of the Working Class in England* (1892).

30. For a discussion of this development see David Beetham, 'Reformism and the "bourgeoisification" of the labour movement' in Carl Levy, ed. *Socialism and the Intelligentsia 1888–1914* (London, 1987) esp. pp.123–29.

31. Ibid., pp.109–23.

32. Ibid., pp.114–16 citing sources from Michels' syndicalist period.

33. Sidney and Beatrice Webb, *Industrial Democracy* (London, 1897) footnote pp.197–9 for an examination paper.

34. *The Miners' Next Step* (London, 1972 edn; introduction by by Merfyn Jones). For background documentation see David Egan 'The Unofficial Reform Committee and the Miners' Next Step', *Llafur* (1978), pp.64–80.

35. L.J. Williams, 'The Road to Tonypandy', *Llafur* (1973), pp.41–52; also Dai Smith, *Wales! Wales?* (London, 1984) ch. 3.

36. *The Miners' Next Step*, p.15.

37. Ibid., pp.18–20.

38. L.J. Williams, 'Road', p.41.

39. For Mill see his 'Chapters on socialism' in Geraiant L. Williams, ed., *John Stuart Mill on Politics and Society* (London, 1976). For Marx see the discussion of the Paris Commune in The Civil War in France.

40. The Miners' Next Step, p.21.

41. Ibid., p.27.

42. Ibid., p.27.

43. Ibid., p.29.

44. Ibid., p.30.

45. Ibid., p.32.

46. Ibid., p.32.

47. Ibid., p.24.

48. For the formation of the NUR see Philip Bagwell. *The Railwaymen* (London, 1963), ch. 13, and the discussion of syndicalist influences in Holton, *British Syndicalism*, chs 6 and 12.

49. Robert Michels, *Political Parties* (New York, 1959 edn), part 5, ch.3.

50. *The Miners' Next Step* p.30.

51. See for example Ray Evans, *Loyalty and Disloyalty: social conflict on the Queensland home front* (Sydney, 1987).

52. The classic presentation remains James Hinton, *The First Shop Stewards' Movement* (London, 1973).

53. For a lucid analysis that locates this moment In a broader context, see Alan Campbell, 'From independent collier to militant miner. Tradition and change in the trade union consciousness of the Scottish miners', *Scottish Labour History Journal, 24* (1989), pp.8–23.

54. See Dubofsky, *Big Bill Haywood* pp.86–94.

55. On this see Emmet O'Connor, *Syndicalism in Ireland 1917–23* (Cork, 1988) and *A Labour History of Ireland 1824–1960* (Dublin, 1992) ch.5.

56. For material on this see Bird, Georgakas and Shaffer, *Solidarity*, pp.125–36.

57. Ian Turner, *Sydney's Burning :an Australian political conspiracy* (Sydney, 1969).

58. See Childe, *How Labour Governs*, ch. 11.

59. See Hinton, *First Shop Stewards' Movement.*

60. See William Preston Jr., *Aliens and Dissenters. Federal suppression of radicals 1903–1933* (Cambridge Mass., 1963).

61. There is still a need for work on this critical year, not least on the containment of radical challenges within the coal industry. For a discussion of one theme which links to the argument of this paper see M.G. Woodhouse 'Mines for the nation or mines for the miners: alternative perspectives on industrial democracy 1919–1921'. *Llafur* (1978) pp.92–109.

62. See O'Connor, *Syndicalism* and *A Labour History*, op.cit.

63. See G.D.H. Cole, *Labour In The Coal Mining Industry 1914–1921* (Oxford, 1923), esp. pp.217–18. For railway union deliberations in 1921 see David Howell *Respectable Radicals: studies in the politics of railway trade unionism* (Aldershot, 1999) pp.315–21.

64. Robin Page Arnot, *The Miners Years of Struggle* (London, 1953) pp.117–18.

Housing the Masses
Ideas and experiments in the US in the 1920s

Rosalyn Baxandall and Elizabeth Ewen

In the United States as opposed to Europe, the suburbs are places where the wealthy live and the middle class aspire to. Or so the myth goes. Our book, *Picture Windows: How the Suburbs Happened* examines the historical development of suburbia in relation to pivotal issues of twentieth-century American life. Unlike conventional cliches which see the development of suburbia as a post-war phenomenon, our book shows how suburbia arose from nearly a century of heated social debates over the American standard of living, and the need to provide people with decent housing regardless of social class. This article focuses on how visionary planners and architects during the 1920s and 1930s, in an attempt to solve the 'housing crisis', created experimental communities that prefigured a suburban way of life that took hold after the Second World War. These communities pioneered modern architectural and production methods and were affordable to those exluded from the private real estate market. After the Second World War there was a serious debate influenced by these visionaries about whether the government, or the private builders subsidized by the government, would construct mass suburban housing. Unfortunately the commercial master builders like William Levitt seized the day, eliminating the democratic and communitarian aspects the visionaries thought so essential. The only housing the government was allowed to build by the commercial giants was housing for the extremely poor and these massive unattractive blocks were built largely in the inner cities.

Filene and Ford

If the housing industry was only interested in building houses for the upper middle class and the wealthy, who would consider the housing needs of the masses? During the suburban boom of the early 1920s and the later housing bust, a range of social critics—socialists, utopians, communitarians, social workers, progressive architects, members of the arts and crafts movement, trade unionists and enlightened businessmen—argued that housing was the burning social issue of the era. Whether 'the people' had decent places to live, they felt, was the true measure of whether the new consumer economy could live up to its promise of endless bounty, mitigate the old misery of the working class and lay to rest the class conflict that haunted the industrial age. As part of their larger social and aesthetic agenda for the machine age, visionaries in the 1920s sought to put into practice inventive ideas about housing working- and middle-class people, advocating methods of mass production methods and innovative designs.

The ideas of Edward Filene had a great impact on the social thinkers and planners of the period. Filene was a progressive department store magnate who pioneered radical employment practices such as good wages, a profit-sharing plan, a 40-hour working week and medical benefits. His famous department store Filene's in Boston was a model of the new consumer economy; opened for all classes who shopped on different floors depending on their wealth.[1] Filene was also a writer and social thinker. In 1925, he wrote a highly influential book, *The Way Out*. From his vantage point as both businessman and progressive, he recognized that a capitalist society that retained the conditions of what he called 'the first industrial revolution', marred by class conflict and a growing disparity between rich and poor, risked massive social unrest. Filene argued that the benefits of the 'second industrial revolution' should be extended to the working class. He believed that an enlightened, humanitarian consumer capitalism could content the masses, defusing working-class militancy and discrediting socialist ideas.

Filene's vision stemmed from Frederick Winslow Taylor's scientific management ideas and entrepreneurs like Henry Ford who put these ideas into action, making mass production possible and profitable. Taylor's labour method re-organised the workforce and the workplace by allowing management to take the production process out of workers' control. Assembly lines that broke down the labour process into simple individual tasks no longer required skilled workers in the way old industrial factories had. Managers were trained to plan and supervise, increasing speed and production.[2] Ford showed how the application of Taylorism could speed up production and pay workers higher wages simultaneously. Filene argued that the challenge to American businessmen of the 1920s was: '*Fordize or fail....We can repeat the causes or reverse the results of the old Industrial Revolution*'.[3]

How would Ford's assembly line make this second industrial revolution different from the first? 'The business man of the future must produce prosperous customers as well as saleable goods', asserted Filene. 'His whole business policy must look forward to creating great buying power among the masses. The business man of the future must fill the pockets of the workers and the consumers before he can fill his pockets.'[4]

Filene argued that workers needed higher wages, shorter hours, quality machine-made products, new housing and mass education—in short, more economic 'freedom'—before they could become consumers. And Filene predicted that a consumer society with its perpetual cycle of abundance, of mass production fuelling mass consumption, would be a peaceful society:

> Economic freedom [would] actually change men's interests and motives. Today the minds of the masses are centered on the getting of economic necessities. If we can make getting the necessities of life a much smaller part of men's lives—as we can under a regime of mass production and mass distribution—men's minds will inevitably turn to other higher issues...Most of the social and economic issues that now keep the world on edge will disappear. Men who can take care of the whole material side of life by working, say six hours a day, simply won't be interested in socialism or communism.

Instead, workers would 'have a wider margin of money and leisure, and as their taste and sense of values grow in that freedom, we shall see a new competition for beauty and refinement'.[5]

Filene believed that modern workers would express their new sense of freedom in the consumer marketplace. He cited the automobile industry as a perfect example. Henry Ford's assembly line workers were paid at the then incredible wage of five dollars a day. In turn, workers poured their money back into the economy, buying cars, taking vacations, going to the movies. Mass production made cars, and the leisure pursuits they encouraged, affordable for the masses, even for car workers. Thus, Filene redefined democracy as people's freedom to consume. What was important for citizens, he thought, was not the right to vote or participate in the politics, but rather a democracy consisting of vast choices of mass-produced goods, including houses. 'Make houses like Fords', he insistently urged. The slogan drew immediate attention from housing reformers and innovators, eventually making its way into business thinking, New Deal goverment philosophy, and ultimately, the popular press.

Mumford and the RPAA

The Regional Planning Association of America (RPAA), a small, informal but influential group, based in New York City, took Filene's ideas seriously.[6] The organisation brought together visionary intellectuals, activists, architects, planners and financiers who were interested in creating democratic communities based on social rather than commercial principles. The group included the influential urban theorist Lewis Mumford; the housing author and activist Catherine Bauer; and social architects Henry Wright and Clarence Stein. It exerted considerable influence, directly shaping the policies and priorities of the New Deal[7] and indirectly inspiring the emergence of post-war suburbs, especially, Levittown. In particular, the RPAA believed in the necessity for the modernisation of housing. They based their theory and practice on the idea that the machine age had fundamentally altered the relationship between people, houses, technology and the environment. The group proposed building communities with well-made, efficient, affordable houses and space for both pedestrians and cars, places where civic life would be structured around new forms of work and leisure.[8]

Members of the RPAA had a broad vision of housing for the modern age. They criticised past urban housing reform movements for concentrating only on legal reform of overcrowded tenement dwellings. As Mumford argued in a 1911 article in *The Nation*: 'Housing reform by itself has only standardized the tenement. City planning by itself has only extended the tenement....It is fatuous to suppose that private interests will correct this condition, for it is for the benefit of private interests that it exists.'[9] They also criticised the earlier municipal housing reform for restricting its vision to the slums of the city. Henry Wright argued, 'The housing problem could not be kept in the slums; it has become universal'. The twentieth-century dream of home ownership seemed to be bankrupt, Wright observed:

> In housing we are torn between an intolerable reality and an impossible ideal. All the while we are lulled by the fancy that we will someday be able to realize the home of our dreams. We see it pictured in the house and garden periodicals and in our Sunday magazine sections. We hear it praised and boosted in Better-Home Weeks and in Own-Your-Own-Home Drives. It is the dream of a picturesque house standing free and independent on its own plot—a whole country estate if we have any luck, but at any rate an independent and isolated plot.

Wright argued that this dream had come to nothing but an advertised illusion based on Gold Coast fantasies. The real suburban homes being constructed delivered neither freedom, nor independence, nor happiness:

Within the limits of New York City no less than 50 miles of new small framed houses have been built, in long monotonous rows with a single repetitive design, closely crowded together on poor land, usually without proper public facilities or fire protection, and often with the barest provisions for health and sanitation. Practically no recreation areas have been set aside in these districts. The houses are of the flimsiest construction and the cost of up-keep will be excessive and will fall on purchasers just when they are least prepared for it.[10]

Some were not quite as sombre. Mumford, for instance, agreed with Wright's critique, but still believed that the idea of the suburbs held great promise. Suburbanisation, he argued, was the most recent migration spurred by America's great social and technological transformations. The first, westward expansion had dispersed a farming population across the continent. The second, industrialisation, propelled by water power and the railroads, carried people from farms to small factory towns. The third, urbanisation, was the migration of people to large industrial and financial centres. Suburbanisation was the fourth migration, made possible by new technologies and giving working- and middle-class people the opportunity to move from congested cities to spacious suburbs. In particular, Mumford believed that electricity was an essential prerequisite for this current migration. Unlike coal or water, it could be dispensed anywhere inexpensively. People no longer had to reside near older sources of energy for work. And the automobile would make it practical for people to live in this new decentralised society.[11]

Like Filene, Mumford believed that these changes represented progress. The second industrial revolution, he argued, was:

An attempt to spread the real income of industry by decentralizing industry...Far sighted industrialists like Dennison and Ford are already planning this move, and business men like Edward Filene feel that business is at an impasse unless decentralization is followed as 'The Way Out'. Regional planning is an attempt to turn industrial decentralization—the effort to make the industrial mechanism work better—to permanent social uses. It is an attempt to realize the gains of modern industry in permanent houses, gardens, parks, playgrounds and community institutions.[12]

The fourth migration would be qualitatively different from the previous ones. A regionally dispersed population could reap the benefits of both the city and the country, living a life both cosmopolitan and planned, democratic and healthy. Communities would be built on a human scale surrounded by the beauty of nature. Mumford believed that community planning would bring to the suburbs 'a more exhilarating kind of environment—not as a temporary haven or refuge—but as a permanent seat of life and culture, urban in its advantages, rural in its situation'.[13]

This vision, articulated in the press and in academic, government and business circles by Mumford and other members of the RPAA, was an ambitious one requiring a massive restructuring of society. As historian Carl Sussman explained, 'Instead of working in the name of pragmatism on meaningless civic improvement projects, [the RPAA] argued for a dedication to a new social order where people have decent homes, a stable community life, a healthy and varied environment, and a genuinely urban culture'.[14] Or, as Mumford said, 'A full realization of our ideas required a complete reformation of our dominant personal incentives and social objectives, a change from a Money Economy to a Life Economy'.[15]

Clarence Stein, an influential architect and planner, described the goals of the RPAA and how they represented a radical departure from the past. 'To build a substantial setting for neighborhood and family life, rather than to control and regulate, requires a completely different kind of planning. That is why I intend to call it community development or new town planning to differentiate it from the procedure that is generally called city planning in America.' Because the RPAA believed in building real communities in the suburbs, not merely containers for living, they argued that parks, woods, hiking trials, baseball diamonds, tennis courts and swimming pools were as important for communities as stores or houses. Creating community centres and tenant associations was equally vital.

Wright argued that creating these kinds of communities meant abandoning market-driven building for building based on the principle of community. He explained the distinction: 'There is actually an antithesis between the two procedures. The prime objective of one is to assist in the marketing and protection of property, of the other to create communities. The latter deals with the realities of living rather than with trading. The two are at cross purposes: preserve and protect, in contrast with devise and produce.' Four principles defined the building of non-market driven communities:

> Coordinated, not disorganized
> Communities, not lots or streets
> Contemporary, not obsolete
> Dynamic, not static.[16]

Mumford saw New Town Planning as the integration of people, land and industry. 'The housing problem, the industries problem, the transportation problem, and the land problem cannot be solved one at a time...they are mutually interacting elements and they can be effectively dealt with only by bearing constantly in mind the general situation from which they have been abstracted.'[17] Thus, the RPAA believed that planning should reflect a multi-disciplined approach and be coordinated by professionals, activists and ordinary people working together.

Experiments and achievements

RPAA members promoted their ideas through books, articles, exhibitions and, most importantly, by building real communities. These were, as Stuart Chase, economist and Consumer Union founder, said, 'definite achievements; something you could kick with your feet'.[18]

The first experiments in planned housing on a national level took place during the First World War, when the government created the first federal housing institutions—the Emergency Fleet Corporation and the United States Housing Corporation—to deal with the lack of housing for munitions workers and shipbuilders living in new military towns. The question was— how to do it? Inspiration came from Raymond Unwin, a co-founder of the English Garden City movement. The federal government hired RPAA member, architect and writer Frederick Ackerman, to go to Britain to investigate Unwin's new housing approach, which had attracted international attention. Back in America, Ackerman and Henry Wright worked under government auspices to design 176,000 low-cost, substantial, attractive housing units. The wartime housing communities they generated like Blackrock in Bridgeport, Connecticut and Yorkship Village near Camden, New Jersey were models of enlightened architecture and planning, proof that government planning and funds could produce modern, liveable communities.

Political leaders adamantly insisted, however, that these developments should not set a precedent for government financed low-cost, modern public housing. As they would for years to come, politicians and the real estate lobby argued that the government should not compete with private builders, and that any mass housing projects the government undertook should definitely not waste resources on aesthetic concerns. In 1920 the Senate Committee on Public Buildings and Grounds declared that: 'Congress certainly did not intend...to enter into competition in architectural poetry with any nation or private organization...We do not believe that this was necessary for the mechanics who were to be housed.' In response to these attacks, influential housing reformer Edith Elmer Wood proclaimed that public wartime housing 'proved that government housing could be produced and administered in the United States without scandal, without the sky falling, or the Constitution going on the scrap heap'.[19]

After the war, to avoid the criticism that the government was constructing mass housing, reformers refined an old philanthopic idea first developed in mid-nineteenth century Britain and arriving in the United States by the end of the century: the limited-dividend fund or cooperative. Early housing experiments relied on philanthopic investments but had no stockholders and paid no dividends. The issue facing reformers in the 1920s was how to expand the limited-dividend model to increase the supply and diminish the cost of capital available for non-speculative housing. To do so, the RPAA proposed that limited-dividend companies should sell shares but limit dividends to six per cent and be exempt from state and local taxes. This would eliminate the bane of the private housing industry—speculation—and allow investments to come from private businesses, charity organisations, labor unions or individuals.

Clarence Stein was pivotal in these efforts. Stein served as the first and only chairman of the New York State Commission of Housing and Regional Planning from 1923 to 1926. He was instrumental in the passage of the inventive New York Housing Law in 1926 which was based on the RPAA limited-dividend concept: restricting dividends on housing projects approved by the State Housing Board, exempting those approved from state taxes and authorising municipalities to free such projects from local taxation. The New York State Board of Housing established to administer America's first limited-divided law, engaged in extensive research on housing design and costs to demonstrate the superiority of large-scale devopments and defended its research based on the chronic shortage of decent housing whose rooms rented for under $15 a month. [20]

Using limited-dividend companies, housing could now be built on a non-profit basis. Designed by socially concerned, well-known architects like Ackerman, Stein, and Wright, new communities, based on limited-dividend societies, financed either by progressive businessmen like Marshall Field, Julius Rosenwald (owner of Sears) and Henry Buhl Jr., or by progressive unions like the Amalgamated Clothing Workers, provided an alternative to both tenement slums and slipshod, speculative suburban homes.

One of the best examples of such well-made, modern, planned housing was Chatham Village in Pittsburgh. Built for people of moderate means, it was constructed complete with garages and stores. At the same time its layout reflected the notion that houses should blend into the natural surroundings: the houses climb gracefully into the hills. Similarly, success-ful developments included the Rosenwald apartments, Marshall Field's mammoth low-cost garden apartment houses in Chicago, and the Metropolitan Life Insurance housing in New York City.[21] A few housing experiments were built specifically for African-Americans: the Paul Lawrence Dunbar apartments in Harlem, financed with Rockefeller money, Rosenwald's Michigan Avenue apartments in Chicago, the Douglas apart-ments built by Prudential Life Insurance in Newark, New Jersey, and the Cincinnati Model Homes.[22]

Most of the new housing developments were located in and around New York City. New York was home to many housing reformers, trade unions and enlightened capitalists and it housed a huge tenement population. Also, the New York Housing Law ignited interest in large-scale non-profit hous-ing projects. New York City was the only city in the state to take advantage of the new law. In 1927, the city enacted a measure which exempted from taxation new buildings or improvements approved by the State Board.[23] The Amalgamated Clothing Workers were the first to jump in. Between 1927 and 1931, the union built two cooperative apartment complexes, one on Manhattan's lower East Side and the other in the north Bronx. Contemporaries praised these cooperatives as 'a first step in remaking the entire lower East Side, replacing dank, crowded tenements block by block with modern housing for the working class'.[24] Unlike older tenements, which were built up against each other with only narrow airshafts in the center, the Amalgamated dwellings were built around a large landscaped court yard. Elaborate brickwork patterns marked their exteriors, while their interior con-tained three to five ample rooms with modern bathrooms and kitchens. Each building also included a library, a nursery, a roof deck, a gym and an audi-torium. The apartments were affordable to working and lower middle-class employees.

Other builders also made use of the limited-dividend housing concept. Progressive real estate tycoon Alexander Bing working with Clarence Stein, joined to form the City Housing Corporation [CHC]. The CHC was capi-talism with a socialist face. It sold $100 shares to teachers, social workers and others in the same moderate salary range as well as to wealthy capitalists who believed that profit and humanitarianism were compatible. The CHC board of directors exemplified this combination of social reform and business. It included Felix Adler, founder of the Ethical Culture Movement; Richard Ely, progressive educator and economist; Henry Wright and Frederick Ackerman; settlement house directors; Mary Simkhovitch and Lillian Wald; Eleanor Roosevelt, whose husband was then serving as Governor of New York; and philanthropic capitalists like William Sloan Coffin, John Agar and V. Everit Macy.[25]

One of the most significant communities the CHC financed was Sunnyside Gardens in Queens, one subway stop away from Manhattan's bustling streets and business districts. Finished in 1928, Sunnyside Gardens was intended to provide low-cost, low-density housing for urban workers seeking a more countrified refuge from crowded tenements. Although close to the city's employment, recreational and cultural opportunities, the well-constructed homes were priced substantially lower than other newly constructed houses built in New York City at the time.[26]

This was possible because Sunnyside was a large-scale operation, built with efficient mass-production methods on a large tract of underdeveloped land bought at a reasonable cost. It was these Fordist principles, CHC head Alexander Bing argued, that made moderate home prices possible. Unlike other construction projects, building at Sunnyside continued on a year-round basis, which created additional savings. Planners made sure labour practices maximised efficiency: when a construction worker finished one job, he went on to another, assuring him a steady wage and contributing to high productivity.[27]

Handsomely designed by Ackerman, Stein and Wright, the Sunnyside community consisted of traditional row houses—but with a twist. Still constrained by the urban street grid, 'Each house was given broad frontage and constructed only two rooms deep. Instead of pushing the design into the interior of the block, the designers turned the frame 90 degrees and stretched it along the perimeter of the street.'[28] This allowed for more air and light and for the large interior courtyard. Unlike in conventional subdivisions, the courtyards were not cut up into little back yards but were left open for common use. A green space where children could play and neighbours socialise was a welcome change for city residents used to cramped grid-iron streets. The necessity for residents to decide together how to use the common court yards fostered the creation of block associations and civic spirit generally.

Sunnyside apartments cost more than the planners would have liked, but still attracted a cross-section of working- and middle-class residents.[29] A 1927 survey discovered that its denizens included skilled or semi-skilled mechanics (20%), office workers and small shopkeepers with moderate incomes (24%), a smattering of restaurant workers, domestic servants, and chauffeurs (3%). Business people (32%) and professionals (17%) made up the rest, including, 'a sizeable proportion of young artists, writers and liberal intellectuals who were fascinated with the concept of a planned community and found Sunnyside both an exciting and convenient place to live'.[30]

Lewis Mumford himself lived in Sunnyside for 11 years.[31] He recalled, proudly, the economic diversity of the residents. 'In the block where I lived, there was a grocer's clerk who earned $1,200 to $1,500 a year and a physician who earned $10,000...So this effort at an acceptable minimum in housing achieved something even more important; a mixed community, not the economically segregated kind that the higher costs of a well-planned middle class suburb demand.'[32] Indeed, one principle of new community planning was that the planners themselves would live in the community. As Clarence Stein explained, 'The planner cannot discover the needs of people merely by asking them what kinds of home and town or community they want to live in. They do not know beyond their experience. However, with their assistance—not their guidance—he must discover their requirements....He should live in the places he helps to create.'[33]

In the late 1920s, the CHC, again under the direction of Stein and Wright, undertook their next and more ambitious project: the town of Radburn, New Jersey, a suburb of New York City. Unlike Sunnyside, Radburn was not built on a city grid-iron and therefore presented new design possibilities. Built again on a large scale—1,300 acres of land that would house 1,500 residents—Radburn was designed as a suburban community of single unattached modernised homes, complete with shopping centres and schools, and advertised as 'a town for the motor age'.

In 1920, Frederick Lewis Allen tried to imagine how life dependent on automobility would alter the shape of physical space from its vertical, urban lines, marked by the skyscraper, to new, horizontal, flat, sprawling suburban contours. The car was the medium for this alteration. It became the connective tissue between home and work, play and, most importantly, consumption. The problem was that cars required much more space than people. The designers of Radburn offered an answer.

Using Central Park as a model, Wright and Stein planned two road system for Radburn—one for pedestrians and another for vehicular traffic. The large roadways, called 'super blocks', contained narrow cul-de-sac streets which led to houses facing large interior parks, and a footpath system.[34] Each house was turned so that kitchens and service rooms faced the street and living rooms faced inward toward the garden. The Radburn idea, said Stein, 'was to answer the enigma of how to live with the auto: or if you will, how to live in spite of it'. 'We met these difficulties with a radical revision of the relation of houses, roads, paths, gardens, parks, blocks, and local neighborhoods.'[35]

Radburn was designed for middle-income, white-collar families with a car and children. It provided its residents with twenty acres of parkland, swimming pools, tennis courts, baseball fields, basketball courts and summer houses. The CHC encouraged recreation and cultural activities such as nursery schools, playgrounds, sports and day camp for the children and amateur theatre groups, courses in psychology, current events and literature for the adults. New residents were urged to participate in the town's many activities by Citizen Associations.

In 1929 author Geddes Smith described Radburn as 'a town built to live in—today and tomorrow. A town "for the motor age". A town turned outside in—without any backdoors. A town where roads and parks fit together like the fingers of your right and left hands. A town in which children need never dodge motor trucks on their way to school. A new town—newer than the garden cities, and the first major innovation in town planning since they were built.'[36]

Demonstration samples and the New Deal

Limited-dividend housing experiments like Sunnyside, Radburn and Chatham were important because they demonstrated that middle- and working-class housing could be affordable, innovative and liveable. They also showed that large-scale housing developments could be socially conscious, civic-minded and planned. But however visionary, they could not solve the giant problem of housing: one-third of a nation still remained ill-housed in tenements and slums.

Lewis Mumford noted the limitations inherent in these utopian-like experiments. He argued that 'to improve the housing of the workers while preserving intact the institutions that infallibly produced slum housing was impossible. All that could be done, at best, was to produce demonstration samples which partially showed what might be achieved on a larger scale if the entire economic basis were radically altered.' The institutions that blocked this radical alteration were, Mumford exclaimed, 'free enterprise, private land speculation, and building slums for profit'.

The solution, he argued, lay in a dramatic reversal of priorities:

Modern housing is a collective effort to create habitable domestic environments within the framework of integrated communities. Such housing demands not merely an improvement of the physical structures and the communal patterns. It demands such social and economic changes as will make it available to every income group. In the larger processes of reconstruction, housing, sustained by public authorities and supported by public funds is a means for overcoming gross inequalities in the distribution of wealth, for producing more vital kinds of wealth, for restoring the balance between city and country and for aiding in the rational planning of industries, cities, and regions.[37]

If Mumford was interested in the macro political and economic causes of the housing crisis and understood that the experimental communities he helped create were inadequate to address these causes, Catherine Bauer saw the enemy in more particular terms and specified a concrete solution:

> The jostling small builders in the front foot lots and the miserable strangling suburbs and the ideology of individual Home Ownership must go. And in their place must come a technique for building complete communities designed and administered as functional and constructed by large scale methods. And finally, that only government can make the decisive step and set up the new method of house production as a long time social investment to replace the wasteful and obsolete chaos still prevailing.[38]

Although they differed in their analytical approach, both Bauer and Mumford understood that the housing crisis could not be solved in a piecemeal, philanthropic manner. Like Filene, they argued that the capitalist system had to develop a new consciousness in order to deliver the social benefits the second industrial revolution promised. But it would take the depression to make this apparent to the society at large. The housing projects of the RPAA, isolated experiments in the 1920s, proved to be critical models for New Deal policies and programmes. As Mumford said, 'Without this (RPAA) leadership, the Roosevelt administration would not, in all probability, have been able to evolve the comprehensive national housing policy that it actually embarked on with such readiness'.[39]

Notes

1. Edward Filene (1860–1937), an important commercial figure and social thinker, has been largely ignored by historians of the twentieth century. To date, there is no major biography of Filene, whose thought influenced the evolution of modern consumerism. In the 1920s he became famous for the creation of a new kind of department store where all classes could shop: the fifth floor was for the wealthy, the fourth, the upper middle class; the next, the middle class and the basement contained goods at prices affordable for the masses. He also helped found the consumer union movement, the US Credit Union movement as well as funding cooperative stores and starting the 20th Century Foundation.

2. Robert Kanigel, *The One Best Way: Frederick Winslow Taylor and the Enigma of Efficiency*, (New York, 1997).
3. Edward A. Filene, *The Way Out: A Forecast of Coming Change in Business and Industry* (New York, 1925) pp.176, 184.
4. Ibid., p.201.
5. Ibid., pp.203–5.
6. Its membership over ten years may have reached 25.
7. RPAA members were disproportionately influential in the New Deal's policies and projects, particularly the Tennessee Valley Authority, the Civilian Conservation Corps, the Rural Electrification Administration and the Greenbelt Communities.
8. Members of the RPAA drew inspiration from a range of sources. They were influenced by Ebenezer Howard, the father of the English Garden City Movement. Howard believed that the reformation of the physical environment could contribute to the transformation of the social environment. They looked to American ideas as well, drawing from Henry David Thoreau's emphasis on nature, Thorstein Veblen's critique of conspicuous consumption and John Dewey's ideas of participatory democratic culture.
9. Lewis Mumford cited Carl Sussman, ed., *Planning the Fourth Migration: The Neglected Vision of the Regional Planning Association of America*, (Cambridge Mass., 1976), p. 13. For an excellent history of the RPAA see Roy Lubove, *Community Planning in the 1920s: The Contribution of the Regional Planning Association of America* (Pittsburg, 1963).
10. Henry Wright, 'The road to good houses', *Survey Graphic* 7, May 1925, pp.165–8.
11. Mumford, cited in Daniel Schaffer, *Garden Cities for America: The Radburn Experience*, (Philadelphia, 1982), p.61.
12. Mumford, *Survey Graphic*, 151–2.
13. Ibid.
14. Sussman, *Planning*, p.45.
15. Mumford cited ibid., p.44.
16. Clarence Stein, 'New towns for new purposes' in Lewis Mumford, ed., *Roots of Contemporary American Architecture*, (New York, 1952), p.336.
17. Mumford, cited in Sussman, *Planning*, p.13.
18. Stuart Chase, cited ibid., p.23.
19. Schaffer, *Garden Cities*, p.114.
20. Lubove, *Community Planning*, 67–82
21. Stein, 'New towns', p.339. Gwendolyn Wright in Mumford, *Roots,* pp.205–7.
22. 'Limited dividend roll call', *Architectural Forum*, January 1935, pp.98–103. Most businessmen who invested were involved in major department store and retail trade, like their contemporary, Edward Filene.
23. Lubove, Community Planning, p.79.
24. Christopher Gray, 'Amalgamated housing still works', *New York Times*, 3 July 1994.
25. Schaffer, *Garden Cities,* p.106.

26. Ibid., p.123.
27. Ibid. Henry Wright in Mumford, *Roots*, p.205. This pioneering large-scale building method in housing was a forerunner to Levittown where speed was essential: 1,200 units were erected in four years.
28. Schaffer, *Garden Cities*, p.124.
29. A Sunnyside house cost between $4800 and $17,000 depending on size, the average house or co-operative apartment, with a 10 per cent down payment, cost a minimum of $42 a month or $504 a year to maintain, 'necessitating an annual family income of $2500, an amount earned by only 40% of all urban families' (ibid, p.127).
30. Ibid., p.127.
31. *New York Times*, 26 June 1994. According to a 1994 *New York Times* article, Sunnyside is still, in the 1990s, considered one of the most successful planned communities in the United States.
32. Mumford, cited Schaffer, *Garden Cities*, p.127.
33. Stein, 'New towns'. p.345.
34. Wright in Mumford, *Roots*, pp.205–6.
35. Clarence Stein, *Towards New Towns For America*, (Liverpool, 1951). p.46. For a useful bibliography on the new town movement, see Susan L. Klaus, *Links in the Chains: Greenbelt, Maryland, and the New Town Movement in America: An Annotated Bibliography on the Occasion of the Fiftieth Anniversary of Greenbelt, Maryland* (Washington: George Washington Studies, 195).
36. Geddes Smith cited Stein, *Towards New Towns*, p.44.
37. Lewis Mumford, 'America Can't Have Housing', *New Republic*, 1934, pp. 15–19.
38. Catherine Bauer, *Modern Housing*, (New York, 1934), p.242. It is interesting that Catherine Bauer was the daughter of Jacob Bauer, the New Jersey Highway Commissioner who initiated the modern super highway that by-passed major towns. See *Notable American Women. Modern Period, A Biographical Dictionary*, (Cambridge Mass., 1980).
39. Mumford cited Stein, *Towards New Towns*, p.15.

The Other Future
The British left and America in the 1920s

Kevin Morgan

In the early to mid-1920s, the British labour movement took what was in many respects a distinctive stance on international affairs. Most obviously and controversially, while comparatively untroubled by active communist allegiances, the British movement was more generally supportive or tolerant of the Bolsheviks than almost any of its major continental equivalents. In several cases, prominent leaders or institutions took up strongly pro-Bolshevik positions which the greater discipline and cohesiveness of continental social democracy rarely allowed. Even among more moderate figures there were many who saw in NEP Russia a striving, in altogether different circumstances, after something akin to their own aspirations. Sometimes referred to as labour's 'Russia complex', this sense of being somehow on the Bolsheviks' side reflected a division between social democracy and communism that was far less sharply defined in Britain than in many other European countries.

In a larger study, I have explored these themes through the now largely forgotten figure of A.A. Purcell: variously a syndicalist, Furnishing Trades' official, guild socialist, Communist Party foundation member, twice Labour MP and leading TUC 'left'. As president of the International Federation of Trade Unions (IFTU), Purcell's robust advocacy of pro-Bolshevik causes aroused intense debate internationally, notably when in December 1924 he led a TUC Russian delegation which reported fulsomely on the regime's successes. Emma Goldman and Friedrich Adler were among those who fired off stinging replies, communists lionised him as one of their own and even the first Tin Tin adventure featured a credulous Russian touring party of British trade unionists. In reality, there was far more to the attraction than mere gullibility, and an exploration of Labour's Russian attachments raises intricate questions as to the particular characteristics that may have given rise to it. These are the subject of the larger study.

This article tackles some of the same questions from the rather different perspective of the other possible future which the America of the 1920s represented. In this case too, a comparative approach confirms not the old bugbear of exceptionalism but the variousness of national labour movements whose local quiddities, as well as basic common purpose, were expressed through international networks. Like the young Soviet republic, the dynamism of 1920s America provided a magnet to overseas visitors and, in Britain at least, the ideological battle over the future of industrial society was seen by many commentators in terms of a contest between the two. That was Beatrice Webb's theme in a series of diary entries; it was Bertrand Russell's when he lectured to London Fabians in 1926; and it was Tom Mann's when, four years earlier, he prefaced one of numerous publications on the same topical subject. 'Both creeds, though they differ in all else, look to the future', the book conceded, and that was their common attraction. It was the vision of a capitalism rejuvenated which prompted the *Daily Mail*, on a suggestion thrown out by Stanley Baldwin, to send a 'trade union' delegation to the States just a year or so after Purcell's to Russia. That same year, 1926, Baldwin's government sent its own industrial commission, with what one of its trade union members, Ernest Bevin, thought the same object of 'boosting' US industrial achievements. Bertram Austin, an engineer whose report on the 'new industrial gospel' of high wages had a great *réclame* the same year, showed every solicitude in trying to impress its merits on the TUC secretary Walter Citrine. As with every form of mass tourism, itineraries soon became regularised. Willingly, visitors trailed around East Coast efficiency showpieces, whose virtues were promoted almost as assiduously as the Bolsheviks did theirs. American trade unionists, themselves no detractors of Americanism, warned their British confreres of the great efforts made by the big industrial managements to direct foreign observers towards the desired conclusions. Subliminally assisted by Mary Pickford and the Charleston, America thus cast its own beguiling spell as the capitalism of the future and the answer to the class war. 'There are two ways of acquiring a political reputation as a foreign affairs specialist in the present day political world', noted the *Socialist Review* in 1928. 'If one is conservative one goes to America, spends three hectic weeks being pump-handled by enthusiastic Americans and then comes back and writes a book proving that capitalism is the only possible system, etc, etc. In the other political camp one goes either to Russia or to Geneva.'[1]

Americanism and Fordism

In its American almost as much as its Russian aspect, that was very much a

British way of looking at things. Habitually though Americanism has been identified with the right, in the Europe of the 1920s it also exerted a palpable fascination for many socialists. In her lucid study of the German case, Mary Nolan distinguishes productivist, consumptionist and ideological readings of Fordism, and though the last of these clearly buttressed business values, its economic readings were equally accessible to sections of the left.[2] To those in the Marxist tradition, the productivist rationale which Fordism carried on from Taylorism had its own 'progressive' validity irrespective of its temporary mechanisms of control and distribution. Most famously nowadays, such arguments will be found in Gramsci's essay 'Fordism and Americanism'. Predicating social advance on the development of productive forces, Gramsci hailed, as necessary steps towards a planned economy, the defeat of customary working practices and the principle of 'coercion' in the ordering of work. The future he envisioned was Fiat, symbol even beyond Italy of the new Americanism, but Fiat now planted with a red flag above its famous test track.[3]

Though written in isolation and published only posthumously, Gramsci's essay was nevertheless but the most sophisticated example of the widespread communist enthralment with American productive technique. In America itself, even W.Z. Foster, home-grown version of a Pollitt or Gallacher, expressed his admiration for Fordist methods. Where Gramsci spoke cryptically to the new 'psycho-physical equilibrium' of mass production becoming internalised under new social forms, Foster was able to invoke more directly the appropriation of its own future by workers' Russia. That was fully in accord with the Bolsheviks' own infatuation with America, and the wonder is only that it was so little commented upon by British observers like Purcell. With the Fordist gospel *My Life and Work* running through eight Soviet editions, with Ford's name even borne with Lenin's on processions and fordizatsiya proclaimed the escape-route from backwardness, the moment has been described by one historian as Russia's 'rediscovery of America'. Never had a country so much to learn as well as teach, and with the inauguration of the Five Year Plans, as US technicians flocked to make real the fantasies of Soviet power, the strange symbiosis of Bolshevism and Americanism seemed complete. Personifying the link with Detroit was Albert Kahn: chief architect at Ford's, inspiration for the Fiat design office and now described by a Corbusian detractor as 'God-engineer and pig-architect to the Soviets'.[4]

In its Soviet and Gramscian renditions, Fordism, like its elder sibling Taylorism, was thus essentially a philosophy of rationalised production.[5] That alone, however, could not explain its spell over a Europe whose plight, the very reverse of Russia's, was the inability to work even its existing productive resources. The issue for the old world was demand, and what made Fordism such a compelling social doctrine was its marriage of technique and organisation to the consumptionist mantra of High Wages. The power of this vision was nowhere more evident than in Weimar Germany. It was not just that Germany sent more investigators to America than any other country, that *My Life and Work* sold 200,000 copies there, or that Berlin even more than Moscow seemed to the Russian writer Ehrenburg 'the apostle of Americanism'. What distinguished this from the milder but comparable British contagion was less its intensity than its identification with a broadly social-democratic vision of modernity, and specifically with the German Social Democratic Party (SPD). Deriving like Gramsci from the same bifurcated Marxist tradition, the SPD too was characterised by a heady technological optimism and the belief that enhanced productive capacity must inevitably conduce to the eventual benefit of the workers. Also like Gramsci, who envisaged a work-process so undemanding as to free the mind to explore its own higher reaches, SPD socialists looked beyond the performance of work functions for the flowering of personality. Following Kautsky's unambiguous theoretical lead, even trade unionists aspired to what the woodworkers' leader Tarnow called 'joy in life'—'life', that is, as leisure and consumption—and not fulfilment in work.[6]

Ford and Weimar alike, from such a perspective, represented broadly progressive tendencies already embodied in the eight-hour day.[7] Indeed, with its works councils, its corporatist Federal Labour Council and its progressive labour legislation, the 'German model' itself, in the early 1920s, was presented to British labour as far in advance of any other.[8] The content and control of those eight hours were thus the more readily conceded to managerial imperatives, whose survival was anticipated even under socialism. Concerns with 'quality work', in Britain an issue with guilds enthusiasts like Purcell, were derided by Gramsci and often identified in Germany with the political right. Even the *Bauhütten* or building guilds, though a far greater success in Germany than in Britain, achieved that success as social building corporations accountable not to their workers but to their consumers and (social) investors. Through their managing director, the SPD architect Martin Wagner, they actively preached and even practised industrialised building methods. It was not in these circles, therefore, but more typically on the right that were to be found the craft values of the *Berufsethos*, extolling the skill and dignity of manual labour but harnessed to traditionalist and usually hierarchical visions of society. 'The left thus not only rejected the right's construction of the problem of modern work, but also abandoned any possible discourse about alternative technologies and job satisfaction', writes Mary Nolan. 'Work as reality belonged to the proletariat; work as ideology became the distinct preserve of the right.'[9]

While deeply rooted in national habits and alignments, such attitudes both predisposed German socialists to Americanism and drew further sustenance from its example. Where the TUC sent its delegates to workers' Russia, its German equivalent, the ADGB, provided what was virtually an American counter-delegation just months afterwards. The superficial similarities were unmistakeable. First attending the convention of the AF of L, just as Purcell and his colleagues had that of its Russian counterpart, the German delegates then fanned out across the USA before compiling a report almost as favourable to its subject as was its British precursor. Perhaps, too, the Germans like the British were a little flattered by their welcome, including an audience with President Coolidge. Like the TUC party, they warned against the easy transference of lessons from one culture to another, though without disturbing the dominant impression their report made of a tremendous enthusiasm. 'By the book's conclusion all…caution had been thrown to the wind', Nolan sums up. 'America was held up not only as a model for Germany's economic future, but as a textbook from which one could read the revised laws of capitalist development.' As a final irony, the report's trade union section was written by Purcell's direct counterpart, the woodworkers' leader Fritz Tarnow. No less impressionable in his own way, Tarnow was to publish a Fordist tract whose very title, *Why Be Poor?*, was lifted from a chapter in Ford's *My Life and Work*.[10]

Americanism in Britain

It would have been surprising had British labour remained entirely unaffected by such enthusiasms. Though fitful suggestions of an American Labour delegation came to nothing, many individuals were in a position to make the journey. Often they were drawn by lucrative lecturing engagements, described by one visiting British socialist as 'great resource of the intellectual unemployed' and an indication of the close cultural and linguistic ties between the two countries.[11] A particularly impressible traveller was Oswald Mosley, who went with his wife on a US fact-finding mission early in 1926. 'Perhaps like the Webbs in Russia eight years later, they went in search of a new civilisation', Mosley's biographer writes, and Mosley himself was to describe the tour as one of his most formative experiences. Though he holidayed with Roosevelt, politics, as was usual with such visitors, was entirely secondary to his purposes. Instead, his tour inevitably climaxed with the sight of the Ford works, churning out the powerful message that high wages not only sustained domestic purchasing power but commanded efficiency through the need to circumvent high labour costs. That mass production methods made for miracles of monotony as well as output, Mosley made no attempt to deny. Nor, on the other hand, did he see any viable alternative to such methods, but looked instead to the reduction of hours and development of leisure for the compensations of a fuller life.[12] Ideologically, if not socially, that would have made of him a very unexceptional member of the SPD. It also fitted perfectly with the Living Wage demands which signalled a broader undercurrent of Americanism within the ILP which in part reflected Mosley's own influence.[13] The question nevertheless remains as to why such a response was so much less typical of the British labour movement as a whole.

Several reasons may be suggested, some occurring in combinations that again reveal the unusually tortile alignments of the British left. Undoubtedly, the contingencies of party competition played a part. Labour's America, like the SPD's, was filtered through the prism of domestic politics, but the defining cleavage in this case was not with communism but conservatism. Precisely because the break of 1917–21 did not have the same intense significance as in Germany, a common left-wing discourse was thus able to persist of Americanism as threat or cautionary tale. American success, conversely, was not a card to use against the communists, but one deployed against the Labour movement itself by its traditional enemies. Hence, like Russia, America did not provide a field for detached investigation but one that was already clearly marked out by domestic rivalries and solidarities. Arguably, Americanism in its dominant reading was simply not available to Labour, at least until the shocks of 1926 began to persuade it that rationalisation and industrial partnership were its only realistic alternatives. Why Labour should not have produced its own alternative reading of Fordism nevertheless takes us beyond the crude logic of adversarialism. What it reveals, in both its moderate and militant guises, was an ethos of emancipation, or regulation, which did not exclude the world of work and which produced in Britain a deep ambivalence as to the values of mass production.

As early as the turn of the century, America in Britain was marked as an employers' refrain, buttressing managerial prerogatives against countervailing 'restrictive' practices and the very existence of an effective trade unionism. For the active trade unionist, the same associations resonated with aggressive forms of competition and a pattern of industrial relations that sometimes seemed unbelievably violent. Here and there, among older trade unionists and co-operators, there lingered a breath of a radical-democratic Americanism of a much earlier vintage. In the shape of the octogenarian E.O. Greening, it even survived through sheer longevity to confront the Bolshevik sympathies that surfaced in the co-operative movement.[14] For most of its partisans, however, it was no longer politics but economics, not 'liberty' but industry, that explained the allure of the West.

At least from the turn of the century, America provided a significant site of contest and disputation, exactly as did the industrial issues with which it was identified. More subtle than most, the South African mineowner, Alfred Mosely, sent a commission of union officials to America to impress upon them a more positive view of the American experience. One of them, the Engineers' secretary George Barnes, was later to provide the *Daily Mail* party with almost its only credible working-class sponsor, the other being its 'industrial adviser' William Mosses, former Patternmakers' secretary and, like Barnes, an aged union stalwart long since lost to Labour.[15] Potentially, the Mosely commission might have encouraged an understanding of America which need not prove unpalatable to trade unionists and did not depend on their subjection or extinction. Nevertheless, this positive reading, of high wages linked with advanced technology, never became the dominant one in Britain. The obviously diminished credibility of the *Daily Mail*'s party, as against Mosely's, suggests if anything a distinct stiffening of attitudes.

Most critically, perhaps, on the issue of control that was central to British labour relations, Americanism appeared to furnish merely a threat without a pay-off. The threat became the more tangible with its codification as 'Scientific Management', and the Taylorist ideal of the 'trained gorilla' seemed little calculated to allay trade unionists' concerns over workplace status and authority. Even advocates of scientific management, at least those of a 'progressive' outlook, were concerned to distance the method itself from its American examplar.[16] Already in 1911, the Singer strike at Clydebank provided an early set-piece battle over 'American' methods. William Weir, another goad to Clydeside militancy, personified the same challenge. Himself a disciple of Ford and proselytiser for the machine, as both employer and public figure Weir indicted custom, skill and workers' organisation with brutal homilies of transatlantic derivation. In 1926, he was one of the employers to provide a worker for the *Daily Mail*'s party, and cannot have been disappointed to have him declare his every craft prejudice dispelled and the Fordist production line as pleasantly undemanding as drawing one's breath. Weir's very factory, the famous Cathcart Foundry, borrowed one of the Detroit designs of Albert Kahn, pig-architect indeed to Ford, Weir and Stalin alike. It was a lineage unattractive to any budding Stalin or Gramsci closer to home. 'Surrounded by a retinue of "scientific managers"—those modern prototypes of the early court favourites of the crown—workmen are regarded by him as so much raw material for manufacturing *pumps*!', ran a leaflet of the Glasgow Ironmoulders in 1919.

> The refractory human element that separates the moulder from the pig-iron, or the mechanic from the machine, he would fain repress....with apparently cheap overalls, and Weir's special dope in the shape of a monthly bulletin, added to the 'Clubs' and such-like 'Welfare' work, honest men are expected to be robbed of their character and reduced to the category of worms!

For the leaflet's author, Tom Bell, it was not productive advances which led toward socialism, but socialism alone which provided against the human costs of such advances. The modernity of Americanism, unconstrained by such considerations, seemed as new and attractive as a return to feudalism.[17]

Embedded in the culture of British labour were thus concerns with independence and control that were rooted in craft values even where craft was rejected as a basis of organisation. This commitment to 'work as ideology'—work, that is, as a source of identity and site of contestation that went beyond its mere exchange value—was at least as evident in the new 'producer' ideologies of syndicalism and guild socialism as in the older craft traditions they repudiated. Inevitably, how far that commitment proved effective or merely ceremonial was critically bound up with the sectional expediencies which it helped to articulate and legitimise. Probably in no industry was it better matched to present utility than in Purcell's sector of the building and allied trades. Nor, because of the political saliency of housing between the wars, was there any other case in which the issue between craft and technology was so widely represented beyond its particular industrial context. For that reason, as both an example and a wider point of reference, building graphically illuminates the general debate then taking place over the issue of production.[18]

The defence of craft

To his detractors, who were numerous, the bricklayer was to the 1920s what the car worker was to the 1970s: a symbol of obduracy, restrictive practices and the dogged refusal of any higher public or corporate spirit. Housing statistics suggested a gaping shortfall by American or pre-war standards of productivity, and even so friendly a critic as G.D.H. Cole was to record the impression of this period that 'hardly anybody was doing a reasonable day's work'. Nothing so infuriated 'middle' Britain as the sight of the British brickie resting with his trowel; or, to point the contrast supposedly witnessed by that model of industry, a Conservative MP, of his French equivalent laying some 3,000 bricks a day, or six and a half a minute. As housing needs loomed large in both national and local politics, the reputed indifference of organised labour to the wider 'community' was provided here with its most visible and well-publicised demonstration.[19]

Labour, both politically and industrially, contested that argument on its own terms, and produced its own reconciliation of housing needs and building livelihoods in the shape of the 1924 Wheatley Act. Beyond its rejoinders as to output and efficiency, however, there was also a qualitatively different perception: that of building as process at least as much as product or service. Still discernible, at least at a rhetorical level, were the notions of the builder as archetypal craftsman which a whole generation had absorbed from such staple labour readings as Ruskin, Morris and Tressell. It was in the spirit of this tradition that both craft and guild philosophies, the latter not so much obliterating craft values as generalising and democratising them, had perhaps their greatest contemporary resonance in the industry.[20] Even the bricklayers' secretary George Hicks, a TUC 'left' and a figure somewhat dismissive of romanticised views of craft, described this same craft spirit as a 'form of self respect' that was ultimately irrepressible. Denouncing dilution in 1924, he advanced what was almost an ideal-type definition of the Webbs' Doctrine of the Vested Interest. 'Would doctors, lawyers, architects, or even dancing masters, look upon "dilution" favourably?', he asked with some justice (except perhaps with regard to dancing masters). 'Believe me, our craft is one of no mean respect, and it is our livelihood.' That protest followed proposals at the previous year's British Association for conscripted 'Housing Battalions' to deal with the industry's under-performance: just as if, Hicks protested, labour were 'an indifferent sort of merchandise, to be handled like so many bags of mails'. 'I do not know how many years it takes to make a professor', he pointedly reminded his interlocutor, a professor in civic law, 'but strangely enough it takes some time to make a qualified bricklayer, joiner or plasterer'.[21]

If phantom housing battalions convey something of the wide frustration felt at the building industry's performance, the more serious challenge to the building trades was not the prospect of quasi-military methods but the shaking up of organisation and technology that was usually referred to by its German cognomen of 'rationalisation'. Against such a threat, even a more moderate union leader than Hicks, such as the Building Trades' president Thomas Barron, invoked the prospect of a 'twentieth century John Ludd'.

He did so, however, on grounds not just of displacement but of degradation:

> The ordinary Capitalist idea of rationalisation is to reduce costs, to speed up production, to displace men by machines, to remove all semblance of craftsmanship and those things which give men joy in their labour, and to make the few remaining human beings who are left employed into mere mechanical Robots, who, provided they are kept stoked, oiled and trimmed, will give no more trouble than their counterparts which are made of metal...

In some form or other, Barron acknowledged that the tide of technology was unstoppable. Nevertheless, against even a socialist version of rationalisation, which secured its human discards against the scrap heap, he made an impassioned defence of craft as expressing the humanity of labour:

> We believe that a nation or an industry which extinguishes or loses the spirit of craftsmanship is, or might as well be, dead. Especially is this so in an industry such as our own, which ought to provide an example of the highest expression of man's creative mind, imprinted on his handiwork. We want men trained in mind and hand; men who, because their faculties have been so trained, can carry out their work, however common, in that spirit of conscious freedom and power which still distinguishes Man from the Machine.

The same year, 1930, a Building Trades' Federation commemorative brochure invoked the same 'spirit of craftsmanship', and with a characteristic emphasis looked to see rekindled 'the vital spark of genius responsible for the magnificence of the past'.[22]

It hardly needed America to crystallise such attitudes, and 'rationalisation', without any special stress on its German origins, was the term more commonly used in British industry. Nevertheless, as a German commentator put it, 'the word rationalisation is without exception linked to the expression "Americanisation" in the European literature', and the connotations of the two phrases were virtually identical.[23] Even in building, more obviously sheltered and vernacular than most major industries, the challenge of an untransliterated Americanism was occasionally made explicit. Appropriately it was Weir who provided the outstanding instance. A critic not just of the unions but of the whole cossetted building industry, in the mid-1920s Weir undertook with government encouragement the mass production of prefabricated houses on transparently American precedents. A brief cause célèbre, this Weir steel house, with its Fordist franchise, even generated its own small trickle of overseas admirers. One of them, Julius Hirsch, merits special mention as the German author of *The American Economic Miracle*, a figure ideologically close to the SPD who now lavished on Weir's dumpy little bungalows the same extravagant praise as he had on its American prototypes. His report, for the liberal *Berliner Tageblatt*, made a by-now familiar case equating mass production with mass enrichment, even at the expense of general deskilling. 'The German workpeople will scarcely oppose such an experiment', he concluded. 'If it succeeds, it means, like every economic improvement, both the increase in purchasing power of the masses and the increase in employment...Moreover, the German trade union—and that is exactly what is noted again and again in England—has never yet resisted economic progress.'[24]

The 'English' unions—and this was noted even more frequently—took a very different attitude, and with the broad assent of the labour movement as a whole successfully defeated the new methods. In these, their respective experiments in industrialised building, the two countries manifested a whole world of cultural and institutional difference. In Weimar Germany, it was the progressive architect, employed by socialist administrations and drawing on the building guilds, which pioneered the use of new, cheaper and faster methods of construction. The Bauhaus itself—a 'guild' in inspiration, but one essentially of design and not production—was universally identified with the left and had the support of the socialists and even communists.[25] How different the situation in Britain, where Weir's debased variant of modern construction methods was pushed by a conservative industrialist, eased by a Conservative government, and successfully resisted by the generality of the labour movement.[26]

Egon Wertheimer, London correspondent of the SPD's *Vorwärts*, explained such a marked difference by the German trade unionist's early induction into Marxist concepts. 'It is true that often his Marxism has become mere lip-service', he conceded:

> but he has learned from it to think thoroughly and to see beyond the immediately practical in the problems that confront him. His British brother, whose mind is unburdened by theoretical convictions, has a far greater appreciation of immediate realities. Marxist training has given the German leaders ability to counteract in his union those medieval craft tendencies that have hampered the British trade union movement even to this day and to approve rationalisation as an inevitable process in capi-

talist development at a time when to the Englishmen...not only the concept but the process itself seemed more than suspicious.

A similar claim was made for his own compatriots by Gramsci, insisting that, far from their impeding rationalisation, in Italy it was 'precisely the workers who brought into being newer and more modern industrial requirements and in their own way upheld these strenuously'. Nobody wrote such things of the British trade unionist. Marxism, even for those who professed it, was understood in terms of the class struggle, not of productive forces, and it was to the former that they looked for the promotion of working-class interests. Conversely, it was with 'outworn theories of class conflict' that they were reproached by defaulting pro-Americans like George Barnes. What Gramsci called the 'inherent necessity' of productive development was thus subordinated to a hardier trade-union tradition whose deficiencies in theory, or theorists, was at least in part a mark of its greater independence.[27]

If the endorsement of the building unions' position on housing attests the influence of the smaller craft-based unions within the 1920s TUC, the misgivings as to Americanised work processes went far beyond such craft milieux. The doubtful virtues of *Rationalisierung*, for example, were especially associated with the German coal industry, to whose example the British miners' unions proved fully as resistant as the coal owners. Again, it was only after the General Strike that the case for such rationalisation, as opposed to generalised indictments of capitalist disorganisation, began to find its way into the socialist press.[28] Even Ernest Bevin, embodiment of the new, no-nonsense general unionism and singled out by Wertheimer as an exception to his overall characterisations of British labour, was singularly unimpressed by America, which he visited with the government commission of 1926. In particular, he was little enamoured of the 'hard cruel city' of Detroit. 'The Lancashire of the last century, excepting labour is more difficult to get and they have to pay higher wages', he wrote to his secretary. 'No one talks to you except in dollars and mass production and the way they boss labour.'[29] Similar views were expressed beyond the immediate sphere of trade unionism, and though argument persists as to whether Labour's intellectuals shaped, voiced or appropriated the movement's values, there is no disputing a certain commonality of outlook to which they gave their own expression.[30] Fabian socialists, for example, though their ordering of work and leisure apparently resembled the SPD's, evinced a sense of the humanity of labour that could not be reduced to managerial calculation. In a Fabian lecture on 'Ford and socialism', W.A. Robson, youthful epigone of the Webbs, indicted Ford for having 'robotised' his workers while oblivious to the strain, monotony and subjection in their work that this imposed upon them. Herman Finer, another Fabian lecturer who had spent a year in America as an academic fellow, found like Robson that the language of industrial 'tyranny' came to him almost as a matter of course.[31]

In the same way, although Americanism flavoured the ILP's undercon-sumptionism, it was not even there the only or even predominant flavour. Just a week prior to Mosley, another Midlands Labour candidate, Wilfred Wellock, had described for the *New Leader* his own very different impressions of America. A convert to the ILP via the alternative ethical waymarks of Morris, Tolstoy and even Gandhi, Wellock described the miracle of American production exactly as they might have: as merciless, tyrannical, autocratic and impatient of workers' rights. 'It casts aside men like bricks or tools at a moment's notice', he wrote, rather like Hicks or Bell. 'Quantity, cheapness and speed are its gods, on whose altars human nature and human welfare are daily sacrificed.' What perhaps is more remarkable is that the following year Wellock also visited Russia, but brought back on this occasion a very different image in which humane social provision was accompanied by a pervading sense of joy, purpose and anticipation. 'Here', he reflected in his memoirs, 'was human nature at its best!'[32]

The *Leader*'s editor Brailsford, while a proponent like Mosley of the Living Wage, broadly accepted the same dichotomy. 'It is evidently possible for capitalism, with the aid of an intelligent technique and the advantage of great national resources, to abolish poverty', he conceded of the American miracle.

> But it survives only by infecting the masses with its own materialism. They remain, in spite of their comparative prosperity, powerless to govern their own lives, more helpless under the dictatorship of capital than any impoverished proletariat in Europe which struggles and keeps its own soul. We march to defeat, if we allow our own army to suppose that our purpose is merely to win for it an easy material life. Our purpose is to change the motive of work. Our goal is the conquest of power.

Like Wellock, and for much the same reasons, Brailsford was far more impressed by his trip to the USSR for the ILP in 1927. Ironically, it was to an American public that he addressed his case for the Russian experiment.[33]

These concerns with the quality and dignity of labour went beyond the work process to the standing of labour in society as a whole. In contrast with the more statist traditions of classical social democracy, British socialists had envisioned their goals in terms of the advance to control and broadening self-government of Labour's own institutions. Syndicalism, Guild Socialism, co-operation and even Webbian collectivism had all in their different ways given expression to such an outlook. Perhaps, like Perry Anderson, we could call this outlook 'proletarian positivity', and no doubt it reflected that 'distinct hermetic culture' which Anderson felt had thwarted socialism through very excess of class consciousness.[34] Aspirations for a better society were thus identified with the progress of organised labour, whose ostensible predominance in Russia was first among the causes of the solidarities which Bolshevism engendered. Perhaps it was symptomatic of this 'corporatist class consciousness' that in the three-volume *Encyclopaedia of the Labour movement* and its world view published in 1927, the entries on the major industrial powers—Russia, significantly, was the exception—concentrated exclusively on the character, strength and legal standing of their respective labour movements. The section on the USA, contributed by Finer, thus failed even to mention Fordism in either its productivist or consumptionist readings, but attributed the success of US capitalism to the weakness of legal regulation and collective bargaining procedures. 'On the whole American labour purchases its extra prosperity by more strenuous labour conditions', Finer concluded, not at all extolling efficiency at such a price.

> The important question to be asked by the Labour Movement in any country is what general welfare and security is it willing to sacrifice for a few extra shillings in wages per week? The American worker has shown a disposition to strive for shillings, and to sacrifice for them some of the general independence and social amenities of life.[35]

That, nevertheless, was still a Fabian gloss. More directly, trade unionists looked to the weakness of union bargaining rights and the sheer brutality meted out to strikers by the American employing class. W.T. Colyer, a veteran of seven years' activities in the New England labour movement, likened the 'terror' of US capitalism to that of Horthy or Mussolini, but directed in this case against 'one of the feeblest and most docile Labour organisations in the world'. Through Colyer's book, *Americanism: a World Menace*, this blend of contempt and indignation became the version of its subject most widely circulated in British Labour circles. Long notices in the *Socialist Review* and the official *Labour Magazine*, the latter by so mild a class warrior as Norman Angell, endorsed Colyer's basic emphases. In the *Yorkshire Factory Times*, a series of features drew heavily on the same source to depict this other future under such headings as 'Mammon and murder' and 'The American capitalist frame-up'.[36] There were notable exceptions, such as the Railwaymen's secretary C.T. Cramp, TUC delegate to the 1924 AF of L convention, and the British secretary of the miners' international, Frank Hodges. As well as reporting favourably on American values, Cramp went on to provoke controversy by his apparent endorsement of the Weir house. Intriguingly, he owed his initial conversion to socialism not to *Merrie England or News from Nowhere*, but to Edward Bellamy's *Looking Backward*, the somewhat chill and technocratic blueprint which had prompted Morris's own more pastoral counter-utopia.[37] Such exceptions should not be overlooked, and were later to become more influential, but for the time being generally negative conclusions and preconceptions as to Americanism were all but pervasive on the British left.

Cultural critiques

Imparting an extra vigour to such antagonisms were instincts of moral and cultural repugnance such as are more widely familiar from the writings of historians like Martin Wiener and Correlli Barnett.[38] The selectivity of this so-called 'cultural critique' has long been recognised, while its productivist obsessions, oblivious to concerns with the character, purpose or intensity of work, betray a technocratic and almost Darwinian conception of modernity which the socialists of the 1920s would rightly have found bleakly one-dimensional. Nevertheless, it is also undeniable that British anti-Americanism, though largely identified with the left, included a strain of cultural pessimism or conservationism which in other countries was more congenially and perhaps appropriately propounded by the right. In the vivid phrase of one of Brailsford's correspondents, the novelist Richard Church, there was hanging over Europe a 'tidal wave of American barbarism', the back-wash of laissez-faire and a leviathan of 'arrogance, megalomania & vulgarity'.[39]

Even the Fabians, though traditionally as concerned with efficiency as trade unionists were with high wages, looked askance at its realisation in this abject salesman's paradise. Though themselves so often accused of philistinism, the language they used differed little from Church's. While it is therefore notable that America and not Russia provided the staple of Fabian lectures, it is equally notable that only one of the lecturers, S.K. Ratcliffe, avoided the generally prevailing note of dislike and condescension. This dated from at least as far back as the Webbs' US tour of 1898, when Beatrice noted already the country's obsession with money and its 'tyranny' (again) of conformism. Twenty-five years later, the same ideas seemed almost a condition of membership of the society. St John Ervine, in his 1923 lecture, stressed the 'standardisation' of minds as well as production, and the propensity of Americans to think, move and act 'in a crowd'. Emil Davies, the Fabian authority on nationalisation, contrasted material wealth with a poverty of manners and found consolation only in the Americans' continuing cultural deference to Europe. Finer, fresh back from a year as an academic fellow, was the most damning of all. Along with much else, he complained of the prevalence of stealing ('from trustification to small scale getting by'), the absence of any 'fixed standard of decent individual conduct' and the fixation on earning capacity to the detriment of freedom of conduct or opinion. Overall the picture was one of a deadening cultural abasement and unformity.[40] As powerful a symbol as Ford was George F. Babbitt, eponymous hero of Sinclair Lewis's withering satire on middle America's business values. Published in Britain just the month before *My Life and Work,* the novel ran through editions at a similarly American tempo, and Babbitt and Babbitry rapidly entered the vocabulary of Americanism. C.E.M. Joad even published a book called *The Babbitt Warren.*[41]

Perhaps this reveals the emplacement within the Labour movement of the liberal pedigree of Barnett's '"enlightened" Establishment'. Possibly it represents a variant of Gramsci's 'old European arsenal, bastardised and therefore anachronistic', though that also reminds us that such attitudes were by no means confined to Britain.[42] What is more noteworthy in the present context is that such attitudes were by no means confined to middle-class socialists, and that 'American' qualities of bustle, bigness and bombast were precisely those least likely to impress the unflappable British trade unionist of late-Victorian or Edwardian formation. Even Joe Toole, a Salford MP never described as a snob, remembered America as a landscape blighted by tin cans and a doctor who threatened him with a gun when he demurred at a reference to *Plato's American Republic.*[43]

Similar sentiments are revealed in Colyer's book on *Americanism*, coincidentally published almost simultaneously with *Babbitt* and *My Life and Work.* Possibly the only prominent member of the early British Communist Party to sport a beard, Colyer had worked for several years at the Local Government Board before resigning, a member of the ILP, over the compilation of the war register in 1915. Moving to New England, he then became active in the Socialist Party, was arrested in the Palmer Raids and deported back to Britain in 1922. There he joined the CPGB and was active on its Central Training Committee and as secretary in turn of the Labour Defence Council and the National Left Wing Movement, before resigning from the party in 1926. Despite such militant associations, a Fabian residue, like his whiskered chin, must have remained in Colyer from the LGB. Indeed, his book-length diatribe against Americanism strikingly anticipated the emphases of the Fabian lecturers and provided Ervine at least with one of his sources. Along with the trade-unionist's refusal of an 'industrial feudalism' at once violent and intrusively paternalistic, Colyer railed at philistinism, 'dollar-worship', arrogance, the 'standardisation of human beings' and generally a state of 'besotted ignorance and spiritual degradation unique among civilised nations'. Evidently inclined to the broad picture, among the other sweeping traits he reported were the 'total absence...of what the Old World knows as "honour"', a disregard for personal truthfulness bred of sales ethics, and the intellectual conformism that arose from Europe having sent to America 'chiefly the riff-raff who could be persuaded or obliged to leave home for their country's good'. Most remarkable was his chapter on American religion, a creed 'as unlovely as superstition ever assumed on this planet', which launched Colyer into a curious remembrance of Anglo-Catholic forms which oddly recalls the liturgical enthusiasms of Beatrice Webb. 'Glorious architecture, lovely music, and a stately ceremonial...have undoubtedly associated Christianity...with the satisfaction of human longings after beauty', he wrote, while even to English nonconformity he conceded the qualities of a 'moral and spiritual crusade'. Prefaced by Tom Mann, boosted in the *Labour Magazine* and *Workers' Weekly*, revisited in Plebs League lectures and even—who knows?—communist training schools, Colyer's America once more suggests how strangely interconnected were the different trajectories of the British left.[44]

Purcell in America

Purcell can provide us with a closing scene. In 1925 he made his one and only visit to America, which proved scarcely less controversial than his toasts to the revolution in Moscow the previous winter. The occasion was his selection as TUC fraternal delegate to the AF of L convention in Atlanta. Ordinarily, the main public responsibility of such a delegate was merely an exchange of formal courtesies. Hicks, a close colleague of Purcell's and the delegate the following year, played the part to perfection. Though privately he expressed an engaging scepticism as to whether US achievements really merited 'the energy expended', he paid his hosts effusive compliments in which the skyscraper outdid the Pyramid and the educative force of American efficiency was admissible even by the British bricklayer. 'I am gratified and charmed with...your wonderful Republic', he told them publicly. 'Pro rata I feel confident Gt Britain could easily hold her own', he added in private.[45]

Perhaps that especially overdrawn language was intended to repair an earlier breach, for Purcell the previous year had entirely disregarded such proprieties. There could indeed have been no greater contrast between the reception accorded Tarnow and his German colleagues, delegates at the same convention, and that simultaneously given the former pugilist from Salford. Where Tarnow's address was appreciatively received and reciprocated, Purcell's provoked a bruising riposte from AF of L president William Green that was cheered to the conference rafters. Where the Germans were then welcomed into the White House, and had talks with both President Coolidge and his Secretary of Labor Davis, Purcell spoke only at trade union halls and had no less an organ than the *Washington Post* demand his deportation. That may also be contrasted with the reception given the *Daily Mail* party, which like the Germans was entertained by Coolidge and Davis, and even with the AF of L's leaders, who urged on willing ears a greater efficiency in work and friendlier relationship with capital.

The immediate cause of controversy was Purcell's forthright identification with the Russians and a public demeanour that few Americans knew how to distinguish from communism. 'I say that you, workers of America, have much to learn from Russia', he told the AF of L with his customary directness. 'It has often struck me that while the Americans have been the most advanced...in ideas concerning mechanical invention and business organization, they have been most slow in accepting new social and political ideas.'[46] Beyond such obvious disharmonies, Purcell also tapped into the deep vein of depreciation. To his AF of L listeners, he at least paid the compliment of likening Britain to a US colony, swept by crazes for American hit tunes and business methods. Back with his Forest of Dean constituents, he hardly even conceded that much. Instead, like Hicks, he made sport with the American cult of 'bigness' and insisted on what a 'very much over-rated place' it was, with nothing to speak of to teach the British worker. His ruling criteria were those of organised labour, and he dismissed the boasts of affluence with a reminder of the 'far greater opportunities of expressing himself and of taking part in the business of appointing his representatives' which were the democratic achievements of the British trade unionist.

Purcell's strongest attack on the AF of L was for its exclusive and even racist craft basis, and he avoided that unsavoury strain in anti-Americanism which attributed the weakness of US labour to its indifferent social or racial composition. On the other hand, one notes again the persistence of concerns with the work process which were themselves rooted in Purcell's own craft tradition. What struck him about America 'as a workman' was not, remarkable as he found it, 'the perfection of industrial technique'.

No, what impressed itself unforgettably on my mind was the spirit of vigorous regimentation, the extreme division of labour which makes a man a mere automaton, performing one monotonous mechanical operation year in year out. The American industrial régime, in spite of its boasted high wages, is even more than its British counterpart a monotonous tyranny, in which the worker is regulated and ordered and disciplined and controlled to the last possible degree. American industrialism is nothing more nor less than a slave system...

Beyond the workplace itself, the same criteria of workers' rights mocked the democratic rhetoric with which the AF of L had replied to Purcell. "'Democracy'", he taunted:

'Democracy'—in the land of the frame-up, the gunman and the spy?...'Democracy'—in the land where negro lynchings and the bludgeoning and murder of workmen striking for their rights have been a part of every-day life these many years? 'Democracy'—in the land where all the forces of the law, the State and the police—the whole machinery of government, legal and illegal—are openly and shamelessly at the beck and call of triumphant plutocracy...? I submit that we must not be deluded by the mere forms of government; and that if we pierce through to the facts behind those forms we see that America is ruled by a capitalist dictatorship. America is the supreme example of the new Tsarism—the Tsarism of monopoly capitalism...[47]

As the IFTU's continental affiliates looked to the Americans, not the Russians or colonial workers as providing its best chance of enlargement, Purcell's performance in the States must surely have contributed to the bad feeling that was soon to tilt him out of the federation's presidency.[48]

Purcell's America both illuminates and complements his Russia. In sharply counterposing these two possible futures, the world-view of much of the British left discounted what were often perceived in other circles as the marked affinities between the two systems. That was the *Socialist Review*'s one real cavil with Colyer's presentation, which portrayed Bolshevism as alternative and antithesis to Americanism. It was a connection also made by the ILP's Clifford Allen when in 1925 he linked the dangers of Bolshevism, Fascism and Americanism, all three 'preaching hate, the denial of liberty, the organising of things that are least important, the destruction of things that are most important'.[49] It was also, as we have seen, an association which the Russians themselves hoped to make real, and which underlay the many contemporary depictions of Bolshevism as harbinger of a new 'collective man' and new machine civilisation.[50] Nevertheless, for its British admirers of the 1920s it was almost invariably what was most unAmerican about Bolshevism which attracted them. Where Russia represented education and culture, America stood not for individualism but a stultifying conformism. Where Russia represented humane welfare provision, America represented a heartless, egotistical 'dollar-worship', and a society bitterly divided on lines of race and class. Where Russia represented the government of the workers, albeit in conditions not yet of political freedom, America was repeatedly described as an industrial autocracy whose democratic 'tissue', to use a Webbian phrase, was enfeebled. Russia was a labour activist's, perhaps a New Jerusalemist's utopia, its calls on extenuation and solidarity only strengthened by its pariah status as international underdog and outsider. America, again by contrast, loomed across the Atlantic as both rival and threat, and it was entirely apt that Ben Tillett should have interpolated a note of fierce anti-Americanism into his own reflections on the Russian TUC delegation.[51] Again that might be contrasted with the more benign view of American investment as well as culture taken in Germany. What one notices above all, if once compares the British left's picture of Russia with an account like Fülöp-Miller's, is the essential *familiarity* of the former. Whatever Bolshevism represented for the British labour movement, it was not the transformation of that movement's values on the basis of technocratic rationality.

In many ways that was to change even within the decade. Quite apart from the projection of the Russia of the plans as a productivist utopia, there were already by the late 1920s distinct shifts in the attitudes of the British left to America. G.D.H. Cole, erstwhile ideologue for the 'producer', in his book *The Next Ten Years* embraced the managerial imperatives of the 'new capitalism' and the world of private satisfactions that increased productivity seemed to open up. Dismissing his earlier work-centred philosophy as 'cant', he was now so free of such cant as to propose the formation of a National Labour Corps whose tasks would have included the building of Weir houses, 'if we cannot build better'. George Hicks, though he could hardly have been receptive to that idea, had by this time delivered the 1927 TUC presidential address which opened the door to the Mond-Turner talks, in which Weir himself was one of the participating employers. These too marked a willingness to adapt to the 'new capitalism', for Mond, like Weir, was a professed admirer of American methods and his undisguised objective was the Americanisation of British industrial relations. The General Strike, for Cole, Hicks, and the currents of opinion they represented, had proved a decisive turning point. 'Rumours of the new departures in Trusts and Syndicates in Germany and in the USA, of the penetration of Russia and of the control of Europe by American financiers, are rife...and are spreading a sort of defeatism and desire to come quickly to terms with the Mammon of Righteousness', Beatrice Webb wrote already from the 1926 TUC. Cometh the hour, and there came, to stay, Walter Citrine.[52]

Nevertheless, the issues of the 1920s were to survive the passing of their immediate context and leading personalities. Though abruptly foreshortened by the Wall Street Crash, the America of the 1920s may be regarded as the first of the 'affluent societies' which extended across the West from the 1950s. It is therefore not surprising to find an echo of these earlier debates as Labour came to terms with Britain's own post-war 'age of affluence'. The ascendant revisionists, chief among them Gaitskell and Crosland, were, crudely speaking, Atlanticists in social philosophy as well as in their international loyalties. Theirs was the world of Cole's *Next Ten Years*, a world of expertise in power and workers brought to life through consumption, and their lineage can be traced directly to Cole himself and the 'Cole group' of the late 1920s. The left in return offered a rhetoric heavily weighted to foreign policy issues, and a solidaristic ethos which its opponents portrayed with some success as anachronistic and self-denying.

Notoriously, the left was nothing if not anti-American, and superficially the lines seemed drawn as in the 1920s. Nevertheless, the allure for the left of Wilson's and other bastard forms of technocracy suggests that there was also something that had been lost. Part of that something was the notion of 'work as ideology': the critique of alienation that had assumed the forms of anti-Americanism but also raised more fundamental issues as to the nature of any possible good life. No doubt its postulates were utopian, or else served to dignify more basic material interests. But in a world of flexible labour markets and 'human resource' management, a world in which frenetic or contrived consumption justifies a length and intensity of work barely dented by new technologies, that concern with the nature of work, shorn of its contingent antipathies, continues to strike a chord.

Notes

1. Beatrice Webb *Diaries* (LSE), 8 November 1926 and Bertrand Russell, 'The danger of creed wars', *Socialist Review*, May 1927, pp.7–19; *The Daily Mail Trade Union Mission to the United States. Full story of the tour and members' report*, (London, 1926), p.3; Alan Bullock, *The Life and Times of Ernest Bevin. Volume one. Trade union leader 1881–1940*, (London, 1960), pp.357–62; TUC archives, MSS 292/973/35, B. Austin to Citrine, 7 April 1926; Bertram Austin and W. Francis Lloyd, *The Secret of High Wages* (London, 1926); Warwick University, TUC archives, MSS 292/973/36, W. Green, AFL, to W. Citrine, TUC, 30 July 1926; C.R. de Gruchy in *Socialist Review*, April 1928, cited A.J. Williams, *Labour and Russia. The attitude of the Labour Party to the USSR 1924–33* (Manchester, 1989), 65–6.

2. Mary Nolan, *Visions of Modernity. American business and the modernisation of Germany* (New York, 1994), p.32.

3. Antonio Gramsci, 'Americanism and Fordism' in *Selections from the Prison Notebooks*, eds Quintin Hoare and Geoffrey Nowell Smith (London, 1971), pp.279, 285–6, 301–3, and, for Gramsci and Fiat, Jean-Louis Cohen, *Scenes of the World to Come. European architecture and the American challenge 1893–1960* (Paris, 1995), p.80.

4. Edward P. Johanningsmeier, *Forging American Communism: The life of William Z. Foster* (Princeton N.J., 1994), p.181; Richard Stites, *Revolutionary Dreams. Utopian vision and experimental life in the Russian revolution* (New York, 1989), pp.146–9; Jeffrey Brooks, 'The press and its message: images of America in the 1920s and 1930s' in S. Fitzpatrick, A. Rabinowitch and R. Stites, eds, *Russia in the Era of NEP. Explorations in Soviet society and culture* (Bloomington, IN, 1991), pp.239–44. For Kahn, see Jean-Louis Cohen, *Le Corbusier and the Mystique of the USSR. Themes and projects for Moscow 1928–1936* (Princeton, NJ, 1992), p.198, citing O. Storonov, and Cohen, *Scenes*, pp.79–83.

5. Gramsci's essay does include a short section on high wages, but this was incidental to his main argument; more so, for example, even than prohibition.

6. Nolan, *Visions*, pp.76ff; John Willett, *The New Sobriety. Art and politics in the Weimar period 1917–1933* (London, 1978), pp.98–9 citing Ehrenburg. For Kautsky, see Peter Beilharz, *Labour's Utopias. Bolshevism, Fabianism, Social Democracy* (London, 1992), pp.98, 103.

7. See Detlev J.K. Peukert, *The Weimar Republic* (Harmondsworth, 1993 edn), pp.174–7, and David R. Roediger & Philip S. Foner, *Our Own Time. A history of American labor and the working day* (London, 1989 edn), pp.190–4.

8. See Dr Aldred Streimer's two articles on the German works councils, *Labour Magazine*, October 1922, pp.275–7 and November 1922, pp.324–5, and the encomiums in Arthur Henderson, 'An industrial parliament', *Labour Magazine*, July 1922, pp.116–19.

9. Nolan, *Visions*, p.100. For the *Bauhütten*, see IFTU Press Reports nos 99, 169 and 178, September-October 1922 (International Institute for Social History, Amsterdam); also Barbara Miller Lane, *Architecture and Politics in Germany*

1918–1945 (Cambridge MA, 1968), pp.51, 246–7.

10. Nolan, *Visions*, pp.50–4, 65–7, 251 n.30.

11. M.A. Hamilton, *Remembering My Good Friends* (London, 1944), p.225.

12. Of course, the Webbs visited Russia in 1932; see Robert Skidelsky, *Oswald Mosley*, London, 1981 edn), pp.146–50; Oswald Mosley, *My Life* (London, 1970 edn), pp.185–209, and for his contemporary impressions, 'Is America a capitalist triumph?', *New Leader*, 2 April 1926.

13. See the summary in the *Daily Herald*, 1 October 1926 which closely follows Mosley's view of America.

14. See the poem 'To E.O. Greening' by S. Gertrude Ford, *Co-operative News*, 15 January 1921:

    > *There shall the People win their quest*
    > *As Peace advises:*
    > *Not in the East but in the West*
    > *The new star arises!'*

15. For Mosely and its context, see Henry Pelling, *America and the British Left. From Bright to Bevan* (London, 1956), chs 5–6; for Barnes and Mosses, *Daily Mail Mission*, pp.4–5.

16. For example, the employer Charles Renolds and the engineer H. W. Allingham in their Fabian Society lectures, *Fabian News*, May 1917, p.23 and June 1917, p.27.

17. For the Singer strike, see Glasgow History Workshop, 'A clash of work regimes: "Americanisation" and the strike at the Singer Sewing Machine Company, 1911' in William Kenefick and Arthur McIvor, *Roots of Red Clydeside 1900–1914? Labour unrest and industrial relations in West Scotland* (Edinburgh, 1996), pp.193–213. For Weir see W.J. Reader, *Architect of Air Power. The life of the first Viscount Weir of Eastwood 1877–1959* (London, 1968), pp.29–30 and 110–14; for the patternmaker Thomas Murray, given leave of absence for the *Mail* party, see *Daily Mail Mission*, pp.97–101; for his foundry, Elizabeth Williamson et al, *The Buildings of Scotland: Glasgow* (London, 1990), p.541; for the Ironmoulders' leaflet, Tom Bell, *Pioneering Days* (London, 1941), pp.140–6.

18. In studying resistance to scientific management in the workplace, there may be a case, as Kevin Whitston argues, for focusing on the engineering industry, where these managerial practices were devised and perfected. Nevertheless, engineering cannot be assumed to be representative of other industrial sectors, nor was it necessarily the most significant determinant of wider labour movement responses as discussed here. See Kevin Whitston, 'Worker resistance and Taylorism in Britain', *International Review of Social History*, vol.42, no.1 (1997), p.4.

19. G.D.H. Cole, *Building and Planning* (London, 1945), p.93; Herbert Williams MP, House of Commons *Debates*, vol. 180, col. 499, 12 February 1925. The translation into a minute rate was Wheatley's idea.

20. For the guilds and craft, see e.g. G.D.H. Cole, *Self-Government in Industry* (London, 1917), pp.206–8: 'There will be no standardisation or centralisation of production...The individual worker will be a free and self-governing unit, and in the works the individual craftsman will find his freedom.'

21. George Hicks, *The ABC of Housing* (London, 1924), pp.9–10; *Daily Herald*, 20 September 1923; Hicks, 'Craft or class. The future of trade union organisation', *Labour Magazine*, November 1922, p.303; 'Problems of Amalgamation', *Labour Magazine*, July 1923, p.114. The debate was continued in *Plebs*, April-June 1924. For the 'Doctrine of the Vested Interest', see Sidney and Beatrice Webb, *Industrial Democracy* (London, 1897).

22. National Federation of Building Trades' Operatives, *Thirteenth Annual Conference Report* (London, 1930), pp.12ff; *A Brief Account of the National Federation of Building Trades Operatives* (London, 1930), pp.6–7.

23. M. Rubenstein cited Nolan, *Visions*, p.6; see R. Palme Dutt, *Socialism and the Living Wage* (London, 1927), p.201, and G.D.H. Cole, *The Next Ten Years in British Social and Economic Policy* (London, 1929) for examples of the words being used interchangeably.

24. Glasgow University archives, Weir papers, DC 96/2/23, translation of article from *Berliner Tageblatt*, 5 June 1926. For Hirsch, see Nolan, *Visions*, pp.19, 68–9, 91.

25. Lane, *Architecture*, pp.50 ff. and passim; Magdalena Droste, *Bauhaus* (Köln, 1990).

26. This crude summary neglects distinctions which would be crucial in other contexts, such as that between flexible prefabrication on Gropian lines and Weir's crude Model T approach.

27. Wertheimer, *Portrait of the Labour Party* (London, 1929), pp.7–8; Gramsci, 'Americanism', pp.279, 292; *Daily Mail Mission*, p.5.

28. For example, an article by Walter Meakin, written at John Strachey's invitation: 'The German coal industry: its lessons for us', *Socialist Review*, August 1926, pp.12–22. Meakin's book *The New Industrial Revolution* was published in 1928.

29. Bullock, *Bevin*, p.360.

30. See H.M. Drucker, *Doctrine and Ethos in the Labour Party* (London, 1979), p.27, for the view that the unions provided Labour's ideas while its intellectuals were merely allowed 'to provide the details and "take the minutes"'.

31. Finer, 'Impressions of America', *Fabian News*, February 1926, pp.9–10; Robson, 'Henry Ford and socialism', *Fabian News*, May 1927, pp.26–7.

32. Wilfred Wellock, 'America as a school for socialists', *New Leader*, 26 March 1926; Wellock, *Off the Beaten Track. Adventures in the art of living* (Tanjore, 1961), pp.60, 94–5, 102ff; also his article 'Gandhi: as revealed by himself', *Socialist Review*, December 1924. Wellock was elected MP for Stourbridge in 1927.

33. Brailsford, 'Can capitalism save itself?', *New Leader*, 26 March 1926. For his Russian trip and the book *How the Soviets Work*, see F.M. Leventhal, *The Last Dissenter. H.N. Brailsford and his world* (Oxford, 1985), pp.205–7.

34. Perry Anderson, 'Origins of the Present Crisis' (1964) in his *English Questions* (London, 1992), pp.33–6.

35. H.B. Lees-Smith, ed., *The Encyclopaedia of the Labour Movement*, vol. 3 (London, c. 1927), pp. 266–73.

36. Walker, *Bloody American Capitalism. Its murder of labour* (Bradford, 1924); Colyer, 'American capital and British Labour', *Labour Monthly*, October 1922, pp.230–1.

37. C.T. Cramp, 'Impressions of America', *Labour Magazine*, February 1925, pp.435–7; Philip S. Bagwell, *The Railwaymen. The History of the National Union of Railwaymen* (London, 1963), p.535. See also Frank Hodges, 'Aims and ideals of the miners' international', *Labour Magazine*, June 1925, pp.64–6.

38. Martin Wiener, *English Culture and the Decline of the Industrial Spirit 1850–1980* (Cambridge, 1981), pp.88–90 and passim; Correlli Barnett, *The Audit of War* (London, 1986), ch.1.

39. National Museum of Labour History, Brailsford papers, Church to Brailsford, 19 October 1926.

40. Norman and Jeanne Mackenzie, eds, *The Diary of Beatrice Webb. Volume two: 1892–1905. All the good things of life* (London, 1983), pp.137–45; *Fabian News*, April 1923, pp.14–15; March 1925, pp.10–11; February 1926, pp. 9–10.

41. Published in October and November 1922 respectively, *Babbitt* went through twelve editions and *My Life* thirteen during the 1920s.

42. Gramsci, 'Americanism', p.286.

43. Joe Toole, *Fighting Though Life* (London, 1935), pp.145–9.

44. Colyer, *Americanism*, esp. chs 1 and 6–8; for biographical details, see *Workers' Weekly,* 12 September 1924.

45. TUC archives MSS 292/973/20, AF of L 55th Convention, *Report of Proceedings*, 6 October 1926, and Hicks to Citrine, 14 October 1926.

46. *Trade Union Unity*, November 1925, pp.126–7; AF of L, 54th Convention *Proceedings,* October 1925, pp.139–43, 151–2; see also Philip Taft, *The American Federation of Labour from the Death of Gompers to the Merger* (New York, 1959), p.430.

47. AF of L, 54th Convention *Proceedings; Dean Forest Mercury*, 4 December 1925; Purcell, 'Capital and Labour in the USA', *Labour Monthly*, February 1926, pp.93–6.

48. For this issue, see the exchange between Swales and Oudegeest in TUC archives MSS 292/947/15, minutes of joint meeting of IFTU and TUC GC, 1 December 1925.

49. Allen, 'The ILP and revolution', address to ILP summer school, *Socialist Review*, October 1925, pp.148–9. Russell too regarded Bolshevism as 'really an Americanising process', but again from a position of considerable ambivalence about both; see Barry Feinberg and Ronald Kasrils, eds, *Bertrand Russell's America. His transatlantic travels and writings. Volume one: 1896–1945* (London, 1973), p.104.

50. For one of the most influential see René Fülöp-Miller, *The Mind and Face of Bolshevism* (London, 1927).

51. Tillett, *Some Russian Impressions* (London, 1925), pp.17–18.

52. G.D.H. Cole, *The Next Ten Years in British Social and Economic Policy* (London, 1929), pp.56–62 and passim; Beatrice Webb, diaries, 12 October 1926.

'New-fangled Men' and 'New-fangled Forces'

Reflections on the revolutions of 1848 and 1968

Alan Hooper and Michael Williams

'There have only been two *world* revolutions...1848...1968. Both were historic failures. Both transformed the world. The fact that both were unplanned and therefore in a profound sense spontaneous explains both facts—the fact that they failed, and the fact that they transformed the world.'[1] This paradoxical claim presents a challenge to consider the significance of these momentous years, for while the essay in which it is made, by Arrighi, Hopkins and Wallerstein, is suggestive rather than conclusive as to what the years heralded, their claim that the 'political ground-rules of the world-system were profoundly and irrevocably changed as a result of the revolution' seems indisputable. If Europe and the world failed to 'turn' in 1848 and 1968, as the protagonists intended, there is no doubt that both were radically different in the decades that followed the 'events' and that comparing their impact is likely, as Wallerstein and his collaborators suggest, to prove historically illuminating and politically instructive for the contemporary left.

1848 and 1968 were climacterics within epochs of transformation which, either side of those dates, were generational in scope. Each involved the development of new forms of popular social and political activity in response to accelerating processes of capitalist industrialisation, in particular the accumulating powers deriving from what Marx described as the twin but conflicting processes of capital centralization and labour socialization. It was the second—labour's socialization—which was key to the challenge of 1848 and 1968 and to the formation of a popular politics. Marx analysed the processes in detail in his chapter 'On Co-operation' in the first volume of *Capital*. Noting that co-operation 'ever constitutes the fundamental form of the capitalist mode of production', Marx stressed that co-operation brought not only a process in which the worker 'strips off the fetters of his individuality and develops the capacities of his species' but also the 'creation of a new power...the collective power of the masses'.[2] It was this new power, 'new-fangled men' seeking to master the new-fangled forces of society', that appeared in 1848 and 1968 and whose release or containment defined the politics of subsequent decades.[3]

A sense of the scale of the challenge in 1848 (and of 1968) can be found in the writings of Moses Hess. Today a neglected figure, Hess was a major, if unacknowledged, influence upon Marx during the 1840s and his writings in the years preceding 1848 capture the spirit of the period. In 'The Holy History of Mankind' (1837) he identified the temporal and spatial transformations foreshadowing a new society. Describing the American and French Revolutions as signs of a 'new age' he stressed that it was in America 'where the free communities developed...[that] the new age has achieved its first victory', while the French Revolution was the first, comprehensive attempt to shape the world in the image of this new age. Equally striking was Hess's characterisation of the social content of this era as one in which 'man should associate with his fellow men, live in society',with a 'community of property' as a necessary feature of what one recent intrepreter has called Hess's sense of an emerging 'socialized humanity'.[4] Here was a conception of a transformation encompassing the world created by the Atlantic revolutions of the previous half-century.

Hess's new epoch, radically original both in social content and in geographical scope, was one which the mid-nineteenth century would come to recognise as 'modernity'. For Matthew Arnold, whose sensibility registered these changes as spiritual loss and cultural challenge, it was the moment at which there began 'the dialogue of the mind with itself'; for Hess and Marx, free from theological despair and buoyed by the optimism of the *vorMarz*, it marked the possibility of a new 'social man' or, as Marx put it, 'the development of human power which is its own end'. Whatever the local circumstances there was a sense in both Western Europe and North America in 1848 and 1968 of socio-economic formations that were changing gear, with transitions from manufacture to modern industry and from country to city during the decades 1830–70, and from Fordist industry to post-Fordism and from a national to a global consciousness in the period 1930–70.[5] Both processes necessarily resulted in profound social and political—or class and human—reorderings, with the 'revolutions'/'events' of 1848 and 1968 their most spectacular manifestation.

Only democracy, in all its originality and ambition, could meet the challenges of a modernity which expresed itself collectively as 'mass society' and aesthetically as modernism. Democracy involved a claim for political participation 'as a function of...(one's) humanity' and for forms of sociability involving new modes of cultural expression. In America, as Michael Lind notes, by the 1850s 'the *real* national religion, it sometimes appeared, was democracy itself' while in western Europe, despite the defeats of 1848, democratic institutions—liberal in form, if conservative in inspiration—were to be adopted during the 1850s and 1860s; by 1950, with the Cold War adding urgency, it seemed, as Lind observes, that 'the democratization and Americanization of the entire human race was possible'.[6] Cultural practice was also informed by a sense of mass involvement and modern promise, the mid-nineteenth century seeing the emergence of cultural forms and practices—'metropolitan press, department store, ball park and vaudeville house' in America—which were to remain popular until the twentieth century when they were reshaped or superseded by the world of 'tabloids and movies, radio and television' which constituted the cultural context for the movements of the 1960s.[7]

It was America and its democratic prospects that provoked a sense of opportunity and of anxiety amongst contemporaries. While it prompted Matthew Arnold in the 1860s to ask 'what influence may help us to prevent the English people from becoming, with the growth of democracy, *Americanized*?', a question that looked back to de Tocqueville's troubled reflections in the 1830s and forward to the cultural anxieties of the American Dwight MacDonald a century later, it also produced an equally defining statement of optimism concerning the cultural possibilities of the masses. Writing in 1846, of a 'democratic feeling...becoming more and more powerful', Walt Whitman claimed that this was true not only of America but 'across the Atlantic...on the shores of Europe, [where] a restless dissatisfaction [is] spreading wider and wider every day' with the cause of 'freedom' in the Old World linked to the 'fate of our American Union'. While 1848 did not fulfil Whitman's hopes, his injunction to pursue a cultural practice that was democratising and which embraced mass concerns—'Imagination and actuality must be united'—was to define the work of modernist artists, both American and European, in the following century. It was an imperative for C.L.R. James when, in the 1940s, he reflected upon the cultural and political implications for mass struggles of 'American Civilization', written in the spirit of de Tocqueville and effectively a response to Arnold's challenge to Americans, and defenders of popular culture, to 'tell me if your civilisation is interesting'.[8]

The release of mass energies also prompted questions as to the institutional outcomes of such developments. While conservatives, cultural and political, looked to a redeployment of the state as the political form most likely to secure controlled change, the left—as befitted movements whose impetus was, as George Lichtheim has stressed, romantic and even anarchistic in spirit—looked beyond the state, either against it or, at best, in association with it. This proved the case in the aftermath of 1968 as in the decades which preceded 1848, as Sheila Rowbotham has reminded us in her examination of associationist activities—of work and leisure together—on both sides of the Atlantic in the latter year. These involved an exploration of ways of achieving a 'combination of autonomy and solidarity'—new forms of productive sociability through which to organise emergent material forces—which, she implies, is also the key to 1968.[9]

The left's desire to deepen democratic practice through novel agencies (parties and movements; associations and communities) encountered the challenge of renewed states and resourceful rulers. Both de Tocqueville and Marx stressed the manner in which, in Marx's words, all previous revolutions had 'perfected the [state] machine' and this proved to be true, though in different fashions, in the years following 1848 and 1968. While Ralph Miliband suggested that this perception was a 'main theme' in Marx's thought, Bernard Moss has recently argued that a shifting perspective in response to the changing fortunes of the revolution of 1848 not only revealed an ambiguity in Marx's evaluation of the state but highlighted lasting dilemmas for the left concerning its relationship to the state. Marx, Moss argues, fluctuated between a state-centred perspective prior to the movements of the mid-1840s and following Louis Napoleon's coup, and a society-centred one in response to the revolutionary energies of 1848; in the second case, he suggests, Marx adopted an 'engaged' materialism which stressed 'the open-ended development of humans in their productive relations' and a 'proletariat...transformed through revolutionary practice, without the help of theoretical anticipation and guidance'.[10]

Moss queries whether such a description of the movements of 1848 is historically accurate and, more pertinently, whether it was politically prudent, leaving as it did 'little room for...theory and the relative autonomy of the state', and the latter charge is one that can be made concerning the movements of 1968. Nevertheless, a stress upon the energies released in 1848 and 1968, above all the desire to reclaim the powers of the state for society, would seem to come closer to capturing the spirit of those years and the decades which spanned them than a narrowly conceived ideological perspective. For in both years the left, in attempting to define its objectives, was compelled to criticise existing institutions in the light of new possibilities: neither a democracy restricted to white males nor a state form that excluded 'non-historic' peoples could encompass the unfolding potentialities of modernity.[11] In what follows, therefore, we seek to explore the implications of the cultural and political energies which emerged in the revolutions of 1848 and 1968. We do so through the analyses of two pairs of contemporary observers of the revolutions—Alexis de Tocqueville and Karl Marx on the first and Dwight MacDonald and C.L.R. James on the second. While each was concerned with the implications of new forces, both political and cultural, and their significance for state and society, their responses reveal the differing political perspectives provoked by the impact of modernity in America and Western Europe in the decades surrounding 1848 and 1968.

1848 and after: revolution and reaction

1848 saw the second of five great waves of revolutions which have punctuated European history over the last couple of centuries: 1789, 1848, 1917, 1968, 1989. Looking further back one can detect other great upheavals—at the time of the Reformation in the 1520s, then during the last decades of the sixteenth century, and again in the 1640s—but none so synchronised as in the last couple of centuries. Not long afterwards the revolutions of 1848 became a byword for futility, as did those of 1968. This section tries to look deeper, taking its departure from the reflections of Marx and de Tocqueville on the course of revolution and reaction in France, still—for the last time— the epicentre of European politics.

Raymond Aron has remarked that France between 1848 and 1851 experienced 'a political conflict which, more than any other episode in the history of the nineteenth century, resembles the political conflicts of the twentieth century....[I]n this period one can observe a triangular conflict between what are known in the twentieth century as fascists, more or less liberal democrats, and socialists'.[12] Similar patterns can be observed in central Europe in what amounted to a struggle for the succession to a series of bankrupt dynastic states epitomised by Metternich's Austrian Empire. Both the socialists represented by Marx and the liberals represented by de Tocqueville went down in defeat in 1848 but, as Eric Hobsbawm observed of the most recent wave of revolutions which swept away the Soviet Union and its satellites, 'there is nothing which can sharpen the historian's mind like defeat'.[13] How did Marx and de Tocqueville interpret the events of 1848–51 in the light of the comprehensive defeat of the causes for which they contended?

C.L.R. James, whose anticipations of 1968 we shall be examining in the next section, has remarked on the parallels between Marx and de Tocqueville's responses to the earlier wave of revolutions: 'Tocqueville looked at 1848 and *he came to much the same conclusions as Marx did*, only he was on the opposite side'.[14] First of all, both predicted the coming upheavals. Marx (and Engels, let us not forget), in what has become known as *The Communist Manifesto*, completed in late 1847, described Germany as being 'on the eve of a bourgeois revolution that is bound to be carried out under more advanced conditions of European civilisation, and with a much more developed proletariat, than that of England was in the seventeenth, and of France in the eighteenth century, and because the bourgeois revolution in Germany will be but the prelude to an immediately following proletarian revolution'.[15] Addressing the French Chamber of Deputies in January 1848, de Tocqueville warned his audience of 'the disorder in men's minds', an increasing concern among the working class about 'social questions' rather than politics: 'can you not see that little by little there are spreading among them [the working class] opinions and ideas which are not concerned just with overthrowing this or that law, this or that administration, even this or that government, but society itself, shaking the very foundations on which it now rests....Do you not believe that I think that we are slumbering now on a volcano'.[16]

Second, both men (in common with other observers like Flaubert and Herzen) noted the extent to which the revolutionaries of 1848 drew on images and themes from the French Revolution of 1789. Marx observed that 'the Revolution of 1848 knew nothing better than to parody, now 1789, now the revolutionary tradition of 1793 to 1795....From 1848 to 1851 only the ghost of the old revolution walked about....An entire people, which had imagined that by means of a revolution it had imparted to itself an accelerated power of motion, suddenly finds itself set back into a defunct epoch'.[17] Marx himself was not immune to this tendency: 'the Jacobin of 1793 has become the Communist of our own day', he pronounced in February 1848.[18] Recalling the events of February 1848, de Tocqueville commented that '...the tepid passions of our day were expressed in the burning language of '93, and the names and deeds of illustrious villains were continually on the lips of men who had neither the energy nor even the sincere desire to imitate them'.[19]

Third, both recognised the workers' rising in Paris in June 1848 (the June Days) as a crucial watershed. Marx described it as 'the tremendous insurrection in which the first great battle was fought between the two classes that split modern society....a fight for the preservation or annihilation of the bourgeois order. The veil that shrouded the republic was torn asunder'.[20] De Tocqueville, who helped to organise the sanguinary suppression of the revolt and witnessed the savage street-fighting that ensued, recognised it as quite different from previous revolts: 'its object was not to change the form of the government, but to alter the organisation of society. In truth it was not a political struggle...but a class struggle'.[21]

Fourthly, both noticed the way in which universal suffrage could be used for counter-revolutionary purposes. Marx learned from the election of a predominantly conservative National Assembly in May and the election of Louis Bonaparte as president in December 1848 that 'universal suffrage did not possess the magic power which republicans of the old school had ascribed to it....Bourgeois rule as the outcome and result of universal suffrage...that is the meaning of the bourgeois constitution'.[22] De Tocqueville, who was elected to the National Assembly in May, noted that landowners of all sizes had united against the working class of Paris: 'By establishing universal suffrage [the revolutionaries of February] thought they were summoning the people to support the revolution, whereas they were only arming them against it'.[23] Louis Bonaparte showed how universal suffrage combined with fear of the working class could be used to sustain a new kind of authoritarian regime. That demonstration would not be lost on others.

Finally, both Marx and de Tocqueville noted the increasingly important and independent role played by the state and its masters. Marx's analysis of the French state and the emergence of Bonapartism will be too familiar to require elaboration or illustration. What might be worth remarking upon is the extent to which Marx saw the emergence of the Bonapartist state—'this executive power with its enormous bureaucratic and military organisation'— as the culmination of developments originating under the absolute monarchy of the seventeenth and eighteenth centuries.[24] De Tocqueville took a similar view in his last work, *The Ancien Régime and the French Revolution*, in which he analysed the development of the French state which he saw as 'a vast, centralised power', more so than any other government since the fall of the Roman Empire. This process began under the absolute monarchy, reached a climax under the Jacobins and Napoleon, and continued under each of the subsequent regimes.[25] France above all illustrated de Tocqueville's general argument, first advanced in *Democracy in America* (1835 and 1840), about the way in which the revolutionary road to democracy, and the attendant social conflict, could open the way to a new despotism, based on a passive, atomised populace.[26]

De Tocqueville died only three years after publishing *The Ancien Régime*. Marx, however, would have a lifetime to reflect on 1848. Speaking before an audience of working men in London in 1856 he described 'the so-called revolutions of 1848' as 'but poor incidents—small fractures and fissures in the dry crust of European society. However, they denounced [sic] the abyss. Beneath the solid surface they betrayed oceans of liquid matter, only needing expansion to rend into fragments continents of hard rock. Noisily and confusedly they proclaimed the emancipation of the proletarian, i.e. the secret of the nineteenth century, and of the revolution of that century'. He went on to describe 'steam, electricity and the self-acting mule' as 'revolutionists of a rather more dangerous character' than the men of 1848. He concluded by arguing that 'new-fangled men' were needed to master these 'new-fangled forces of society' and asserted optimistically that 'working men' were such men.[27] A couple of years later he took a more pessimistic line, commenting to Engels that 'the reaction is carrying out the programme of the revolution'.[28] Looking back from 1895, in an introduction to Marx's *Class Struggles in France*, Engels commented that when Marx was writing in 1850, 'the period of revolutions from below was concluded for the time being; there followed a period of revolutions from above....The grave-diggers of the Revolution of 1848 had become the executors of its will'.[29] Who, and what, did he have in mind when he wrote those lapidary words?

The upheavals of 1848 and the next few years saw the disappearance of one generation of rulers shaped by the French Revolution and Napoleonic Wars—Metternich (born 1773), Louis Philippe (1773), Nicholas I of Russia (1796), Frederick William IV of Prussia (1797)—and the emergence of a new generation of conservatives capable of mastering the 'new-fangled forces of society'. Louis Bonaparte (born 1808) was perhaps the prototype of other, more formidable figures including Bismarck (born 1815), Cavour (1810) and Alexander II of Russia (1818). A similar pattern can be discerned even in Britain, where the 1850s and 1860s were dominated by Palmerston (albeit born 1784) until his death in 1865. Asa Briggs has compared his victory in the 1859 election to a plebiscite by Louis Bonaparte.[30]

The 1850s and 1860s can be seen as an extraordinary period of state-building, not only in Europe but around the world. Louis Bonaparte promoted the industrialisation of France and prepared the ground for the relatively stable bourgeois republic built on the ruins of the Commune. Bismarck engineered the creation of the German Empire under Prussian leadership following the example of Cavour's unification of Italy under Piedmontese leadership. Alexander II ended serfdom and strove mightily, if unsuccessfully, to build a modern Russian state. Gladstone modernised Britain's public finances and its army and civil service and Disraeli, in the Second Reform Act of 1867, discerned the way in which extending the vote to the urban working class could be used for conservative purposes. Further afield, Lincoln ended the grotesque anomaly of slavery and consolidated the American Union in what has been characterised as an advance comparable to the English Revolution of the 1640s and the French Revolution of 1789. These decades also saw the beginning of another 'revolution from above' in Japan and the establishment of the British Raj in the aftermath of the Indian Mutiny. China and the Ottoman Empire saw abortive attempts at modernisation from above.[31]

From this longer perspective, the revolutions of 1848 can be seen as crucial over much of Europe in clearing the ground for the construction of the modern bureaucratic and democratic state which Marx and de Tocqueville discerned in the making in France. In response to this process the working class movement would be obliged to abandon the tactics inherited from the French Revolution and still deployed in 1848, and to develop the mass party seeking to use universal suffrage in order to conquer the state.[32] Thus 1848 was pregnant with future.

1968: anticipations and outcomes

An important clue to the significance of 1968 and the 1960s is to be found in Dwight MacDonald's essay 'Masscult and Midcult' which appeared in *Partisan Review* in 1960. Recalling how he had given a talk on mass culture at a *Universities and Left Review* forum in London in 1959 MacDonald admitted that he had found himself unprepared 'for the reaction to my attacks on mass culture...[which] were resented in the name of democracy'. In particular he admitted to being 'rather dazed' by this 'proletarian defense' of Hollywood— 'our peculiar institution'—which his audience chose to regard not as an 'exploitation' of popular tastes but rather a 'genuine expression of the masses'.[33] Here, before an audience of the emergent new left of the 1960s, a key figure of the left of the previous generation—one indeed who had once thought of calling the magazine 'Politics' which he founded in the mid-1940s *New Left Review*—was confronted by barriers that were not simply geographical and generational but cultural and political.[34]

The encounter was a portent not just of a new mood but of a political divide: the new left's concern with mass culture as an expression of demo-cratic potential was fundamentally alien to the sensibility which MacDonald had cultivated since the early 1940s. Some reconciliation was to be achieved between the left of the 1960s and that of the previous generation when MacDonald's earlier writings, especially his 1944 essay 'The Root Is Man', came to be regarded by the American new left as a formative text, while MacDonald was a prominent supporter of the anti-Vietnam War movement. Nevertheless, significant barriers, both of belief and, more importantly, behaviour, remained even when MacDonald supported the students during the Columbia University protests in 1968. It is another figure, one who even more than MacDonald took the culture of the Atlantic region as his intel-lectual frame of reference, to whom we must look for an understanding of the mass energies and aspirations of the 1960s.

That figure is C.L.R. James. His path had crossed that of MacDonald at a number of points, though direct encounters seem to have been few.[35] In particular, both shared the wrenching experience of those intellectuals and political activists in the New York of the late 1930s who struggled to come to terms with the implications of that 'midnight in the century' whose most dispiriting expression was the Hitler—Stalin pact. As members of one of the largest—and, as time was to show, most distinguished—sections of Trotsky's infant Fourth International, both MacDonald and James were involved in the increasingly fraught debates within the movement concerning the significance of Stalin's regime. In 1941 both followed Max Shachtman out of the Socialist Workers' Party and into the Workers' Party. These developments, as Edmund Wilson noted in 1941, marked 'the end of a phase of American intellectual history', signalling a profound crisis for Marxism in the US; the Cold War in the late 1940s was to complete the marginalisation of Marxism within American life which the disarray of the early 1940s had precipitated.[36] When a new left emerged in the 1960s it had little sense of theoretical continuity with the left of the previous generation. Nevertheless, affinities could be discovered: while MacDonald's pacifist and anarchist beliefs and personal commitment struck a chord with the new generation it was James's response to the crisis of Marxism in the US that suggested more relevant lessons for the generation of the 1960s.

For though James shared MacDonald's concerns his solutions were radically different: they constituted an attempt not only to renew Marxism but also to make it relevant to the cultural experience of the most advanced capitalist society in the world, the US. During the 1940s James sought to redefine the Marxist tradition and give it renewed temporal and spatial purchase, unlike MacDonald who considered Marxism irrelevant to the conditions of modernity in a country which, after 1945, proclaimed its global supremacy both materially and culturally. Though both shared the decade's concern with an overweening state—given classic expression with the publication of Hannah Arendt's *Origins of Totalitarianism* in 1951—their assessment of possible responses to this phenomenon differed markedly. While MacDonald recommended only acts of individual or, at best, group resistance, James saw in such hypertrophic states the perverted expression of mass aspirations to which mass activity was an inevitable and effective reponse.

While such differences owed much to their contrasting definitions of a post-Trotskyist politics—MacDonald's adoption of Shachtman's bureaucratic collectivism suggested that resistance was a distant prospect, unlike James whose state-capitalist analysis built resistance into the dynamic of capital accumulation—more was involved than political economy. While MacDonald's politics were imbued with a deepening pessimism, his cultural stance was, in principle at least, more defiant. Here he followed Clememt Greenberg whose famous 1939 essay 'Avant-garde and Kitsch', had looked to the artistic exponents of a modernist high culture to sustain a sense of cultural, and thereby political, possibility in the face of the aesthetically and politically enfeebling products of mass culture. It was an improbable perspective, for if the forces of political Trotskyism were divided and few in number, how much truer was this of their artistic counterparts: 'what can fifty do against 140,000,000?' Greenberg asked forlornly in 1947.[37] MacDonald's position on cultural issues registered a wider retreat. Whereas in his influential 1944 essay 'A Theory of Popular Culture' he could still quote Trotsky favourably concerning the possibility of 'a potential new human culture', his 1953 revision, significantly re-titled a 'Theory of Mass Culture', described a 'mob' condemned to a culture that was irredeemably kitsch. His 'Masscult and Midcult' essay completed the retreat, looking defensively and to Europe for the maintenance of 'smaller, more specialized audiences' to sustain High Culture from the Masscult which was all the masses required; above all, he asserted, 'don't fuzz up the distinction with Midcult'.[38]

MacDonald conceded that in adopting such a stance he was turning his back on Whitman's goal of a 'democratic culture'; 'this noble vision', he declared, 'now seems absurd'.[39] But it was such a culture that James reaffirmed and the 1960s radicals practised. James's rethinking of Marxism involved a period of great creativity during the years from the mid-1940s to the mid-1950s, from 'The Invading Socialist Society' (1947) to 'Facing Reality' (1958) and including his extraordinary 'American Civilisation', completed in 1950 but not published during his lifetime.[40] Together they constitute nothing less than an attempt to redefine revolutionary politics, post-Stalin and post-Trotsky, and to relate it to a conception of social and cultural development as original as it is radical. Central to this originality was James's conviction that modern societies in Europe and America exemplifed what he called 'the main theme—socialism and barbarism. The concentration of the means of production and the socialisation of labour...'—a conception derived from Marx but which led James to the original perspective that 'the advancing socialist society compels the capitalist to treat the productive forces as a social force', hence the notion of an *invading* socialist society.[41] In 'American Civilization', or what he had originally intended to call 'The Struggle for Happiness', James explored the implications of this perspective in the world's most advanced capitalist society.

James stressed that though his study had a polemical intent—seeking to destroy 'the great illusion that exists in Europe about the United States, that the working people are so well off that they consider themselves essentially a constituent part of the American way'—it also had a profounder (and Tocquevillian) purpose, for while 'the subject matter is the United States, the ideas are general, a view of modern society as a whole, the totality of the present crisis, its antecedents and the perspectives that arise from it'.[42] He sought to vindicate the mass culture which MacDonald disparaged and to find in it a foreshadowing of new forms of collective expression and action. Thus he argued that totalitarian statism, far from being 'proof of the depravity of human nature', proved the opposite: 'the tremendous hopes, desires, wishes for a truly human existence and the consciousness that it is possible to achieve this'. The 'quest' of modern men 'for universality needs a new sense of belonging to the community', he claimed; the popular arts of America 'film, radio, television, comic strip', whose analysis was central to his study, pointed towards an 'integration of modern life' which could take either a totalitarian form—'a cruel, barbarous but necessary perversion of the instincts and desires for high civilization characteristic of modern man'—or, in the manner of the Greeks, could be the basis of a 'totally new society, an active integrated humanism'.[43]

This perspective reflected James's conviction that popular cultural activities expressed 'an immense social and artistic movement' which, as he argued in a memorable image, points a broad arrow to the future and the integration of the social and aesthetic aspects of life'.[44] Such a comment was the product not only of prolonged consideration of the relationship between individual and community, the artistic and the political—themes evident in his earliest masterpiece *The Black Jacobins* (1937) as in his last, *Beyond a Boundary* (1963)—but also of a profound engagement with American politics and society during the 1940s. More immediately the context for his thoughts was provided by the last, as yet unsurpassed, mobilisation of the American working-class associated with the Congress of Industrial Organisations (CIO) during the New Deal years of the 1930s and 1940s. The impact of this movement has been powerfully documented by Michael Denning who situates it in the context of the cultural and political struggles of the Popular Front as part of what he calls a 'cultural front'—a social movement which lent a 'Popular Front "flavor"' to mass culture through the 'laboring of American culture'. Not everyone will want to go as far as Denning in his generally positive evaluation of the politics of the Popular Front but many will endorse his evaluation of its cultural creativity, thereby aligning themselves with James and against MacDonald, for whom the Popular Front was but one example of the encroaching cultural, and political, debasement of which Hollywood and the regimes of Hitler and Stalin were more flagrant examples. As such the CIO, which James stressed was as much a party as a union and which Denning variously describes as a 'movement culture' like Goodwyn's Populists or a form of 'social unionism' of the sort evident in the most dynamic workers' movements of the 1980s, testifies to that capacity for mass action which was at the core of James's political outlook during, and especially after, his Trotskyist years.[45]

But James's outlook in 1950 is not only vindicated by a movement that had, at the time he was writing, lost much of its radicalism; it is also confirmed by the movements which emerged in the 1960s. Direct influences were limited: some links have been established between James and his circle and the Students for a Democratic Society; more compelling are the connections between James, his close associate Martin Glaberman and the Detroit-based League of Revolutionary Black Workers.[46] But direct affiliation is not the issue; rather what we are suggesting is that James's preoccupations are closer to those of the 1960s than almost any of his contemporaries, certainly more than MacDonald, whose public profile was probably higher than James's in the 1960s. Only the Situationists would seem to be closer to the spirit of the decade but their activities were primarily European, indeed Francophone, in their impact and almost by choice subterranean in their mode of operation.[47] For a sense of the strengths and weaknesses of the movements of the 1960s it is James who captures, both in his advances and his absences, the spirit of that revolutionary decade.

One of the strengths of the movements of the period, and in many respects their most significant legacy, was their cultural radicalism, undermining 'rigid and exclusionary definitions of the cultural tradition' of the sort MacDonald had been at pains to sustain and James to challenge.[48] Such rigidities were, in turn, founded upon social hierarchies of class, race and sexuality, hierarchies which were partly reinforced by the Euro-American or 'Lincoln' Republic which emerged during the New Deal.[49] While MacDonald, in the 1940s, was as radically innovatory as James in questioning the last two of those discriminations, his increasingly conservative cultural stance in the 1950s led him to accept class hierarchies, especially those of Britain, as the necessary price of cultural distinction and high modernism. Moreover MacDonald's modernism had become increasingly beleaguered as his own preference for the period of classic modernism (1890–1920) was overtaken by Greenberg's preferred abstract expressionism, an art which MacDonald condemned as the visual equivalent of rock'n'roll. By the begining of the 1960s this stance was looking increasingly unsustainable as political elites worldwide began to embrace a modernising rhetoric of social and political transformation, albeit one that was 'technocratic rather than humanistic, elitist rather than participatory'.[50]

The new left's response was to seek to radicalise and democratise the potentialities released by the elites: to embrace the technological and material possibilities of the booming global economy for human emancipation, redefining personal and social relations, reconnecting modernism with everyday life. Such aspirations were already prefigured by the Popular Front culture of the 1930s, one of whose key concerns, Denning argues, was the 'politics of mental labour' and the 'role of symbol producers in a society dominated by mass communications'. The political perspective which James had formulated in response to that movement—of mass movements, radically self-determining in their objectives and operations—was now a defining feature of the movements of the 1960s.[51] Such movements encouraged not only new conceptions of culture but new constituencies of identity—of ethnicity, gender and sexual preference—whose impact has continued to be felt through to the century's end. In contesting the 'line between high culture and popular culture' so that on 'some fronts [it] was erased entirely', it redefined conceptions not only of value, a seminal text here being Susan Sontag's 1964 'Notes on "Camp"', but also, and more significantly, notions of human capability and creativity; in short, new people for new times.[52] Such were the democratising impulses which the new left released and which James had discerned in his analysis of 'American Civilization'.

Insofar as the decade failed to achieve its political objectives, however, that too could be related to James's thinking, as the absences in his analysis exacted a heavy, but perhaps unavoidable, cost. In particular, the failure of James and his associates to provide a credible answer to the question of political organisation for popular movements restricted their effectiveness. *Facing Reality*, the pamphlet co-authored by James, Cornelius Castoriadis and Grace Lee in 1958, betrays the initial optimism stirred by the Hungarian revolution of 1956 in its celebration of mass insurgency and council democracy and as such is wholly consistent with the perspectives James had been developing since his rejection of the vanguard party in the late 1940s. However, the section on Marxist Organisation, allegedly the work of Castoriadis, is noticeably vague on the purpose and likely impact of such as organisation which at best is defined as an information-gatherer and catalyst to the mass movement.[53] This deficiency goes to the heart of James's political analysis, revealing a stance that developments in the last quarter of the twentieth century would call into question.

For James's claim that the 'proletariat is always increasing in numbers and is united, disciplined and organised'—the basis both of his optimism concerning its political creativity and his neglect of specific organisational issues—was looking less convincing by the 1970s and 1980s.[54] Not only was labour ceasing to be socialised in the forms which Fordism had seemed to make inevitable but capital seemed to be less centralised, if not concentrated, in the new, 'flexible', post-Fordist regimes that were now its preferred mode of operation. These developments were the product of a new political regime which also called into question the conceptions of state and society which James had formulated on the basis of American experience in the 1930s and 1940s. While the role of the state was redefined to secure a significant divestment of its productive, if not its punitive, role—a reduction in collectivist or corporatist modes in the West which foreshadowed the much more spectacular collapse of the authentic state capitalisms of the East and which in both cases called into question the relevance of 'totalitarianism' as a concept—society was becoming disorganised or diversified to such an extent that the categories of mass society, never unproblematic, looked increasingly irrelevant in what many saw as a new pluralism. That the insurgencies of the 1960s, both in their results and in the reaction they provoked, had made no small contribution to this outcome was not the least of the ironies that confronted late-modern, or increasingly 'post-modern', society.

Amongst the many ironies of that allegedly post-modern condition two were especially troubling for the left and suggested that MacDonald's chastened pragmatism might have greater relevance than James's undimmed optimism. The first concerned the cultural transformation of the 1960s. If the decade had achieved a revaluation and potential democratisation of cultural categories—embracing 'Shakespeare and Ginsberg, literature and movies, Beethoven and rock'—that achievement threatened, as a result of the renewed ascedancy of corporate capital from the 1980s onwards, to resolve itself into an 'easy pluralism' in which each segment of cultural taste would indulge its own preferences—or worse, a manipulable populism in which commercial pressures would define much of the agenda. MacDonald had once been willing to countenance something like the first, in defence of 'high culture', but the latter required the continued exercise of a more stringent critical judgement if culture was to be sustained as an exacting and liberating human resource.[55]

The second involved an even more fundamental challenge—the political promise of modernity itself. Paul Goodman was not alone in the 1960s in warning that an elitist 'quack' modernism which emphasised bigness and waste could have perverse consequences, producing not only natural disasters but also undermining the very sense of human agency and capability that underpinned the modernist project. By the late 1960s in the turn to spiritual and anti-rational attitudes just such a reaction was underway and we can see the beginnings of one important strand of post-modernism in this development. MacDonald had sensed such a possibility in the 1940s and in an essay of 1952 had asked whether it was possible to 'understand politics and history any more...find the theoretical key that will lay bare the real forces that shape history—indeed, can we believe there is such a key at all'.[56] This essay concerned C.Wright Mills, who was himself querying the capacity of liberalism and socialism to make sense of the contemporary condition and, in one of its first usages, was to employ the term 'post-modern' to describe this uncertainty in 1959; even James could express doubts as to the capacity of criticism to achieve any 'coherent system or method' for the 'mountains of information' which had been accumulated.[57] It is to MacDonald, however, that we must turn for a possible remedy to this sense of dissolution and enfeeblement, as in his call on the front of his journal *Politics* in August 1945 for '[e]very individual...[to] begin thinking dangerous thoughts about...the fraternity of all men everywhere'. In displaying what one of his readers described as a 'feeling of fraternity' MacDonald had provided a salutary reminder of the need for the third term of popular politics in 1848, and 1968, to be taken as seriously as that modernist equality whose pursuit he had come to distrust and that post-modern liberty he would quite properly have deplored.[58]

Global perspective

In the preceding sections we have attempted to interpret the paradox identified by Wallerstein and his fellow authors that the revolutions of 1848 and 1968 were at once globally transformative and historic failures. We have done so by placing both years in the perspective of a modernity which involved the emergence of novel challenges and modes of engagement—'new fangled forces', material and organisational, and 'new fangled men' and their cultural and political resources. We have described the origin of these forces in the world that was 'civilized' and capitalist: the world of an unfolding capitalist industrialisation in the epicentres of that phenomenon, Western Europe and North America. The product of revolution, whether national, political and economic; or American, French and Industrial, they released revolutionary forces which required the 'constant revolutionising' of society and brought with them the periodic revolutionising of politics, 1848 and 1968 being two key instances. We have explored how the challenges of both years reshaped state and society—politics as institution building and as cultural discovery. We have explored the contrasting perspectives concerning these transformations of sceptics and advocates: de Tocqueville and MacDonald; Marx and James. It was a process that each saw in global perspective and it is with a consideration of the scope and import of these events—their world-transformative significance and their world-historical 'failure'—that we will conclude.

Such questions turn upon a sense of the relevant span of history and its co-ordinates, temporal and spatial. Much recent scholarship, under the impact of the Cold War, has explored the geo-cultural links between societies and in particular the US as a major protagonist in that conflict and Europe as a key arena. There can be no doubt that the US sought to use cultural activities and agencies as weapons of political influence in the struggle against communism. There is much less agreement as to their effectiveness in doing so. Similarly, there is no dispute as to the extent of the geo-political power which the US mobilised during the Cold War but once again little agreement as to whether this was the primary source of trans-Atlantic convergence. In this essay we have stressed more wide-ranging and deep-seated connections between America and Europe based upon their shared experience of modernity and the promises and problems to which it gave rise. Our four writers took the two continents as their frame of reference—de Tocqueville more than Marx and James more than MacDonald—and each displayed a lively sense of the interconnections between the two continents to which Whitman had referred and whose origins may be found in the great revolutions of the late eighteenth century.

If the spatial span was the product of a sense of a shared fate it was a sense of common experience, based upon the forces of modernity, which suggested the temporal links between conditions in the mid-twentieth century and those of a century earlier. James and his circle, especially his one-time collaborator, Raya Dunayevskaya, looked back to the abolitionist movement during the Civil War and the impact of its struggles as a model for political organisation and as the key to their activist and humanist interpretation of Marx; James in 'American Civilization' considered it the 'vital question...today' whether a movement like the Abolitionists was 'bound to end in the vast oppressive bureaucratic militarist structures which mean...the end of civilization'.[59] MacDonald drew different conclusions but was no less convinced of the importance of the mid-nineteenth century's legacy, finding the origins of cultural decline in the destruction of the New England tradition during the Civil War period.[60] 1848 spoke to 1968, America to Europe and vice versa, for reasons that owed more to the challenges of modernity than to the manouevres of power, whether geo-political or geo-cultural.

These deep-seated affinities also explain the strengths of the two revolutions and the nature of their failure. Both James and, in his revolutionary years, Macdonald, stressed the essentially humanistic impulse of Marx and radical politics. James and his circle, as part of their attempt to renew Marxist politics in the mid-1940s, provided one of the first translations and interpretations of Marx's 'Economic and Philosophic Manuscripts': it became the basis of their stress upon the 'subjective factor, man as man, and not as the slave of capital' which informed James's analysis of contemporary, and especially American, political developments.[61] MacDonald, in seeking to salvage an ethical dimension for radical politics from the debris of Stalinism and war, had stressed the imperative of human responsibility. This return to the spirit of the 1840s to replenish energies in the 1960s can be seen as part of that wider embrace of utopian energy that marked both decades. George Lichtheim has written of that 'alliance between socialism, romanticism and feminism...[that] became a reality in the 1840's'; a later observer has described the politics of the 1960s as a 'Romantic socialism' seeking 'the libertarian socialist dream of a community of redeemed selves'.[62] Both periods sought to realise that 'socialized humanity' which Hess had discerned and which formed the basis of those associationist and modernist currents which continued to reverberate during the years between 1860 and 1960.[63] To participants the revolutions of 1968 and 1848 take their place in a deepening dynamic of democratic practice which was modernity's greatest promise, an ambition evident in a Sorbonne appeal of 1968: 'The bourgeois revolution was judicial; the proletarian revolution was economic. Ours will be social and cultural so that man can become himself'.[64]

If this 'revolution in the revolution'—of democratic association and sociability—is the great achievement of 1968 it also suggests the source of what Wallerstein and his fellow authors describe as its failure. For like the movements of 1848, those of 1968 underestimated the scale of their ambitions and the resistance they would encounter. 'The sign that the present crisis is at last up for resolution will be the appearance of...[a] new mass political organisation which will seek to make politics an expression of universal man and a totally integrated personality', James had written at the end of 'American Civilization'.[65] If an such organisation has appeared—and its nearest embodiments would seem to be the 'social unionism' which James had celebrated in the CIO and which he was to live to see in Solidarity in the 1980s—it has not been able to supplant the logics of state or capital against which 1848 and 1968 were directed. Rather, the forces linked to those two monoliths were able to redeploy them, as a state-led capitalism post-1848 and a market-dominated statism post-1968, against the forces of sociability and associationism.

The political modes appropriate to such sociability—the historic challenge of 1848 and 1968—remain unclear: to the optimistic James they were a matter of anticipation, predictable only in their purpose not their pattern; to the more pessimistic MacDonald they meant a form of witness, personal as much as collective. For both, however, there was a recognition of the need for a new 'social man', for new sensibilities to match new possibilities. Each looked to the release of sentiments and energies whose expression had been endangered by an overweening state, both in the rationalising bureaucracies of de Tocqueville's West and the developmental ones of the 'Marxist' East. The release of such energies was, however, made more problematic by that post-modern bafflement of modernist aspiration which was not the least of the unintended consequences of the 1960s and which continues to perplex the left at the century's end.[66] Nevertheless, only those disposed to believe that the placing of the prefix 'post' before the word modern signals the annulment of the energies that modernism and socialism once harnessed will conclude that the 'long revolution' whose span and scope we have explored in this essay is at an end.

Notes

1. G. Arrighi, T.K. Hopkins and Wallerstein, 1968: *The Great Rehearsal in Antisystemic Movements* (London, 1989), pp.97–8.
2. K. Marx, *Capital*, Volume 1 (1867; Moscow, 1965 edn), pp.326, 329, 335.
3. K. Marx, 'Speech at the Anniversary of the People's Paper' (1856), in K. Marx, *Surveys from Exile. Political Writings: Volume 2* (Harmondsworth, 1973), pp.299–300.
4. S. Avineri, *Moses Hess: Prophet of Communism and Zionism* (New York, 1985), pp.32–4.
5. M. Dickstein, *Gates of Eden. American culture in the sixties* (Cambridge, Mass., 1997), p.249; R. Dunayevskaya, *Philosophy and Revolution. From Hegel to Sartre and from Marx to Mao* (New Jersey, 1982), p.290; T. J. Clark, *The Painting of Modern Life. Paris in the art of Manet and his followers* (London, 1985), pp.3,63.
6. G. Williams, *Karl Marx and Alexis de Tocqueville in the revolutions of 1848* (Milton Keynes, 1976), p.122; M. Lind, *The Next American Nation. The new nationalism and the fourth American revolution* (New York, 1995), pp.55–6.
7. G. Barth, *City People. The rise of modern city culture in nineteenth-century America* (New York, 1980), p.234; W.L. Burn, *The Age of Equipoise. A Study of the mid-Victorian Generation* (London, 1964), pp.284–5.
8. M. Arnold, 'The Popular Education of France' (1861) in P. J. Keating, ed., *Selected Prose* (Harmondsworth, 1982) pp.111–12; B. Erkkila, *Whitman the Political Poet* (New York, 1989) pp.57, 76; R. Hughes, *American Visions. The epic history of art in America* (New York, 1997), p.215.
9. G. Lichtheim, *The Origins of Socialism* (London, 1968), pp.71 and 165; S. Rowbotham, *Threads through Time. Writings on history and autobiography* (Harmondsworth, 1999) p.228; F. Lenger, 'Beyond Exceptionalism: Notes on the artisanal phase of the labour movement in France, England, Germany and the United States', *International Review of Social History*, vol.36 (1991), p.18.

10. K. Marx, *The Eighteenth Brumaire of Louis Bonaparte*, (1852; Mosow, 1954 edn), p.105; R. Miliband, 'Marx and the state', in G. Duncan, ed., *Democracy and the Capitalist State* (Cambridge, 1989), p.97; B. Moss, 'Marx and the permanent revolution in France: background to the Communist Manifesto' in L. Panitch and C. Leys, eds, *The Socialist Register: The Communist Manifesto now* (London, 1998), pp.154, 155.

11. M. Lind, *The Next American Nation* (New York, 1995), pp.73–4;. A.M. Schlesinger Jr, *The Cycles of American History* (Harmondsworth, 1989 edn), p.120.

12. R. Aron, *Main Currents in Sociological Thought*, Volume 1 (Harmondsworth, 1968), p.233.

13. E. Hobsbawm, 'The present as history' in *On History* (London, 1993), p.239.

14. C.L.R. James, *Modern Politics* (1960; Detroit, 1973 edn), p.34.

15. K. Marx, 'Manifesto of the Communist Party' (1848) in *The Revolutions of 1848. Political Writings: Volume 1* (Harmondsworth, 1973), p.98.

16. A. de Tocqueville, 'Speech in the Chamber of Deputies, January 27, 1848' in *Democracy in America* (1835 & 1840; New York, 1988 edn), pp.752–3.

17. Marx, *Eighteenth Brumaire*, pp.10–12.

18. Marx, 'Speeches on Poland', in *The Revolutions of 1848*, p.102.

19. A. de Tocqueville, *Recollections* (New York, 1971 edn), p.93.

20. K. Marx, *The Class Struggles in France, 1848 to 1850* (1850; Moscow, 1952 edn).

21. De Tocqueville, *Recollections,* p.169.

22. Marx, *Class Struggles*, pp.48, 121

23. De Tocqueville, *Recollections*, pp.109–10.

24. Marx, *Eighteenth Brumaire,* p.104.

25. A. de Tocqueville, *The Ancien Regime and the French Revolution* (1856; London, 1966 edn).

26. A. de Tocqueville, *Democracy in America.*

27. Marx, 'Speech at the Anniversary', pp.299–300.

28. K. Marx in *Surveys from Exile*, p.31.

29. Marx, *Class Struggles,* p.14.

30. A. Briggs, *Victorian People* (Harmondsworth, 1965) p.93.

31. B. Moore Jr, *Social Origins of Dictatorship and Democracy* (Harmondsworth, 1967), pp.183, 229, 353; J. A. S. Grenville, *Europe Reshaped 1848–1878* (London, 1976), pp.220, 321.

32. G. Eley, 'Reviewing the Socialist Tradition' in C. Lemke and G. Marks, eds, *The Crisis of Socialism in Europe* (Durham, NC, 1992), p.36.

33. D. MacDonald, *Against the American Grain* (New York, 1992), pp.64–5.

34. D. MacDonald, *Discriminations. Essays and afterthoughts* 1938–1974 (New York, 1974).

35. M. Wreszin, *A Rebel in Defense of Tradition. The life and politics of Dwight MacDonald*, (New York, 1994), pp.80–1.

36. S. Biel, 'Freedom, Commitment and Marxism. The predicament of independent intellectuals in the United States, 1910–41' in J. Jennings and A. Kemp-Welch, eds, *Intellectuals in Politics from the Dreyfus affair to Salman Rushdie*

(London, 1997), p.243.

37. Hughes, *American Visions*, p.466.
38. Wreszin, *Rebel*, pp.286–9; MacDonald, *Against,* p.73.
39. MacDonald, *Against*, p.72.
40. C.L.R. James, *American Civilization* (Oxford, 1993).
41. A. Bogues, *Caliban's Freedom. The early political thought of C.L.R. James* (London, 1997), p.62.
42. Ibid., p.2
43. James, *American Civilization*, pp.150, 156–7, 160, 162, 276.
44. Ibid., pp.139–40.
45. M. Denning, *The Cultural Front. The Laboring of American Culture in the Twentieth Century* (New York, 1997), pp.50, 67, 125, 478 n33; Lind, *Next American Nation*, p.81.
46. K. Worcester, *C.L.R. James. A political biography* (Albany, 1996); J.A. Geschwender, *Class, Race and Worker Insurgency. The League of Revolutionary Black Workers* (Cambridge, 1977) p.88.
47. R. Gombin, *The Origins of Modern Leftism* (Harmonsworth, 1975) pp.61–4.
48. Dickstein, Gates, p.5; A. Marwick, *The Sixties. Cultural revolution in Britain, France, Italy and the United States, c.1958–c.1974* (Oxford, 1998).
49. Lind, *Next American Nation,* pp.81–5.
50. Wreszin, *Rebel*, pp.139, 354–5; Dickstein, *Gates*, pp.61, 79.
51. Denning, *Cultural Front,* pp.97, 104.
52. Dickstein, *Gates*, p.186; Marwick, *The Sixties*, pp.154–5, 191; G. Cotkin, 'The tragic predicament. Post-war American intellectuals, acceptance and mass culture' in Jennings and Kemp-Welch, *Intellectuals in Politics*, p.250.
53. G.C. Lee, P.Chaulieu and J.R. Johnson, *Facing Reality* (Michigan Ill., 1958); Worcester, *C.L.R. James*, p.140.
54. Bogues, *Caliban's Freedom*, p.125.
55. Dickstein, *Gates*, pp.5, 186.
56. Ibid., p.79; MacDonald, *Discriminations*, p.298.
57. Worcester, *C.L.R. James*, p.135.
58. Wreszin, *Rebel*, pp.122, 162.
59. James, *American Civilization*, p.226; also R. Dunayevskaya, *Marxism and Freedom from 1776 until Today* (New Jersey, 1982) pp.84–5; R. Dunayevskaya, *Women's Liberation and the Dialectics of Revolution: Reaching for the Future* (New Jersey, 1985), pp.35–8.
60. MacDonald, *Against*, p.34.
61. Bogues, *Caliban's Freedom*, p.100.
62. Lichtheim, *Origins*, p.234; Dickstein, *Gates*, p.21.
63. Rowbotham, *Threads*, pp.206–8; T. Crow, *Modern Art in the Common Culture* (New Haven, CT, 1998), p.3.
64. Dickstein, *Gates*, p.267.
65. James, *American Civilization*, p.323.
66. P. Anderson, *The Origins of Postmodernity* (London, 1998).

Reviews

Suburbs and society

Mark Clapson, *Invincible Green Suburbs, Brave New Towns : social change and urban dispersal in postwar England* (Manchester University Press, Manchester, 1997), 224 pp., ISBN 0 7190 4135 X, £ 35.00 hbk.

When Mark Clapson repeats the title of his book as the heading to his final chapter, he adds appropriate question marks. He reminds us that changing family sizes and population increases will require four million new houses over the next decades. For this reason, the trials, tribulations and successes of aspects of post-war housing and planning policy which he explores represent a store of useful information to those who will be building those new homes, as well as, and perhaps more importantly, to the people who will become the residents.

Suburbs and new towns had their problems for residents who moved there from dense inner city streets, some of which were slums, but the 'suburban neuroses' and 'new town blues' which were sensationalised in the 'popular' press were not primarily caused by architects and town planners. Difficulties such as loneliness and feelings of jealousy and isolation linked to class differentiation were part of the wider problems of postwar English society, particularly those associated with the inequality of women.

Clapson shows that families went willingly to the new towns and the suburbs because of their desires to obtain modern houses in rural surroundings free from the dirt and pollution of town and city life. For many working class people who had been living with in-laws or in cramped rented accommodation, the change led to them feeling 'like royalty'.

> Never before had we the luxury of a bath, hot water on tap and, best of all in the childrens' eyes, our own stairs, They run up and down them ...

and they all kept flushing the toilet.

The numbers involved in the dispersion from city to suburb and new town were considerable. Between 1919 and 1944, 1,691,000 houses were built for owner-occupation in the English suburbs. And in the following period to 1990 a further 4,137,000 were built. With local authorities providing some two million units of housing in suburban estates, and a further million across the thirty-two new towns, the context was created for over eight million people to become residents in such new surroundings. This investment in housing was linked to developments in transport policy which saw the advent of the mass use of rail and—in London—the underground, as well as the bus and, increasingly, the private car.

The author criticises the jaundiced view that new town 'settlers' lost the close-knit family life which had shaped working class experience in the inner-cities. Whilst it is true that there was often a break until settling-in had occurred, relationships were usually re-established, with kinsfolk sometimes also moving into the new towns.

Trade union activity may have diminished in the later new towns, but this was not the result of some planners' plot against 'traditional' working class life either. It was more due to the change from manufacturing to service industries being experienced across society.

In launching the New Towns programme in 1945, the Labour government hoped that it would help to bridge the gap between and overcome the prejudices of working class and middle class residents. But by the time the New Towns programme was wound up by Peter Shore during the 1974–79 Labour administration, the deep roots of class consciousness within British society had shown little sign of abating.

New town origins

Clapson's book is well researched and it is a positive addition to our knowledge of the suburbs and new towns. However, its particular focus does not allow for a discussion of the origins of the processes which led the post war Labour government to produce a policy for the building of new towns, and the remainder of this review sketches these processes.

The rise of industrial capitalism in the 1770s also saw the emergence of organisations which opposed the taking of profit from other peoples' labour. Trade unions arose alongside co-operative manufacturing and retail societies. Some people popularised the idea that those using land should pay rent for its use to the community.

Robert Owen's New Lanark community was an experiment which synthesised some of these views. The industrial village, which operated from 1800 to 1829, showed that good working conditions, and a corresponding educational and social life, could still produce a handsome profit. New Lanark spoke of an alternative to the mass misery and unemployment prevalent within capitalist society.

Other Owenite settlements followed during the rest of the nineteenth century. The model community described by Ebenezer Howard In his 1898 book 'Garden Cities of Tomorrow' built on Owen's ideas, but incorporated new ideas which meant that this pioneering effort was more sustainable. Howard and his supporters collected sufficient money to purchase 4000 acres of industrial land and started to build Letchworth Garden City in 1903. Howard ensured that there was a belt of farmland around Letchworth, but stressed the policy of collecting ground rent from all users of land. Today, Letchworth is a town with a population of 35, 000 which has an annual meeting to discuss the ways the town can be improved using the profits from the rents collected from farmers, and the other users of its lands and properties. The profits for 1996–97 were £2,137,000.

The garden city idea and Letchworth became the focus for support and campaigning which led to the New Town Acts of 1946–47. It was intended that when new towns were completed, the land and assets would be transferred from the development corporations building them to the respective local authorities. Harold Wilson's government failed to carry through this policy, leaving the way clear for the Thatcher government to arrange for their sale to the private sector.

The differing histories of garden cities and suburbs suggest that they have different political logics. Garden cities can be seen as embryonic forms of socialism developing within capitalist society. Suburbs, on the other hand, are purely capitalistic ventures. Suburbs and garden cities are also wholly different in their built form. Suburbs are fragmentary and haphazard, produced in a speculative way by different individuals and companies as funds, land and planning permissions become available. This leads to 'ribbon developments' of narrow strips of housing outside of towns and cities, in which car ownership is essential.

Garden cities, an the other hand, are settlements in the round. The theory is that schools, shops and services are all in the centre, so that all the city's people have an equal distance to travel. With industry zoned, an agricultural belt, and revenue from the rents of land users, the garden city aims to be a balanced, viable and sustainable community.

Whether people's housing needs will be addressed in future through garden cities remains to be seen. It is certainly an aim worth working for. Particular forms of built environment and living space, however, are not a sufficient condition for the good life. Clapson ends his book with indications of how the fine hopes of the postwar architects of social housing were undermined as unemployment 'struck home'. Once smart and new suburban estates became transformed into the depressed and dangerous locations of those suffering most from systemic social exclusion. The positive contributions which can be made to social life by appropriate planning need to be part of a wider family of projects which address social issues across the board.

Alan Spence
Alan Spence is a member of the Architecture and Planning Group of Democratic
Left.

Mark Clapson, *Invincible Green Suburbs, Brave New Towns: social change and urban dispersal in postwar England*

The 'invincible green suburbs' that take up half of Mark Clapson's title are a coinage of John Major's. They have been lifted from that soppy speech of 1993 in which the Prime Minister invoked the suburbs along with cricket, warm beer and old maids cycling to communion as images of Englishness—roots of an ur-conservatism that seemed to need wooing and lulling after the brash iconoclasm of his predecessor. Major, or rather his speechwriter, was probably targeting deep Surrey or Cheshire, not Milton Keynes or other of the 'brave new towns' that Clapson has sneaked into the tail of his title.

The suburbs, then, are manifold, and we generalise about them at our peril. Clapson's suburb is the working-class estate, neighbourhood or new town—the distillation of a broader dispersal movement from Britain's cities that has been going on in practice for a century, and advocated for far longer. As this wider movement reaches an international flood, goverments are presently taking stock. Can the world sustain suburbs on the Anglo-American model? Do they alienate or fulfil? Must we choose between cramming people into dense cities or letting them sprawl over the shrinking countryside? For those alive to these debates, this book has much that is pertinent and provocative to say.

From the standpoint of class, the key question about suburbanisation is this: Is it voluntary or involuntary? Voluntary and personal flight from the city needs freedom or money, preferably both. Till recently in England this was usually confined to the middle class (though splendid exceptions are explored in Dennis Hardy and Colin Ward's *Arcadia for All*). In the involuntary model an employer moves, or a slum is redeveloped, and a working-class family is 'decanted' out to a new town, district and house. It has little choice in the matter, and may well have roots broken and values dislocated in the process.

It was this passive, negative condition of working-class dispersal which sociologists began to diagnose as a sickness, in reaction to the triumphalism of the decentralising disciples of Ebenezer Howard. Ruth Durant (later Ruth Glass) was the pioneer diagnostician in her study of the London County Council's Watling Estate in 1939. But the chief pathologists of class deracination were Michael Young and Peter Willmott, writing in the palmy days of the New Towns' movement. Their egregious 1957 study of *Family and Kinship In East London* set the nobility of working-class Bethnal Green against the *anomie* of suburban 'Greenleigh' (Debden). Their (for the time) sensational findings of 'Glück in Slum' (thus a delightful German headline quoted by Clapson) still resonate today in the language of Lord Rogers' Urban Task Force.

It would be crude to dismiss Clapson's book as a mere refutation of Young and Willmott. That has been done long since, not least by Peter Willmott himself, whose maturer studies of life at Dagenham and other estates leave little doubt that the 1957 book encapsulated stereotypes about class just as sentimental as John Major's. What Clapson does is to draw together, with great richness of detail, the conspectus of sixty years' historical and sociological work on the English working-class suburb, ever since *Watling*. In the process he rids it of Its clichéd reputation for passiveness and sterility.

The book takes two timescales. One is historical. Over the whole century of suburbanisation, Clapson shows that the working classes were seldom as passive about leaving city centres as many have made them out to be. In the Edwardian period co-operativists, and trades unionists like the remarkable Henry Vivian, actively supported garden cities and suburbs, and built a fair measure of housing. The difficulty at that date was to raise housing finance, and to find local employment that would obviate the cost of commuting. Later studies show that for every young wife who missed her mum, there was a couple aching to get out of the parents' spare room and away—not just across the street, but right away to the space and social independence that the middle classes took for granted. By the late 1960s, patterns of dispersal and living at greater distances from one another were familiar to working-class communities and 'receiving authorities', and the trauma of the clumsier post-war upheavals seldom recurred over the post-war period. Clapson traces a shift of motives for moving out, from the desire in the early days for a better house, through a period when job-opportunity was the main incentive, to current concerns with a healthy environment and schooling.

The other chronology is personal—that of the arrivals' progress. Clapson's successive chapters about moving out, settling in, the anxieties of the early days, and the development of relationships and communities, recapitulate the order and quality of experience recorded by a bevy of social enquirers. As people differ, the evidence is of course often contradictory. But one consensus seems to be that the new house (being low-density England, it was generally a house, not a flat) seldom disappointed in the first instance. The squeals of delight over decent baths and sinks and WCs still echo off Clapson's pages. Only the tinny terraces of early experimental Milton. Keynes get slagged off here (and these are now getting pitched roofs added). If people were unhappy at first ('suburban sadness', 'new town blues'), that is a common pattern after moving, as Willmott and his friends surely knew; in any case, as *The Lancet* slyly observed in 1958, it was a help to get a new house if you had a medical certificate. Within the bounds of tight funding, the new towns at any rate made great efforts to foster a social life. It was on the less favoured municipal 'cottage estates' that 'blues' was the graver problem.

In due course most people found their feet, and made some sort of 'community'. Another consensus recorded by Clapson is that the neighbourhood idea never worked well as a self-sufficient focus for social interaction, even when people were less mobile than they later became. Ruth Glass had noticed this at Watling, and again during her wartime study of Middlesborough; but the planners, keen on neighbourhoods for environmental rather than social reasons, took no notice of her. It was left to the Californian Melvin Webber, in studies of the late 1980s, to get the message through ,and be taken on board as a consultant for the planning of Milton Keynes. Webber, as Clapson is careful to remark, did not repudiate localism, but he found it overbearing as an excuse for restricting mobility between parts of a city.

The cumulative arguments of this book restate an unfashionable proposition—that decentralized developent for the working classes in England has worked, on the whole, well. There may be ecological or economic reasons for not going on building low-density suburbs for the less affluent, but the socio-cultural argument against it can be dismissed, on Clapson's evidence, as cant and snobbery. Whether the suburbs and towns already thus created can stay as they are is more doubtful. One measure of a new development's success is its ability to relax, mature, diversify and fade into the background. This is a difficulty for Clapson, who as a keeper of the working-class conscience wants his suburban strongholds to be prosperous, busy and happy, but still solidly working-class. Yet many have gone middle-class, or at least consumerist; and others, as he concedes, are getting as rackety now as the more hapless inner city estates. He struggles a bit with this in his 'conclusions and connections', which go beyond his findings to argue that the suburbs and towns he has so ably defended can retain a distinctive 'left' identity. The current electoral Blairism in these places is scant evidence of this. Time alone will tell whether Major's invinciblilty also implies Clapson's solidarity.

Andrew Saint
Professor of Architecture, University of Cambridge

Books Received

Stefan Berger and Angel Smith, *Nationalism, Labour and Ethnicity 1870–1939* (Manchester University Press, Manchester 1999), 0-7190-5052-9, £47 hbk.

Laura Cohn *The Door to the Secret Room: A portrait of Wells Coates* (Scolar Press, Aldershot, 1999), 1-84014-695-8, £25.00 hbk.

Becky Conekin, Frank Mort, Chris Waters editors *Moments of Modernity: Reconstructing Britain 1945-1964* (Rivers Oram, London, 1999), 304pp., 1-85489-105-7, £14.95 pbk.

Mary Davis, *Sylvia Pankhurst: A life in radical politics* (Pluto, London, 1999), xv+157pp., 0-7453-1518-6, £10.99 pbk.

Gregory Elliott *Perry Anderson: The Merciless Laboratory of History* (University of Minnesota Press, Minneapolis, 1998), 336pp., 0-8166-2966-8, $39.95 hbk.

David Foden and Peter Moris editors *The Search for Equity* (Lawrence and Wishart, London, 1998), 247pp., 0-85315-864-9, £14.99 pbk.

Rana Kabbani, *Imperial Fictions: Europe's myths of Orient* (Pandora, London 1994), 224pp., 0-04440-911-7, £7.99 pbk.

Louis Kushnick, *Race, Class and Struggle: Essays on Racism and Inequality in Britain, the US and Western Europe* (Rivers Oram, London, 1998), 256pp., 1-85489-097-2, £12.95 pbk.

Caroline Kennedy-Pipe, *Russia and the World 1917–1991* (Arnold, London, 1998), 235pp., 0-340-65205-5, £13.99 hbk.

Keith Laybourn and Dylan Murphy *Under the Red Flag: A History of Communism in Britain, c. 1849–1991* (Sutton Press, Stroud, 1999), 245pp., 0-7509-1485-8, £25.00 hbk.

Jill Liddington, *Female Fortune: Land gender and authority* (Rivers Oram, London, 1999), 304pp., 1-85489-089-1, £12.95 pbk.

Laura Marcus and Lynda Nead, *The Actuality of Walter Benjamin* (Lawrence and Wishart, London, 1998), 224pp., 0-85315-863-0, £10.99 pbk.

Neil Riddell, *Labour in Crisis* (Manchester University Press, Manchester, 1999), 0-7190-5084-7, £45.00 hbk.

Patricia Morley, *The Mountain is Moving: Japanese Women's Lives* (Pandora Press, London, 1999), 288pp., 0-86353-414-4, £16.99 hbk.

Jo-Ann Mort editor, *Not Your Father's Union Movement: Inside the AFL–CIO* (Verso, London, 1999), xii+237pp., ISBN 1-85984-286-0, £13.00 pbk.

James Ogude, *Ngugi's Novels and African History: Narrating the Nation* (Pluto, London, 1999), 192pp., 0-7453-1431-7, £12.99 pbk.

Morgan Philips Price, edited by Tania Rose, *Dispatches from the Weimar Republic* (Pluto, London, 1999) 240pp., 0-7453-1425-2, £20.00 hbk.

Natalia Pushkareve, translated and edited by Eve Levin, *Women in Russian history: from the Tenth to the Twentieth Century* (Sutton Publishing, Stroud, 1999), 0-7509-2093-9, £14.99 hbk.

Stephen Roberts and Dorothy Thompson, *Images of Chartism* (Merlin, Rendlesham, 1998), 116pp., 0-85036-475-2, £12.95 pbk.

David Rubinstein, *But He'll Remember: An autobiography* (The Ebor Press, York), 365pp., 1-85072-220-X, £5.00 pbk.

W. F. Ryan, *Magic in History: The Bathhouse at Midnight, Magic in Russia* (Sutton Publishing, Stroud, 1999), 510pp., 0-75092-110 -2, £45.00 hbk.

Vidya Sagar Anand, *In Search of Dr Sun Yat-sen, Father of Modern China* (Institute for Media Communication, London, 1999), 108pp., 0-9526-2213-3, £9.95 pbk.

Roderick Stackelberg, *Hitler's Germany: Origins, interpretations, legacies* (Routledge, London, 1999), 0 415 20114 4, hbk.

Jo Stanley editor, *Bold in her Breeches: Women pirates across the ages* (Pandora, London, 1995), 300pp., 0-04440-970-2, £7.99 pbk.

John Walton, *Chartism* (Routledge, London, 1999), 90pp., 0-415-09689-8, £6.99 pbk.

Jeffrey Weeks and Kevin Porter editors, *Between the Acts: Lives of Homosexual Men 1885–1967* (Rivers Oram, London, 1998), 168pp., 1-85489-093-X, £9.95 pbk.

Wendy Wheeler, *A New Modernity? Change in science, literature and politics* (Lawrence and Wishart, 1999), X+173pp., 0-85315-877-0, £14.99 pbk.

Chris Williams, *Capitalism, Community and Conflict: The South Wales Coalfield, 1898-1947* (University of Wales, Cardiff, 1998), 0-7083-1473-2 pbk.

Stanley Williamson Gresford, *The Anatomy of a Disaster* (Liverpool University Press, Liverpool, 1999) 257pp., 0-85323-902-0 pbk.

SUBSCRIBE TO SOCIALIST HISTORY

Annual subscription for individuals is (UK) £17.50 waged, £10 unwaged and (overseas) is £22.50 waged, £15.00 unwaged. Send subscription with name and address to:

> Secretary,
> Socialist History Society,
> 6 Cynthia Street,
> London N1 9JF

Institutional and library subscription is £25 per annum. Send requests to:

> Subscriptions,
> Rivers Oram Press,
> 144 Hemingford Road,
> London N1 1DE

JOIN THE SOCIALIST HISTORY SOCIETY

Membership entitles you to attend all the Society's events, to receive two numbers of Socialist History per year plus two pamphlets, and to participate in its decision making.

Subscription rates are:

waged £17.50 (£22.50 overseas); unwaged £10.00 (£15.00 overseas), £20.00 labour movement organisations

Kevin Morgan
Department of Government
University of Manchester
Manchester M13 9PL

e-mail: Kevin.Morgan@man.ac.uk

Draylon
THE BEGINNING

by

Kenny Balfour

**Grosvenor House
Publishing Limited**

This book is published by
Grosvenor House Publishing Ltd
28-30 High Street, Guildford, Surrey, GU1 3HY.
www.grosvenorhousepublishing.co.uk

A CIP record for this book
is available from the British Library

ISBN 978-1-908105-36-3

The Chapters

CHAPTER ONE

Easter Island

It was a cold night on Tuesday the 4th of January 2011. The sky was a blanket of stars beautifully lit, and all seemed still but for the lapping of the waves against the rocks on the shores of Hanga Roa, a small town on Easter Island. Paul Gabriel looked out to sea and felt his life pause in the tranquillity of this splendid night. He felt at peace, and happy, and wished for nothing more than this moment. Shooting stars had been predicted on this night and Paul watched intently, hoping to witness the spectacular sights. What Paul witnessed was something entirely different.

A light in the sky much brighter than the rest seemed to move slowly. It appeared to be that of a classic saucer shape. Paul supposed it was probably a passenger plane and his mind was just playing tricks on him. Paul never had much of an open mind when it came to UFOs, ghosts, Loch Ness monsters and the like. Something didn't quite add up though, the light was very bright in contrast to the stars, and it was much higher in the sky than a passenger plane would usually fly. All of a sudden, there was an immense flash of light. It shone with awesome brightness, and then the unidentified craft plummeted out of the sky with extraordinary speed out into the deep dark ocean. It struck the surface with a great force that sent ripples to the shore line where Paul was standing.

Paul could not believe what he had just seen. He used his mobile phone to contact the local police. The police said that there were no other reports in as yet, but they would look into it right away. Paul looked out at the sea and all was calm again, as if nothing had happened. He yawned and decided he'd had enough excitement for one night. It was time for bed, and so he made his way home.

Draylon awoke in his craft on the sea bed. He was dazed from the crash, but he knew he had to get out as he was running out of oxygen. He was able to go without air for over ten minutes, but was still anxious to get free. His craft was damaged beyond repair. He had absolutely no clue what had caused the malfunction, but Draylon knew he would have to detonate it as soon as he was free, so that humans could not find the wreckage. He had been observing and collecting intelligence from the planet for some time, he had even been amongst the population, and so had all that was required to get by amongst humans; he had passports and even clothing.

Draylon grabbed all the possessions he could carry and exited his craft. He held his breath and easily made the ascent to the surface. He then swam to the shore and he emerged from the water. He was just over six feet tall and of medium muscular build. His features were chiselled, and he had these piercing blue eyes. He turned to look out to sea and detonated the craft with a remote. There was an almighty burst of water above the surface of the sea and then all was silent.

Draylon was able to convince his peers to let him come to Earth to observe and collect intelligence. His kind have visited the Earth many times over millennia, only his kind are of the classic greys, the Roswell sort, and thus haven't integrated amongst the human population. This was what Draylon had looked forward to all his life. He was intrigued by Earth, by humans, and wanted to witness every aspect of humanity. He did not intend to destroy his craft in the process, but was not overly concerned, as he could be tracked by a chip concealed within his right shoulder, so when his kin realised he was missing, he could always attain a passage home when they visited the Earth next. Draylon looked all human on the outside; he had brown spikey hair, a white complexion and a physique like that of an athlete.

Paul Gabriel was a bit of a loner; he never knew his parents - they died in a tragic car crash when he was only a baby - and he was brought up by his grandparents, who had both passed away by his late teens. As an adult, he went straight to work as a machinist. He saved like crazy and by the time he was 25 years of age, he decided to emigrate to Easter Island; he figured the fewer people, the better. He now lived in rented accommodation in the town of Hanga Roa. It was a small one bedroom flat, but it suited his needs. He worked at the local supermarket stacking shelves and serving customers. In his spare time, he enjoyed time on his own and music. Paul had lived on Easter Island now for 11 years - thus he was now 36 years of age.

Draylon was feeling a little bruised and battered from the crash. He had a nasty cut on his forehead and bruising on his chest and abdomen. He looked about. There was nobody around, so he closed his eyes, slowed his breathing and focused. Within seconds, the wound started to close and the bruising started to fade. He wiped his forehead and the wound was gone. He was as good as new, but hungry. His human side required nourishment, as did any human, and so he made his way into town, hoping to find food and accommodation for the night.

When in town, Draylon came across a cash point. He needed money. Against his morals, he placed his hand on the cash machine and, using his technopathic ability, he drew out enough cash to last him several weeks. He went into a little shop in town and purchased a couple of cereal bars and a bottle of water. Earth food was almost completely foreign to Draylon, and he was excited about every meal to come. There was a hotel at the end of the main street called, The Moai Inn. Draylon went in and rented a room. He gave his name, Draylon Alexander Cross.

Paul was woken the next day by a phone call. It was the local Police. They informed him that there was nothing to report; that what he saw was probably a shooting star, debris entering the atmosphere. Paul never argued the fact and thought, being a sceptic, that they were most probably correct. Paul then took a shower, styled and parted his short brown hair and got himself dressed in his favourite jeans, a fitted shirt and smart black shoes. He looked at his watch. It was 7:30 a.m. He had an hour to have breakfast and get to work at the supermarket.

Paul arrived at work just as Adriana Morales was opening up. He said good morning and then asked her if she had seen the shooting stars from the night before.

4

She said that she was too busy helping her mother and cooking dinner for the family; that she didn't have time to gaze at the stars. Paul smiled, and thought to himself that it must have been a shooting star. He had a quick cup of coffee and then got started stocking up shelves for the day. He put on his mp3 player, which was frowned upon, but he would go insane with his mundane job if he never had his music.

Draylon awoke feeling refreshed, although still a little dishevelled from the night before. He looked forward to his adventures to come. The world is my oyster, he thought to himself with a grin. He missed the closest thing he had to a father, one of the scientists on his planet, a grey, one of the donors of the DNA that had created him. His name was Karlon. Draylon was sure he would see Karlon again one day, but for now he was going to explore, and anonymously try to make a difference on Earth each and every day. Draylon believed that one small good deed a day went a long way to making a world a better place.

Draylon had a wash, and then put on his still slightly damp clothes, which he had managed to retrieve from his craft - they were his favourite, jeans, grey T-shirt and trainers. He loved his outfit and was happy to wear the same every day. He was feeling hungry again and so excitedly left his room in search of a supermarket. His mouth watered at the thought of new food to try.

After a short walk into town, Draylon found a super-market. He started to look around at all of the many foods and drinks, but didn't have a clue what to try first. He made a point of reading all of the labels on the foods

- his planet were solely vegetarian, and to him eating flesh was barbaric, although he didn't discriminate the human race, as humans have always eaten meat. He decided to try a freshly baked bread roll and a couple of cans of energy drink. Monster Ripper, the energy drink was called. It looked very appealing by the nicely decorated can. He went to the counter to pay and was served by a man with the name tag Paul.

"Hello Paul, I would like to buy these please," said Draylon with a smile.

"Yes sir, would that be all?" said Paul, not wanting to make conversation.

"That is all. Did you see the display of shooting stars last night?" Draylon, even at such a great height in his craft the evening before, could clearly make out the image of Paul watching by the shore.

"Yes, I saw a very bright star; I must have been tired because it seemed as if it dived into the sea right before my eyes."

"I saw it too. Would you like to meet for a drink later when you finish work to talk about it? I'm new to the island, so it would be nice to have company."

"I'm busy tonight, thanks all the same," said Paul, nervously, worried about having to make conversation.

"Please. Just a quick drink and chat, I'd be very grateful - I'll pay."

"Um. OK. I finish work at 5, I'll meet you just outside. What did you say your name was?"

"Draylon. Thank you! See you at 5."

Draylon left the supermarket and sat on a nearby bench. He tried his freshly baked roll. It smelled divine, and tasted delicious. He ate it very quickly, and then wished he'd bought two. He then opened his first can of energy drink. He took a mouthful. He couldn't believe how good it tasted, and he imagined he could quite easily become addicted to these energy drinks. Within a couple of minutes he could feel his heart pulsing and he felt more alert - he was thoroughly enjoying this new sensation. Draylon thought he'd take a stroll down along the shore line just outside of town, and maybe run off some of his new found energy, then maybe sit, relax and contemplate. He very much looked forward to meeting with Paul.

It was 5 p.m. and Draylon was waiting outside of the supermarket, Paul turned up shortly after and decided that they would go to the local bar named Rapa Nui Tavern. When they arrived, Paul ordered a cider and Draylon ordered sparkling spring water. Draylon wasn't keen on the idea of alcohol and its effects on the mind and body. Easter Island has a semi-tropical climate and January was summertime, so they both decided that they would sit outside in the warmth of the sun. Paul seemed quiet. Draylon sensed that he was a bit of a loner but was hoping that he'd be able to change that. His instinct told him that Paul was a decent guy and trustworthy, and so he hoped that they could become friends. They found a bench outside the front of the tavern. It had a nice view of the town, and was a perfect suntrap.

"So you saw a shooting star last night then?" Draylon asked to break the silence.

"Yes. It was very bright, though, I thought it may have been something else."

"Maybe a UFO from another planet?" Draylon asked with a smile.

"No, I'm afraid I don't believe in that sort of thing. I did think it could have been a plane at first, but it was maybe a little high for that, could have been a meteor, I suppose. What do you think it was?"

"I think you're probably right, a meteor. Although it would be kind of interesting if it was an alien craft. Then we would know we are not alone in the universe."

"It's just us. I'm afraid - I really don't believe in little green men."

Draylon was enjoying the conversation; he enjoyed the fact that Paul was a sceptic, but hoped if they became good friends he'd be able to share his secret with him. Paul was surprised at how comfortable he felt - he was enjoying the conversation too. Despite avoiding people, deep down he knew he craved friendship and love, two things he knew very little about. They ordered another round of drinks and chatted about the island. Paul promised to take Draylon to see the Moai. The time was fast approaching 8 p.m. and Paul said that he would have to return home. They both arranged to meet at 5 p.m. the next day to visit the legendary stone heads, the Moai.

Draylon turned up at the supermarket at 5 p.m. the next day. Adriana came outside to let him know that Paul was on his way. Adriana was happy that Paul had found himself a friend. She blushed when speaking to Draylon as she found him handsome and mysterious. She found it hard to disguise her feelings and was annoyed at her sensitive nature always giving her away.

Adriana was slim build, average height, with long brown hair. She had beautiful brown eyes, and even Draylon stumbled on his words a little when speaking to her. Paul arrived and Adriana wished them a nice evening. She then bid them farewell and went back inside to finish up. Paul was looking forward to the little trip after his arduous day at work.

Draylon and Paul got into Paul's yellow Suzuki Alto; it was a bit of a squeeze, as they were both tall in stature. They headed off to the other side of Easter Island, to a place named Tongariki. This is where the famous fifteen huge Moai statues are situated, and it is called Ahu Tongariki. Ahu has two meanings; firstly, an Ahu is the flat mound or stone pedestal upon which the Moai stand, secondly, it signifies a sacred ceremonial site, and both are true at the site of Ahu Tongariki.

Draylon was hoping to chat with Paul on the journey, but Paul insisted on playing his stereo very loudly. He loved his music; it was one of his passions. They arrived and Draylon was stunned by the awesome sight; the stone heads known as the Moai were enormous. Fifteen statues, all differing slightly in size, left as shrines to loved ones long deceased. Legend says the spirit occupies the statue watching over their beloved land and peoples. The statues consist of a large stone body, with a large stone head. The head has deep, carved-out features. It is said that the eyes were the last to be carved after the statue was erected, and once the eyes were carved, the spirit that embodies it is always watchful.

Paul gave Draylon the guided tour of the site. He said that the average Moai was 4 metres tall and weighed about 12.5 metric tons, and that there was one Moai at Rano Raraku Quarry named El Gigante that was almost 22 metres high and weighed between 160 and 182 metric tons. Draylon was fascinated; he wondered how on Earth these massive pieces of rock were moved from the quarry to Tongariki. The theory is they were rolled on trunks of wood; Draylon imagined there was a bit more to it than that.

"Would you mind if I took a time out? I wouldn't mind sitting down for a while," Paul asked.

Draylon smiled. "That's fine, thank you for this."

Paul found an area away from the Moai and sat and gazed out at the ocean. He loved to watch the ocean; he found it so peaceful, away from the stresses of life. Draylon felt uneasy - he could hear a high-pitched noise. He hadn't come across it before. It seemed to emanate from the largest of the Moai. He approached the large statue. He held both of his hands several inches away from the rock, and he could sense a power from within it. He looked about. No one could see him. He focused his ability to manipulate matter, and a space appeared in the rock.

Draylon reached in and could feel a cool metallic object. He removed the object and then resealed the space. It was a small rectangular metallic tablet. He held his right hand over the tablet. The information within it flooded into Draylon's subconscious at the speed of light. Then the tablet disintegrated into tiny particles. Draylon could hardly believe it; the language was that of an alien race long since deceased, Draylon stepped back with astonishment at what had just transpired.

Draylon went over to sit with Paul for a while. They both just sat there looking at the ocean. Draylon broke the silence.

"I'm enjoying my time here, thank you! This is a beautiful view point."

"It is nice, I spend quite a lot of my time in the evenings looking out at the ocean."

"Would you mind if I tagged along with you whilst I'm here on Easter Island? It's good to have company." Draylon smiled and patted Paul on the back.

"No problem, we should be getting back now though, some of us have to work tomorrow you know." Paul smiled and patted Draylon on the back too.

Paul dropped Draylon off at The Moai Inn and arranged to meet up again the next day at 5 p.m. and then Paul headed off home. Draylon purchased a couple of energy drinks from the vending machine inside his hotel, then went to his room and sat up in bed thinking whilst sipping on his drink. The tablet he found inside of the large Moai indicated that another alien race had visited Earth, and quite possibly had something to do with the building of the Moai about the island. What intrigued Draylon the most though, was that the tablet gave co-ordinates to a site in South America, in Peru, on the plain of Nazca. Draylon was excited. He hoped he was on the brink of a huge discovery. He wondered if he could persuade Paul to come with him, they were going to need more money though if he was to come. Draylon had a plan.

Draylon woke the next day and decided he'd go for a run. His human side loved physical activity. He never had any jogging bottoms so he ran in one of his pairs of jeans and a grey T-shirt. His trainers were fine though. Draylon, being a hybrid, genetically modified in a lab, had exceptional human gifts; his strength, speed, agility, reflexes and all five senses were well above that of any other human being on Earth. He decided to run for ten kilometres. He loved the feeling of exertion. After the first mile, his aerobic system kicked in and he was running faster and faster. His breathing adapted and slowed, and he felt invincible. It gave him time to clear the cobwebs, metaphorically speaking, and he was feeling charged and energised. He saw his hotel come back into view and he made a sprint finish. He eased to a stop and his breathing slowed to normal in just a couple of seconds.

Draylon decided to take a shower and freshen up a little. He then washed his clothing in the bathroom sink and hung it outside to dry. He was starting to feel a little hungry and so put on another pair of his favourite jeans, a grey T-shirt and trainers and decided to have a look about town to see what other shops were about. He found a tiny shop that sold newspapers, snacks and refreshments; it was called Alonzo's. Draylon found two of his favourite energy drinks and decided on a ploughman's sandwich, after carefully reading its label to see its ingredients.

The store man was Spanish-speaking, which Draylon understood perfectly. He could speak all languages of the Earth, old and new. A lot of Draylon's knowledge of the Earth and its languages was downloaded. Alien technology allows for the brain to be stimulated and a lot of information passed into it quickly and easily. He had an exceptional ability to learn and retain information anyway, but the technology on his own planet could further enhance that on a massive scale. Draylon paid for his refreshments, and thanked the shop-keeper. Before he managed to leave the shop, he found himself drinking some of his favourite drink, he imagined he was getting some kind of addiction to it; he smiled to himself and left the shop.

It was 5 p.m. Paul met Draylon outside of the supermarket. He suggested that they go for a walk to the sea just outside of the town. He wanted some fresh air after being cooped up all day. Draylon enjoyed the exercise, but was starting to feel hungry. He proposed they stop somewhere to grab a bite to eat after their walk. Paul agreed, as he was feeling a little hungry too. As they approached the end of the main stretch of road, a car came hurtling past them. At the same time, a beige Labrador puppy ran out into the road.

The car braked and skidded, but it wasn't enough - it struck the puppy and sent it tumbling down the pavement. Draylon and Paul ran to the little puppy. Its eyes were still open and it was twitching. The driver of the car got out to help. Draylon informed him that he was a vet and that he should go. The young male driver got into his car and drove off. Draylon looked around; luckily no one else witnessed the event other than himself, Paul and the driver. Paul was upset - he asked Draylon if he was really a vet. He prayed that the puppy would be OK, but deep down, he knew that this was the end for the poor little thing.

"I'm not a vet Paul, but I need your trust now," Draylon said, knowing that everything hung on this moment.

"You can trust me," Paul replied. "But what can you possibly do?"

Draylon placed his hands gently on the puppy; he closed his eyes, slowed his breathing, and focused. Time seemed to stand still.

Paul interrupted, "What are you doing?"

At that moment, the puppy startled to wriggle, then got to his feet, barked, then licked Draylon all over his face. Draylon smiled and handed the puppy to Paul. Paul was ecstatic; he kissed and stroked the little puppy. A tear rolled down his cheek. A little boy came around the corner. He became overjoyed at the sight of his puppy. Paul handed him over and ruffled the little puppy's head, and the boy ran off back home. Paul looked at Draylon.

"That was amazing," Paul said in a soft voice.

Draylon smiled. "We need to talk."

"Yes we do," Paul replied.

They found a couple of rocks to sit on fairly close to the shore-line. There was a silence, with both Paul and Draylon deep in thought. Paul broke the silence, not able to keep it bottled up for a second longer.

"What just happened?" Paul said, feeling a bit flustered.

Draylon felt a bit anxious, hoping that Paul would understand. "That bright light you saw wasn't a meteor, it was my craft. This is going to be very hard to believe. I'm from another planet."

Paul interrupted. "From another planet? What are you talking about? I meant the dog, how did you heal the dog? What did you do?"

"I can heal myself and others, it's one of my gifts. I'm not entirely human, I'm an alien-human hybrid." Draylon knew how that must have sounded to Paul.

"That's ridiculous! OK, I'll humour you, prove it!"

"OK."

Draylon pointed at an empty bottle near the shore line, Paul looked over.

"This is telekinesis."

Draylon, using his hand and his mind, caused the bottle to raise three feet off the ground. He held it for a few seconds, and then lowered it back to the ground. Paul's jaw gaped. He couldn't believe what he was seeing. He was a sceptic, he wanted to believe, but had so many doubts, although his doubts were starting to fade.

Paul smiled. "How can I deny that, in the last fifteen minutes I've seen you heal an injured puppy, and now move a bottle with your mind. What are you? Who are you?" Paul felt a little nervous, but also excited.

"I'm from another planet, from another galaxy light years away. I'm an alien-human hybrid; I was created in a lab by leading scientists on my home planet. They created me using superior DNA from my planet, and superior DNA from yours. They can isolate particular traits, they are that advanced. I have numerous alien abilities, and yet look entirely human on the outside. I need you to keep this secret."

"This is a lot to take in." Paul smiled and patted Draylon's shoulder. "I can't believe this is happening, I feel like I need to pinch myself to wake up," Paul chuckled, "I'm a reformed sceptic."

Draylon laughed, and then proposed they go get something to eat, as he was famished.

They went to a local bar in town that did food. The bar was called The Rongorongo Inn. Paul ordered spaghetti Bolognese and a pint of cider. Draylon ordered penne pasta with mushrooms and an energy drink. They found a nice bench outside the front of the bar and they talked at length and shared stories from their upbringing. Paul felt as if he was on cloud nine. He could hardly believe what he was hearing, but he had witnessed the puppy being saved, the bottle being raised off the ground, and that is impossible by Earth standards.

Draylon felt saddened by the knowledge of Paul's lonely childhood and adulthood. He hoped that they could be good friends and fill that void a little that Paul had created for so long. He realised that being brought up without your real parents is tough; Draylon had experienced the same thing on his planet. Karlon never had much time for Draylon on his home planet - he was always at the lab working on new experiments, but Draylon was thankful for the first class education he received, as Karlon was the top scientist on his planet. The conversation was halted as the food was brought out and they ate heartily. When they finished, Draylon thought it was time to confront Paul with his proposal.

Draylon said to Paul that he had something he needed to ask him, something quite big. He thought he might as well just come out with it rather than beat around the bush. He told Paul that when they were at the site of Ahu Tongariki, he had found a metallic tablet, an alien tablet; a tablet from a race of alien life that was now extinct. One of his biological fathers, named Karlon, told him that this alien race had destroyed themselves and their planet in civil war. This tablet not only suggested that maybe this alien race had something to do with the construction of the Moai, but also what intrigued him the most was it gave him co-ordinates to a site in Peru, the Nazca lines.

Draylon asked Paul if he would like to accompany him on an adventure. He said that he wants to visit the Nazca plains to find out what these co-ordinates lead to, but that required money, so he had decided to go to Las Vegas to win enough money to fund the venture. He also planned to stop at Roswell to pay his respects en route. He explained that he would win enough money for Paul to deposit into his bank to cover his bills for at least a year or more. Paul told Draylon it sounded great, but he couldn't plan to win money because it's all about luck, also he had a job that wouldn't hold until he got back. Draylon told Paul that he could count cards, and that he was technopathic, so winning was the easy part.

"I really would like you to come with me Paul." Draylon said, feeling a little anxious.

"If we won one hundred thousand or more dollars, we could pay my rent for many years." Paul seriously considered the idea. He imagined a long break paid for with a friend would be a great opportunity.

"We can win whatever we feel we need. Casinos rob people of many thousands of dollars every day, so my moral obligations don't really affect me in Vegas casinos."

"OK! Let's do it. I must admit, I feel a little nervous about it, but this is a once in a lifetime opportunity, to become financially secure with my alien friend going walkabout around the Americas." Paul laughed out loud. "I never thought I'd ever string a sentence like that together."

"That's great!" Draylon was overjoyed. "When can you be ready to leave?"

"I need to give one week's notice."

"OK, settled, I can arrange flights for Saturday the 15th of January."

"That sounds fine, I'll hand my notice in tomorrow morning."

"Thank you; it wouldn't be the same on my own. Thank you for trusting me, I know I've put a lot on you."

They both decided to head home. Time was getting on and they were both feeling a little drained from the events of the day.

Paul awoke the next day; he had his breakfast, a quick wash and then wrote his letter of resignation. He never saw much of his boss, José Mendez, and so wasn't too bothered about what his reaction would be. He was a little saddened though, about leaving Adriana - he got along with her really well, he thought she was a lovely girl. He made his way to the supermarket. When he arrived, he was surprised to see his boss José there, which made him a little nervous. He approached his boss and explained that he was leaving and giving one week's notice, and to his surprise, José was fine with it. Paul didn't know if that was a good thing or a bad thing, but was happy to get that out of the way - he felt a lot less tense now.

He noticed Adriana stacking shelves at the back of the shop. He approached her and told her that he'd be leaving; she seemed upset at the news. Paul told her maybe he would be back in a few months and get his job back; she smiled and said that she would miss him and that she really did hope he came back because he had been a good friend. He said that he would definitely be back, no doubt about it, as he loved Easter Island and stacking shelves. She laughed. He told her he'd see her Monday for his last five days. He kissed her cheek and then went home to his flat to relax and listen to music.

Draylon woke up excited about his adventures to come. He couldn't wait to head off with Paul to Las Vegas, and he was especially excited about finding out what those co-ordinates led to. He decided to head to the supermarket to get some breakfast. When he arrived, he saw Adriana at the back of the shop, and he approached her.

"Hi Adriana, how are you?" Draylon felt butterflies in the pit of his stomach.

"Hi Draylon, I'm good, thank you, a little sad that Paul is leaving." Adriana felt nervous and also sad that Draylon was leaving, she really liked him.

"Paul will be back. And so will I. And then maybe we could go out, for a meal or something, if you'd like?"

"I would love to, I would really love to, I wish you weren't going away so soon."

"We'll be back before you know it."

They both stood and looked into each other's eyes for a few seconds; they felt drawn to each other. Draylon leaned in and kissed her cheek close to her lips. Adriana kissed him near his lip also. José shouted across the room for Adriana to get on with her work or two people would be leaving. She blushed and bid Draylon farewell. Draylon smiled at her and said he would see her before he left. Then he bought some freshly baked bread and a couple of energy drinks and made his way back to his hotel room.

It was Friday the 14th of January 4:45 p.m. Draylon made his way to meet with Paul and say farewell to Adriana. All the arrangements had been made to fly out from Mataveri Airport in Hanga Roa tomorrow morning, and Draylon was looking forward to it. He had already paid up at his hotel, and was all packed up in his one and only bag - he preferred to travel light. He arrived at the supermarket and Paul was already standing out front.

Paul said that he would wait outside whilst Draylon said his goodbyes to Adriana. Draylon walked in. He saw Adriana behind the counter, and he thought she looked beautiful - she was wearing a fitted red dress that accentuated every curve. He said to her that he was going to miss her. Adriana and Draylon had only met just days before, but both could sense a real chemistry, as if a rush of endorphins coursed through their entire beings when they were near each other.

Adriana said that she would miss him too, and looked forward to meeting up on his return. She told Draylon to have a great time, and to look after Paul. Draylon said, "Don't worry about Paul, he is in the best of care." He smiled, and they both kissed each other very gently on the lips, a soft caress that sent tingles down both of their limbs. They both said goodbye, and parted ways. Draylon looked back several times to catch Adriana's eye, and then she was gone from view. Paul was waiting outside patiently. When Draylon came outside, Paul suggested getting one last meal at The Rongorongo Inn and then getting an early night, for their adventure started the next day at dawn.

Draylon arrived at Paul's flat at 6 a.m. the next day. They had both packed light. The taxi Paul had booked was already there, waiting to take them the short journey to the airport. When they arrived at the airport, they booked in, went through customs, and then awaited their plane. Paul was impressed that Draylon had a passport, birth certificate, driving licence, the lot. Draylon assured him that technology was his friend and that it was all too easy. Then he smiled, easing back on his chair in the waiting bay.

The plane was ready to board. They both showed their boarding passes and then found their seats at the rear. Paul wanted to sit at the back - he believed it to be the safest part of a plane. The plane felt very primitive to Draylon, but he was enjoying the whole experience. The captain made an announcement and then they all fastened their seat belts - they were ready for take-off. The plane left and they finally embarked on their journey, stopping at Santiago de Chile, then Los Angeles and finally Las Vegas.

CHAPTER TWO

Las Vegas

Draylon and Paul felt tired from the journey, even though they had managed to sleep for a short while on the planes. They went through customs, collected their luggage and then left the building to find a taxi to The Strip. The Strip is the name given to the stretch of road in Vegas that hosts some of the most fascinating and beautiful hotels in the world. It is also famous for its casinos and night-life.

Paul managed to flag down a large pink taxi. It appeared to be driven by Elvis himself. He asked Draylon where they were going first, Draylon said that he would like to get checked in at Caesars Palace and then sleep a little to energise, ready for the casinos in the evening. Paul was so excited. He was very glad he'd taken Draylon up on his offer - although he was still getting to know him, he felt at ease, almost like he was with a guardian. Elvis put their luggage in the boot, put his greatest hits on the stereo and drove them into Vegas, destination Caesars Palace.

They arrived at Caesars Palace. Elvis got their luggage from the boot of the taxi and carried it into the hotel for them, and then Elvis wished them a pleasant stay in Vegas and left the building. They were both awe-struck by the magnificent hotel - it was as if Rome had come to Vegas. There was a statue of Augustus Caesar and a beautiful statue of Michelangelo's David. The hotel was of enormous beauty, with Roman replicas everywhere.

Draylon took the liberty of booking their room. He decided on the deluxe room. They were given their key and then made their way to their apartment, both too tired to think of anything but sleep. Paul was very impressed by the room. There were two queen beds, marble dressing tables, a refreshment centre, dark wood furnishings, Caesar-style marble bathroom, dual sinks and an oversized spa tub, LCD television - and they had room service as an option. Draylon put his bag down and climbed into bed. He said to Paul that he'd see him in a few hours - then they'd go and win some money to fund their expedition. Paul decided to get some shut-eye too, but wasn't sure if he could, with all the excitement of the evening to come.

They woke at just gone 5 p.m. They had a quick freshen up and decided to make their way to Bally's Casino. When they got out on The Strip, they both came alive; it was like electricity in the air, and they could feel the energy. And the lights were awesome, like nowhere else on Earth; almost as if all of the lights in the world had suddenly landed on The Strip at Vegas. When they arrived, Paul asked if they were going to win all their money at Bally's or spread it out elsewhere in other casinos. Draylon assured Paul that many high flyers lose many hundreds of thousands of dollars or more in one night - a simple win of fifty thousand dollars or so they would not miss. He said that casinos were immoral and they robbed people on a daily basis; people with addictive personalities, people that had wives and children to support and yet were compelled to keep on gambling for that next pay out which seldom came.

Paul said that he was going to try his own luck on the slots and that he would catch up with Draylon a little later. Draylon put a little money in the first slot machine he came to and used his technopathic abilities to win. Each time he gambled a little higher and his winnings were going up and up. Very quickly, his prize money was up in the fifty thousand dollar region. When he reached sixty, he thought that was enough. He now had enough money for Paul to bank to cover his expenditures whilst away from home; he had enough for all travelling costs and enough for food and any other eventualities. The money should easily last for six months to a year.

Paul put ten dollars in a slot machine. He was shocked beyond belief when he rang up just over a thousand dollars of winnings - he couldn't believe his luck, but he wasn't about to push it, he decided to collect. At that moment, he was approached by a rather large man who looked drunk and very upset. He told Paul that he was playing that machine all night and had gone to get more change, and when he got back his place had been stolen. He exclaimed that the money was rightfully his. Paul apologised for the large man's grief, but explained that he had won fair and square and that he intended on keeping his winnings.

The man was furious. He pulled back his giant fist and took a swing at Paul. Paul closed his eyes and turned. He screwed up his face in anticipation of the hit, but nothing happened. He looked up and he saw Draylon standing there with the man's fist in his hand. He stared the drunk deep in the eyes and said, "Leave." The man panicked and stumbled on his words and then left rather quickly. Paul looked up at his friend in astonishment and thanked him, he assured Draylon all was under control and laughed nervously. Draylon laughed out loud also, and then suggested they go out on The Strip, enjoy the lights and maybe get a meal and a drink or two. He thought to himself that he quite fancied an energy drink, although he was going to try to resist the urge.

They decided that they would try the Eiffel Tower restaurant and bar. It had all of the ambience and spirit of the French capital, and had a beautiful view of The Strip and all of its lights. Draylon ordered baked herbed crepe, artichoke, walnuts, slow roasted tomato coulis and basil. Paul decided on roasted farm raised chicken with fine herbs. They both ordered sparkling water for refreshments. Fifteen minutes later their food and drinks arrived and Draylon reached for his sparkling water, secretly wishing it had caffeine in it.

"You always seem to eat and drink the same sort of things," Paul remarked, thinking to himself how much he enjoyed variety in all of his meals.

"I know. I'm a creature of habit. I'd be quite happy having the same things every day, although I do want to try other things too - maybe tomorrow," Draylon replied, quietly thinking he'd most probably have similar things again tomorrow.

"Changing the subject slightly, I was wondering where you come from?"

"The planet I come from is named Terspheriton, or at least that is the translation into the language you speak. Although different, my planet works in much the same way as yours. We have scientists and governments, we have homes and we have vegetation. We also have the same struggles your planet faces; crime, corruption. But there's something about Earth and the human race. I feel as if this is my home, this is where I belong."

"And what do your kind look like exactly? Do you all have special abilities?"

"On average, I would say that my kind are between 4 and 5 feet tall. Our complexion is a light grey. In general, we are a slender race. Our heads are larger than that of humans, we have larger eyes and our brains are thousands of years in advance of yours - no offence meant. Our arms are long, our fingers reach down to our knees, and we only have four fingers on each hand. Other than that, we're quite similar." Draylon smiled, taking a sip of his drink. He enjoyed sarcasm and dry humour, and found he liked making people smile and laugh. He went on, "as for special abilities, we can all communicate telepathically. It makes it hard to keep secrets though. Some of us can heal and self-heal and some of us can utilise telekinetic powers. There are lots of different abilities on my planet and I was lucky enough to be created using the best of them - only I didn't have a proper family, so my abilities came with sacrifices."

"Why are you here? Why do your kind visit? Sorry about all of the questions," Paul took a large mouthful of his roasted chicken.

"We've been visiting for thousands of years, collecting intelligence and observing. Some of your technologies are very different from ours, so there is much to learn. I wanted to visit because I have this longing, like I belong here. It's hard to explain, but after all, I do look entirely human, so I do kind of stand out on my planet."

"This is really strange. Obviously that you're a hybrid and this is surreal, but also because I've always avoided people in my life - probably because I lost my parents, and my grandparents died when I was still relatively young. Deep down though, I've always been sad; I've wanted friendship and love in my life, but have been afraid that I would lose it again, so I put up this wall around me. Now here I am opening up, and I now have someone I can call a friend. It's been a strange couple of weeks, that's for sure, but I wouldn't change a thing. I feel that something has woken up in me and now I'm finally starting to live."

"This is only the beginning." Draylon finished off his baked crepe and washed it down with his sparkling water.

"Well, I'm tired, so I think I'm going to head back to the hotel. Are you coming?"

"Yes, but I think I may go out for a run in a while though - make sure that the streets are safe for women and children." He said the latter in jest, but wondered if anyone did want any help tonight; he toyed with the idea of being more, helping those in need of help, and maybe anonymously being a beacon for good.

Paul made his way up to their room. He fancied watching a little television, and then getting a good night's sleep. He was exhausted by the events in the last 24 hours. Draylon said goodnight and then went out for his run. He thought he'd run around the outskirts of the city and see what was about. When he finally made his way past the crowds of people on The Strip, he found the air was starting to get fresher. He was taking deep, slow breaths and finding his pace. His pulse slowed and he was running along at a fairly fast pace and felt as if he'd never tire. He was running on the outskirts of the city, weaving around some of the back streets, when he heard a whimpering. He could make out a female voice saying, "Please don't, please, please." He then heard a male voice say, "You might like it, but if you don't shut up, you will never know, understand?"

Draylon darted down the alley-way. A young woman had part of her clothing torn away and the man was trying to rape her. Draylon was horrified, and angry beyond belief. He grabbed the man by his throat and pinned him up high and hard. He stared at the man, his eyes an intense blue. "You will never ever do anything like this again, or I'll be back, and I'll strike you with such vengeance that you'll spend the rest of your life whimpering in a dark sealed room." Draylon touched the man's head, sending a bolt of energy that knocked him clean out. He said to the young woman "Don't worry, you're safe now. Call emergency services and I'll wait with you until they arrive - then I must be off." The woman called the emergency services and within minutes, the police and an ambulance were coming around the corner. Draylon explained that he had to leave. She smiled at him and said, "Thank you, I will never forget this." Draylon replied, "Be safe," and then he ran off around the corner into the night.

Draylon decided to head back to the hotel. After just a few minutes, he came across a homeless man choking on his own vomit. He ran over to him and placed his hand on the vagrant's back. He closed his eyes, slowed his breathing and focused. In seconds, Draylon neutralised the alcohol in the man's body, and the man became responsive again. Draylon told him that the alcohol had nearly killed him. He told him to wait and that he would be back in a short while.

When he returned, he had a bag of food and bottled water for the man. He said to him that money would be better spent on fuel to sustain him, not alcohol - alcohol would poison, corrupt and eventually kill you. Life is precious, he said, and a gift - nurture it. Draylon gave the man 10,000 dollars. He looked the man kindly in the eyes and said, "You have an opportunity now. Get washed up, get some clothes, get a room, get a job, enjoy your life, look around you, smell the fresh air, look at the stars in the sky, there is so much more, farewell." The man shed a tear and replied, "Thank you, I haven't been shown this much kindness in years, thank you, I promise I'll change, I promise."

Draylon ran back towards the hotel. He figured it was about time he got some rest. He felt good about helping those people and decided that was what he wanted to do with his life. He felt that he fits in on Earth. He felt at home, and he believed he could make a difference. He knew he would miss Terspheriton, but Earth felt like his home now. He had always felt drawn to Earth - he thought maybe he was more human than alien, although of course on Terspheriton, humans are the aliens. He arrived back at the hotel and made his way to his room. Paul was already asleep, and Draylon tried not to wake him; he climbed into his bed and went out like a light.

It was Monday 17th of January. Draylon woke at 8 a.m. He got out of bed and stretched. He decided he'd like to go clothes shopping that day and really push the boat out - all he had was two pairs of jeans, two grey T-shirts and a pair of trainers. He woke Paul up and told him his idea. Paul thought it was a good idea but struggled getting up; he had a lot less energy than Draylon and liked his lie-ins. They decided on breakfast at Caesars and made their way down to the buffet, Draylon's personal choice. Paul opted for a fried breakfast and a pot of tea; Draylon decided on two cinnamon bagels, a coffee and an energy drink for a change.

"I think we should win another 50,000 dollars today, just in case our expedition takes longer than you thought, and we should hire a car," Paul said excitedly.

Draylon laughed out loud. "OK! A little more money wouldn't hurt, but who gets to choose the car? More importantly, who gets to drive the car?"

"Well I believe I should choose the car being an earthling and knowing more about cars than you, but we could take it in turns driving if you'd like?"

"That sounds fair. I think we should try Planet Hollywood casino today," said Draylon whilst finishing off his bagel.

"Planet Hollywood it is. I can't wait to get a car, hey - maybe we could go toward Area 51, it's only a few hours from here I believe."

"You bet, so long as you promise not to hand me in."

They finished their breakfast and exited the hotel admiring the fifty-foot Italian cypresses at the entrance as they left. They made their way to Planet Hollywood casino, it was a beautiful day, with not a cloud in the sky, and already the streets were bustling with people. They arrived and were in awe of its nearly three acres of casino. Paul imagined that these places must make a fortune out of people's misfortunes. Draylon decided on a slot machine again so as to avoid drawing too much attention to himself. He put in ten dollars, used his technopathy, and that ten became a hundred, then a thousand. He decided to stop just short of fifty thousand. The accumulative monies now were just over one hundred thousand dollars left. Paul couldn't believe how easy it was. He suggested making a couple of million and retiring. Draylon laughed, saying that although it was a nice idea, a casino was a business. Although it seemed a little immoral at times, people did choose to gamble. He was content with what they had won and suggested doing a little clothes shopping.

They decided to shop for clothes in the Planet Hollywood miracle mile. They found a great store full of jeans, T-shirts, shirts, shoes, trainers - basically everything that either of them could hope for. They spent almost an hour in there trying on clothes and looking about. Paul eventually decided on a smart black fitted shirt, two decorated black T-shirts and some black Doc Martens shoes. Draylon chose three T-shirts, a black, a red, and a blue one. He also chose a new pair of jeans and some Nike trainers. They paid for their new clothes and then decided to get refreshments. They found a nice café outside on The Strip. Draylon ordered two lattes and a cheese sandwich; Paul ordered a pint of lager and a packet of crisps.

Paul said that he quite fancied hiring an American muscle car and could hardly wait; he looked forward to a bit of power after driving his 1-litre Suzuki Alto for seven years. Draylon suggested a yellow one and laughed. Paul said that there was nothing wrong with yellow – it was a happy colour, but said he quite liked the idea of a red or maybe a black one. They paid and tipped the waiter and asked about any hire car companies nearby. The waiter gave them directions to Joe's Car Hire. They thanked him and made their way to the hire company, a couple of miles off The Strip.

They arrived at Joe's. There was an extraordinary selection of large American muscle cars. Paul immediately fell in love with the new 2011 race red Ford Mustang GT.

"This is it, this is the one, let's get it." Paul found it hard to contain his excitement. Adrenalin started to course his body at the thought of driving such an attractive, powerful machine.

Draylon smiled at Paul's enthusiasm. "OK! I think we should get it for a week. We could go to the outskirts of Area 51, come back to Vegas and then head off to Roswell. I'd like to go to Roswell, what do you think?"

"Sound's perfect! Let's go find Joe."

They found Joe in the showroom and asked him if the race red Mustang was available for rental for one week. Joe said that it was available but it wasn't cheap. Paul told him they would take it. Paul paid the deposit and rental for a week and gave Joe his driving licence to photocopy. He couldn't help but be surprised at the fact

Draylon too, had a driving licence. Draylon handed it over and Joe photocopied it also. Joe handed over the keys and told them both to drive carefully; the Mustang was like a rocket. Paul asked if the stereo was mp3 compatible, Joe replied that it was, the only thing the car didn't do was turbo boost.

Paul laughed. He practically ran out to the car. He got in, started her up, and revved the engine. Paul grinned with satisfaction - it roared like a lion. Draylon got in and suggested they fuel up and head out on that highway toward Area 51. Paul agreed. He connected up his mp3 player, selected a play list, turned up the volume and spun out of the forecourt and onto the main road. The car roared as it sped up to 60 miles an hour in what seemed like a second.

They stopped at the first gas station they found. Paul got out and filled the car to the brim. He went into the shop and got plenty of bottled water, some sandwiches, and of course an energy drink for Draylon. He paid for the fuel and the goods and rushed back out to the car, eager to put the Mustang through its paces out on the open road. Area 51, here we come, he thought to himself.

CHAPTER THREE

Area 51

Draylon and Paul headed out north on route 95. Once they were outside of Vegas, Paul put his foot to the floor. The Mustang roared and they were both pinned to their seats. The car shot past 100 mph, still picking up speed. Paul was exhilarated but a little scared too, and so eased his foot off the gas a little. The car slowed to about 70 mph. In just minutes, they were out in the desert - a very quick transition from being in a busy city. The desert was vast and beautiful and there wasn't another car in sight.

Just forty minutes outside of Vegas, they came to a town called Indian Springs. They decided to stop for a while. Paul noticed a store selling Indian artefacts and decided to go in and have a look around; Draylon said that he would wait outside and enjoy the sunshine. Paul was looking around the shop at all of the Indian relics and came across a knife. He felt the blade - it was very sharp. For some reason, he felt drawn to it and decided to buy it. The shop-keeper put the knife in a bag for him and wished him a pleasant day. Outside of the shop, Draylon was sitting by the front wheel of the car. Paul asked if he was comfortable down there. Draylon smiled and suggested they hit the road, as it was already fast approaching five in the afternoon.

Draylon decided it was his turn to drive for a while. He told Paul to fasten his seat belt; he was going to see what the Mustang was capable of. He pulled out of Indian Springs slowly and headed out onto the main highway. There were no other vehicles in sight. He stopped the car and asked Paul for some music. Paul put on his mp3 player. As the music started, Draylon put his foot to the floor. The car roared, the wheels spun on the spot and then there was traction; the Mustang shot off like a bat out of hell, and Paul and Draylon were thrown back on their seats. The car hit 100mph in seconds. It was still accelerating well past 130, and then Draylon decided to ease off. Paul looked white as a ghost and Draylon laughed out loud. Paul took a deep breath and let out a nervous laugh, glad that they were starting to slow down.

"I thought you liked cars and speed?" Draylon mused.

"Yes, I like my life too though," Paul laughed.

They went past a sign saying Mercury, Nevada. Paul explained that's where they did the atom bomb tests in the 50's - a small dirt road was all that connected Mercury to the highway. Draylon stopped the car and stood outside in the sun. It felt like the middle of nowhere, Paul got out of the vehicle also.

"Why did we stop?"

"I was just curious." Draylon closed his eyes and took deep breaths. "As I suspected, this place still isn't safe to inhabit - I can sense the radiation levels. It could be many years until this stretch of land is truly safe."

"Then why are we still here? Let's go!"

"The levels of radiation are very low, we're safe, but long term it could be harmful to one's health."

They got in the car and headed off again. Paul pointed out the radars and listening posts on the mountains. He said that they must be getting close to Area 51 now. They went past a junction for Route 160 and saw a sign for fireworks in a place called Pahrump, but decided not to stop. Draylon could feel the wind blowing off the desert. It caused the car to swerve slightly from time to time and so he kept the speed down to 60 mph. After a short while on the road, Draylon could make out another services in the distance. He decided they were going to stop - he quite fancied a coffee.

When they arrived, Paul pointed out a sign with a picture of an alien on it, saying, "Last service station before Area 51." They parked the car up and went in the little café to get some refreshments; Draylon ordered a coffee and Paul a pot of tea.

"We can't actually go to Area 51; we'd probably be arrested or worse, shot at," Paul mentioned, hoping Draylon wouldn't be disappointed.

"I know. We could just park up when it gets dark though, maybe we'll be lucky and see a UFO. At the very least, the stars will be an awesome sight out here in the desert."

"That's a good idea, a bit like Wayne and Garth in *Wayne's World* sitting on the bonnet of their car."

"I'm not sure what that is, but yes, I suppose."

They relaxed for a while, chatting further and taking their time with their refreshments, and when it started to get dark, they left the café and made their way to the Mustang. They started heading down Route 95 back toward Vegas. After a few minutes, Draylon noticed some lights in his rear-view mirror. The lights were white and in the sky behind them. The electrics in the car started playing up and the lights on the dashboard flickered. Paul turned off the stereo and asked what was up. Draylon told him there were lights behind them from a craft, and the craft was interfering with the electrics in the car. The car stopped, the lights disappeared, and then a saucer was vaguely visible about 100 metres away.

"Is it one of those crafts from Area 51?" Paul said nervously.

"No, I can hear them, be very quiet."

After several minutes, the craft's lights came on. It stayed level for a few seconds whilst revolving and then it shot off into the sky at awesome speed. The car started back up again and the lights came back on. Paul looked over at Draylon nervously. Draylon looked sad.

"What was that? What's up?"

"That was my kind. We communicate telepathically, and I could hear them."

"What did they say?

"My crash was no accident Paul, my craft was tampered with, and they thought I was dead."

"I'm sorry. Where do you think they've gone? Are we in danger?"

"They're probably seeking counsel. I need you to do something for me. It's important, otherwise we are both in danger."

"What? Tell me, you're making me nervous."

"I have a tracking device in my right shoulder. I need you to cut it out, and then we have to destroy it, but you'll have to be fast because I heal very quickly."

"Oh my goodness, I can't."

"You have to my friend. Please?"

Paul got out his Indian blade, he wondered if this is why he was drawn to it, and then he shrugged the idea off, thinking it impossible. Draylon took off his T-shirt and pointed to a tiny scar on his right shoulder blade. He explained to Paul that he needed to make the incision about an inch wide and half an inch deep, so that he had room to lever the chip out with his blade. He warned him to be quick, or else he'd have to do it again. Draylon leaned forward and bit into his T-shirt in anticipation of the pain. Paul got himself into a comfortable position, blade ready, and he slit Draylon's shoulder as quickly as he could. He felt the knife on a foreign object and wedged the blade underneath it. He prised it as fast as he could out of Draylon's body.

The cut healed in seconds, and Paul took a deep breath. He handed the tiny chip to Draylon, and using his ability to manipulate matter, Draylon destroyed the chip. Draylon suggested they leave and head back toward Vegas, although he couldn't be tracked now, they were still in danger whilst on Route 95.

Paul took his turn driving and floored the Mustang all the way into Vegas. They were both glad to be back in Sin City, the city of lights. They parked up at Caesars Palace and made their way to their room. Both of them were shattered and decided on an early night. Tomorrow, they planned on driving to Roswell, which was a full day's drive, so they had to leave early to get there by nightfall.

It was 6 a.m. on Tuesday 18th January, Paul's alarm on his phone woke them both up. They got out of bed, freshened up and went to the buffet for their breakfast. Paul decided on waffles and syrup for breakfast, washed down with a mug of tea. Draylon opted for four pieces of brown toast and a few large coffees. Paul enquired about Draylon's apparent caffeine addiction. Draylon assured him that he could give up at any time but was enjoying it.

Paul suggested he drive the first half of the journey to Roswell and Draylon drive the second half, it was a fair distance so as soon as they arrived, they would have to check into a hotel in town. They finished their breakfast and grabbed a few of their belongings from their room for the trip. Paul was happy to see the Mustang waiting in the parking lot; he couldn't wait to start driving. They got into the car and buckled up. Paul put the key in the ignition and turned it. The car roared and Paul sat there listening to it for a minute before setting off. They stopped at a nearby fuelling station to top up and then set out on their journey, destination Roswell.

CHAPTER FOUR

Roswell

After several stops for fuel, lots of coffee and bagels, Draylon and Paul arrived in the town of Roswell, New Mexico. They booked into a local hotel named The Roswell Inn. They were shown to their room. It was small with two singular beds and an en-suite bathroom. They put down their bags and crashed out on their beds, exhausted by the day's driving.

"Why are we here Draylon?" Paul asked inquisitively.

"Originally it was to pay my respects at the crash site. As Roswell is in driving distance from Vegas, I thought it a good idea."

"So it was a cover up, aliens did crash here?"

"Yes, my kin, you could say." Draylon felt saddened by the revelation near Area 51. "I can't believe my craft was sabotaged, I can't believe my own kind would do that to me."

"It doesn't make sense. How is it you travel from such great distances, it must take years, surely?"

"We're cryogenically frozen and as the craft approaches the designated destination, it activates the thawing process - regeneration if you like."

"That's phenomenal, so your crafts have artificial intelligence?"

"That's correct; we'll make a scientist out of you yet my friend." Draylon smiled at his friend, and then noticed his stomach rumbling again. "I think it's time for some food, I'm feeling a little hungry, fancy coming out for a bite?"

"Absolutely, Just one more thing though, what do you think those co-ordinates will lead us to in Nazca?"

"Answers, I hope. Other than that, I have absolutely no idea."

They went for a walk into town looking for a place for food. They found a diner named The Cup & Saucer Café. Draylon decided to try something different, so he ordered a jacket potato and cheese with a large butter-scotch milkshake. Paul ordered bangers and mash and a large full sugar Coke. When they had finished, they decided to head back to the hotel to sleep. They decided on checking out the Roswell museum tomorrow and visiting the crash site.

They awoke nice and early, had a wash and got dressed. Draylon decided he'd try out his new blue T-shirt, jeans and Nike trainers. Paul tried on his smart black fitted shirt, the jeans he already had and his new pair of Doc Martens shoes. They both looked very smart. Paul enquired as to Draylon's age. Draylon said that years had a different measure on his planet. Also he was cryogenically frozen for long periods of time. He took a minute to work it out and replied, "I am 36 years of age and my birthday is on April 9th." Paul said that was strange, as his birthday was April 1st and he was 36 years old. Draylon thought it strange too - what were the chances of two strangers being born in the same month and year?

They made their way to the UFO museum. When they got there, Paul thought it looked like the entrance to a cinema from the outside. They went in and were greeted by a model alien holding a sign saying welcome. They paid for their visit at reception and started their tour of the museum and research centre. The first place they stopped had pictures of men that worked at the air base in the 40's and 50's. They moved on to the next room, in which there was the Roswell incident timeline. They then went to look at a display of the Roswell dig; Draylon was taking note of the location so that he could find the site later that day.

They went on to the next display, which was full of pictures of sightings of alien craft. Paul asked Draylon if any of them were real. Draylon replied that he recognised a couple of them that were definitely authentic. They made their way around the museum, looking at all of the newspaper articles and then the art gallery. Draylon's interest was piqued when he saw a model of the alien autopsy. Draylon informed Paul that the alien model was accurate, which meant that his kind were captured dead or alive and dissected. He felt saddened by this and hoped that they were indeed found dead and not killed in the name of science. Paul, noticing Draylon's distress, suggested they leave and head out toward the crash site, if they could find it. Draylon agreed, and they made their way back to The Roswell Inn to get the Mustang.

They arrived at the car. Paul opted to drive and suggested Draylon navigate. They stopped off at a fuelling station first to top up the Mustang. Paul bought Draylon some energy drinks and bagels for the journey and bought himself some Coke and tuna sandwiches. They set off on their journey. After a short while, they came across a sign that read UFO Crash Site; they knew they must be getting close. They headed out down a stony road that caused the Mustang to slip several times. Draylon urged Paul to be careful. After almost an hour down the stony track, there were sheep here, there and everywhere. They noticed a sign that read Enter Only. Paul parked up the car and they made their way on foot. After a short while, they came across a shed, an old truck and some stone markers. Draylon could feel tingles up his spine – he sensed that they were getting close. Paul pointed out a large stone in the distance. Draylon shouted, "That's the spot!" They ran over to it, excited to have found the area in which the saucer crashed in July 1947. There was an inscription on top, it read:

WE DON'T KNOW WHO THEY WERE

WE DON'T KNOW WHY THEY CAME

WE ONLY KNOW

THEY CHANGED OUR VIEW

OF THE UNIVERSE

THIS UNIVERSAL SACRED SITE

IS DEDICATED JULY 1997

TO THE BEINGS

WHO MET THEIR DESTINIES

NEAR ROSWELL NEW MEXICO

JULY 1947

Draylon and Paul sat on the large stone monument, contemplating what took place there all of those years ago. Draylon could sense a presence. He walked back away from the rock about ten paces and dug with his hands. After a minute or so, he retrieved a small fragment of metal, almost rectangular in shape, with a smooth, uneven edge on two adjacent sides. He informed Paul that it was a fragment from the craft. Paul took the piece in his hands. Draylon told him to bend it and try to crush it. Paul did as he asked, and it crushed easily. Draylon said to release it now. Paul did as he asked and to his surprise, the metal went back to its former shape without a crease, mark or blemish on it. Paul was stunned. Draylon wondered if their craft too, was sabotaged. He didn't have any answers and it frustrated and upset him. Draylon wanted to get to Nazca now more than ever in the hope that he could find answers to at least some of his many questions. He suggested that Paul keep the piece of metal from the craft as a souvenir, and said he'd like to get something to eat in town, relax a little and spend the night in Roswell. He added that he would like to spend one last night at Caesars, and then make their journey to Nazca. Paul was quite happy - he was having the time of his life.

They arrived back in the town of Roswell. They stopped in a local store and bought some groceries. Draylon bought some pumpkin seed bread, cheese slices and four energy drinks. Paul bought himself a couple of bars of chocolate; a packet of crisps and a 7Up. Draylon remarked that Paul's choice of food wasn't very healthy. Paul pointed out Draylon's growing obsession with caffeine; Draylon laughed and promised he'd give it up soon. They sat outside on a bench in the centre of town, enjoying the warmth of the day; they chatted for hours until sunset, and then decided on hitting the hay and getting a fresh start in the morning.

The next morning they checked out of the hotel. They got in the Mustang and headed off back to Vegas. Several stops later, they arrived back at the city of lights by nightfall, they took the Mustang back to Joe's Car Hire, which broke Paul's heart, and went for one last meal at Caesars.

The following morning, they checked out of Caesars Palace and booked a taxi to McCarran airport, when they arrived at the airport they booked their tickets to Lima Peru; they had a bit of a wait because the plane wasn't flying out until the early afternoon. Several cups of tea and mugs of coffee later Draylon and Paul boarded the plane. The plane took off. It stopped at Mexico City airport for just over three hours and then went on to Lima, Peru. They arrived at Lima early in the morning on Saturday 22nd January.

CHAPTER FIVE

Nazca

The first thing they decided to do once they arrived in Lima was to get a nice hot drink at a café in the airport. When they found a café, Paul went up to order a very large latte for Draylon and a pot of tea for himself. Meanwhile Draylon found a comfy seat and stretched out his legs. When Paul arrived with the drinks, they sat and discussed their game plan. Draylon mentioned that they were going to need another car. Paul's eyes lit up at this and he became excitable again. Paul insisted that he get to choose the car. He suggested a convertible because it was going to be hot and air conditioning wasn't quite the same. Draylon thought that was a good idea, but felt a little distracted at the thought of finding what those co-ordinates led to. They spent a couple of hours relaxing in the café and then decided to go find a car to hire. When they exited the airport, Draylon approached a taxi and asked the driver to take them to a local car hire; somewhere that dealt in classic American cars. The driver said he knew just the place; they put their small amount of luggage in the boot and headed off.

After a short drive the taxi pulled up at Lima Car Hire. Draylon paid the taxi fare; they retrieved their luggage and bid the driver farewell. Paul's jaw gaped, he couldn't believe it - on the forecourt, they had a mint condition 1967 Plymouth Belvedere convertible in black. Draylon laughed at his friend's enthusiasm and clapped him on the back. They went inside to see if the car was still available for hire. The middle-aged man at reception said that it was, although expensive, it was one of their finest. "We'll take it!" Paul interrupted. They sorted out all of the paperwork and paid upfront for a week's hire with the deposit. The man handed over the keys and Paul ran out to the car - he couldn't wait to drive it. He was ecstatic to find out that the old classic had been fitted with a new state of the art stereo, mp3 compatible. Draylon got into the car, Paul started it up and the engine roared out loud. Paul couldn't stop smiling with pleasure. He looked at his friend and said, "Thank you for this Draylon. I really am having the time of my life, I owe you so much."

"Think nothing of it, it's good to have the company, now are you going to drive or what?" Draylon smiled, happy that Paul was having such a good time.

Paul connected his mp3 player, selected his playlist and pulled out of the car park area and onto the main road. The tank was already full, so no need to stop for fuel. Paul put his foot to the floor and the car roared up the road, echoing off all of the buildings as it went. They had the roof down, the sun was shining, the wind was in their hair and it was a perfect day for driving; the sky was blue; the scenery awesome as they headed out onto the open road toward Nazca.

After several stops and a gallon of water, they arrived at the small town of Nazca. They booked a room with a couple of single beds at the Nazca Lines Hotel. Draylon decided to go for a swim, as they had a lovely pool at the hotel. Paul thought he'd just lie out on a deck chair and catch a few rays - he wasn't feeling as energetic as Draylon. One hundred lengths later, Draylon emerged from the pool. His muscles were ripped to shreds, and he looked the epitome of health and fitness.

"Put some clothes on, there are women and children about," Paul laughed.

"Are you not going to do a few lengths? It'll revitalise you. Exercise is essential to a long, healthy life."

"How long do you live anyway Draylon?"

"About two hundred of your Earth years, I would guess," Draylon laughed at his friend. "Get in the pool and maybe you'll add a few years to your life span."

"I'm quite happy with my life span, thank you!"

The afternoon approached evening and they decided to freshen up, get dressed into some clean clothes and have a meal in the hotel. When they arrived at the restaurant, feeling recharged, they found a seat outside and ordered their food. Draylon ordered a large bowl of pasta and pushed his luck asking for a pint of milk, but they acquiesced to his request; Paul ordered rice and chicken and a cold pint of lager. Draylon suggested they leave at six in the morning the next day, to avoid being seen out by the lines of Nazca. Paul thought it was a good idea, although he was missing his lie-ins. Their meals and drinks arrived and they remained silent until they had finished. Draylon finished first and Paul made a comment that he had seen Hoovers work slower.

After their meals, they retired for the evening, ready for an early start the next day.

It was 5 a.m. when Paul's alarm woke them. They got up and washed, grabbed some bottles of water and were out by the car just before six. Paul started the car, put on the mp3 player and headed out on the highway toward the Nazca lines. It was only a short drive, less than 30 minutes, and they pulled up on the side of the highway. They grabbed a bottle of water each and started their hike over the plains. Draylon knew exactly where he was going.

The Nazca lines are a series of ancient geoglyphs, and the area encompassing the lines is nearly five hundred square kilometres. The geogyphs include that of a hummingbird, a monkey, an astronaut, a landing strip and many more. The geoglyphs have been there for many hundreds of years.

They arrived at the famous landing strip and made their way to the end of the runway, the wide end. Draylon could sense an entity below. They both dug with their hands. About two feet down, they came across a hard surface. Draylon, using his power to manipulate matter, cleared the area of rock to reveal a circular metal door. Draylon placed his hand to the door and caused it to open. He looked at Paul.

"This is an old saucer, it's one of ours."

"What are we waiting for, let's take a look around."

Draylon entered first and was surprised to find there was still power, he activated the saucer and the inside lit up. Paul climbed in behind him. They were both shocked by what they saw. Paul especially felt sick, just as Draylon did at the museum at Roswell. There were five incubators. Each one had a failed attempt at an alien-human hybrid. Two looked more human, whilst the other three were more alien, but they were severely deformed. It was clearly not a voluntary experiment, and Paul wondered what sort of race Draylon's kind really were.

Draylon was equally shocked and upset at this revelation. The craft was a very old one - Draylon imagined at least two thousand years old, which meant they had been experimenting with human beings for at least two thousand years, possibly a lot longer. He explained to Paul that the aliens he saw before him were not of the greys on his planet but the pale greens from an entirely different galaxy. He said that the greens looked very similar to his kind; only their skin was of a very pale green, where-as his kind were a very pale grey. He said that as far as he knew, the greens were destroyed in a civil war about six hundred years before and none now existed.

Draylon suddenly heard the high-pitched noise again coming from outside. He said to Paul that they should get out now. Paul followed him, and Draylon sealed the door behind them and manipulated matter to form rock over the metallic ship so that it could not be seen. They quickly filled the hole with the two feet of gravel and made the area look as if no one had ever been there. Draylon ran to the narrow end of the landing strip and dug down; he pulled out a large rock and manipulated matter to open it up. He found another cool, metallic, rectangular-shaped tablet and what appeared to be part of an amulet. He placed his right hand over the tablet.

The information within it flooded into his sub-conscious at the speed of light and then it disintegrated into tiny particles. Draylon placed the piece of amulet in his jean pocket.

Draylon sat down, thinking. Paul asked him what had happened. Draylon explained that when he placed his hand on the alien tablet, all of the information within it flooded into his sub conscious and the knowledge now belonged to him. He went on to explain that the green alien race had not become extinct by civil war, but they had been destroyed by his own race, the greys. Like your government, he said, my government also keeps secrets. Apparently, these pale green aliens nurtured human life and sought to educate and protect them.

One of their exceptional gifts was that of being able to predict future events. They predicted their demise and realised it was unavoidable, but as a legacy they wanted to protect the human race, knowing that my kind would eventually decide to destroy Earth when human intelligence became a threat. They used all of their power and knowledge to create an amulet, an amulet that would bestow power to the protector of the human race, an amulet for an alien-human hybrid, an amulet created for the coming of Draylon - that is me. My being here was predicted by the pale greens over six hundred years ago. This piece of amulet will find the other two pieces that make it whole. There is also information contained within this piece of amulet, and it says that our next destination is The Great Pyramid in Egypt.

"That is a lot to take in. What sort of power will the amulet bestow?"

"That I do not know. What I do know is that I am exhausted - let's get back to the car before we're seen, and go back to town to get some refreshments and something to eat."

"You are always hungry," Paul laughed at his friend. "To be honest, I have a little bit of a head-ache. One minute, I'm on Easter Island isolated from the world, now I'm in the centre of an alien battle."

Draylon laughed out loud, "You always make me laugh - come on, let's go."

They hiked back to the 1967 Plymouth Belvedere convertible, and made their way back to their hotel. They decided to take a stroll into town to find a place to eat. They eventually came across a little diner called Lines Café. The waitress came over to take their order. Paul ordered a large glass of water and eggs on toast; Draylon ordered a large glass of water also and four pieces of wholegrain toast.

"Why do you think this amulet is in three pieces?" Paul was a little confused - he couldn't believe they had visited so many places in such a short period of time, and now they were about to head off again.

"I can only assume to protect it. If one piece had been removed, I could still find it with one of the other two pieces."

"That makes sense. Don't you find all of this a little overwhelming though?"

"Absolutely, I'm just going to take it one step at a time, otherwise I think my head will explode."

Their breakfast arrived and they both ate heartily. Draylon asked Paul what he would like to do next. Paul suggested relax and enjoy the peace and quiet of Nazca, and maybe stay four days and head back to the airport in Lima on Friday. Draylon, although eager to get to Egypt, relented. He had been taking Paul all over the place, without really giving him time to relax and enjoy the break from everyday life. Draylon took the piece of amulet out of his pocket. Its shape was like a semicircle, but a bit smaller, with no markings. It was metallic and shiny. Paul wondered at how such a small insignificant looking thing could retain so much power when whole. Draylon placed it back in his pocket; they paid the bill and then made their way back to the hotel to relax by the pool. The next four days were going to involve lie-ins, relaxing, eating and just enjoying the serenity of the place that is Nazca.

It was Friday, 28th January. Draylon and Paul got up at 6 a.m. refreshed and ready to start their journeys again. They check out of their hotel and head out to their 1967 Plymouth Belvedere convertible, with their belongings. Paul couldn't wait to drive it again. He got into the car, wired up his mp3 player and started the engine. He sat there just listening to it for a minute or so, and then they were off.

They arrived at Lima just after midday. They took the car back to Lima Car Hire and got a taxi to the airport. They went into the airport and booked their flights. The flight wasn't due to leave until early evening, so they decided to wait it out in the café with some magazines and lots of coffee and tea. Finally, it was time to depart. They were on their way to The Great Pyramid of Egypt - first stop, Madrid, and then onto Cairo.

CHAPTER SIX

Egypt

They arrived at Cairo at 8:30 p.m. on Saturday, 29th January. They had managed to sleep on the long journey, but still felt a little jet-lagged. Draylon was intrigued as to the nature of the amulet and couldn't help but wonder if the power within it was for good or for bad. Once bitten, twice shy, and Draylon had been devastated by the knowledge that his own people had wanted him dead. Trust was something that Draylon had become wary of. Paul interrupted Draylon's thoughts and suggested they stop and get some refreshments at one of the cafés at the airport. Draylon thought that a splendid idea.

At the café, Paul found a nice comfy seat whilst Draylon ordered refreshments; a pot of tea for Paul and a ham and cheese toasty, and three lattes for Draylon and two fresh croissants. Paul was very excited about seeing The Great Pyramid, but a little apprehensive about the narrow tunnels within.

"What's our plan of action then?" Paul asked, hoping that an early night was an option.

"I think we should book into a hotel first and unload our luggage and then head off to the pyramid."

"What? At night time? It'll be dark!" Paul felt a little nervous about the idea of walking around a tomb in the pitch black.

"We won't be able to look around during the day with tourists about; it'll have to be at night. Using the internet on your mobile and my abilities, I'll be able to shut down all surveillance in the area. We can then sneak past any mounted police and make our way into the pyramid. We can get a couple of torches in one of the shops before we leave the airport."

"I must admit that makes me nervous as hell. I'll do it though, I think." Paul's adrenaline was coursing at the thought.

"Thank you, I owe you. Tomorrow we relax though, what do you say?" Draylon admired his friend for his courage and felt as if none of this would have been possible on his own. He was lucky to have a friend like Paul.

"Relaxing tomorrow and a long lie-in would be perfect!" He smiled at the thought.

"Agreed then, and just so you know, if this truly was foretold and this journey is destiny, you share that destiny - that's an encouraging thought." Draylon clapped his friend on the shoulder. "Let's head off - this is going to be a long night."

Before they left the airport, they stopped off to buy a couple of torches and batteries, and then flagged down a taxi outside and headed off into the city to find a hotel.

They found a hotel named Hotel Khufu and checked in for several days. They took their luggage straight to their room and decided to relax a little until midnight and then head off to the pyramid. Paul felt a little anxious about the whole thing. Draylon assured him there was nothing to worry about - they'd be in and out of there in no time at all.

It was midnight. They left their hotel room and started their journey on foot towards The Great Pyramid. When they were getting near, Draylon used Paul's mobile phone to access the internet, and using his technopathic abilities, he shut down all surveillance cameras in the area. They saw the occasional mounted officer, but found it easy to stay hidden; they soon made it just inside the entrance to the pyramid.

Once inside, they started descending down the passageway. It was pitch black, but they waited until they had made a bit of ground before putting on their flashlights. Paul was the first to put his torch on. Although in awe of the mighty pyramid, he felt uneasy and claustrophobic, and prayed he never saw any spiders. As they approached the bottom of the descending passageway, Draylon heard the high-pitched noise again. He told Paul and it eased his nerves a little. The passageway brought them out to a very large subterranean chamber; Draylon could sense the noise emanating from the dead centre of the chamber. He approached the area and using his ability to manipulate matter, he opened up the rock to reveal another piece of the amulet; piece two of the three pieces. The piece seemed to be the opposing piece to the one he found at Nazca. It was a semi-circle but slightly smaller than half a circle, which meant the next piece must be the sliver in the middle to complete the circular amulet. This piece had a singular line across it at an angle. Paul suggested it may be part of a hieroglyph that existed on the centrepiece. Draylon agreed. Draylon placed his right hand over the new piece of amulet; he closed his eyes and focused. The amulet gave him the resting place of the third and final piece, Tunguska ground zero, where the alien craft had struck on June 30th 1908.

A scuffling noise came from the descending passageway. The only light was that of their torches, and shadows appeared about the chamber. Paul was becoming afraid. Then he pointed towards the shaft. One of the grey aliens stood before them. It was Karlon.

"You were my greatest creation, but I am afraid you are no longer required. The council see you as a potential threat, and it is bestowed upon me to undo that threat," Karlon communicated with Draylon telepathically, as is the way on Terspheriton.

"What are you saying Karlon? You're the only real family I have." Draylon spoke aloud so that Paul could understand a little about what was being said.

"I am sorry, but you have no family Draylon, I did what I had to, now it must end."

With that, Karlon used his telekinetic ability to strangle Draylon. Draylon was gasping for air - he could not breathe at all, he started to turn white, and his legs gave way. Paul shouted, "Leave him alone!" He ran at Karlon, which caused him to divert his energy and throw Paul against the wall, smashing his head hard against the rock. Draylon recovered. He had a split second. He drew on all of the available energy he could and gave a telekinetic blast, throwing Karlon with incredible force against the pyramid wall. Karlon was dead on impact.

Draylon ran to Paul. He took his hand - no pulse. He slowed his breathing, closed his eyes and focused. Nothing. Draylon shouted aloud, "No! No, no, please no, if there is a God!" He fell to his knees.

An hour passed. Draylon was on his knees. He was in a lot of emotional pain - he had lost his only friend, a friend who trusted him, and he had let him down....

Draylon suddenly came to his senses. He thought to himself that all was not lost – maybe, just maybe, it wasn't too late. Using his ability to manipulate matter, he created a grave for Karlon beneath the rock and then sealed it. He became aware of another passage hidden behind the rock wall. He manipulated matter and opened it. He gently placed Paul in there, and then, after making an oath that he'd be back, he sealed the passage. Draylon moved faster than he ever had in his life. He ran straight out of the pyramid and headed toward the airport. There was no sign of the craft that had brought Karlon. Draylon assumed the other greys in the craft would soon realise what had happened and be out for revenge - he had to move and fast. He managed to flag down a taxi and asked to be taken directly to the airport. The driver made haste.

Draylon booked his flight. It was a mid-morning take off. He couldn't relax; he just kept pacing about. He had to get to Tunguska fast, to the third and final piece of the amulet. He prayed the power within it could help him save Paul. He boarded the plane. Finally it took off - first stop Dusseldorf, then Moscow, and finally Krasnoyarsk in the early hours of Monday, 31st January.

CHAPTER SEVEN

Tunguska

During his stop at Moscow airport, Draylon bought clothing for the extreme weather conditions in Russia. He bought new boots, thermal socks, thermal undergarments, two fleece jumpers, a heavy duty thermal jacket, gloves and a head warmer - he was all set. Draylon went through customs at Krasnoyarsk airport and then found a washroom in which he put on all of his new attire. He left the airport and managed to get a taxi to a local motorbike shop.

Draylon was looking over the bikes, carefully taking into account fuel capacity. He decided on a KTM 690 Rally. Mainly black in colour, the bike was designed to have exceptional handling and agility on any type of terrain and the fuel capacity was 36 litres. He bought the bike outright and also bought a 20-litre petrol can. He had them both filled to the brim, and the can was then strapped firmly to the bike. He was ready. He bid the Russian salesman good day, speaking the language as if it were his own, and then headed out into the cold treacherous conditions of his trek hundreds of miles across Russia.

The bike handled the snow-covered roads awesomely, and Draylon was going as fast as the bike would take him, taking into account the conditions. Draylon was shattered, cold and saddened beyond belief; all that mattered to him now was retrieving the third piece of the amulet and praying that it was enough to bring back Paul. After many hours of travelling, he filled up the tank with his remaining 20 litres of fuel. He thought he had maybe enough fuel for the journey, but had no clue how he would get back. The terrain was getting tough - he was now off-road manoeuvring through forestry, dirt tracks and waterlogged fields, and the snow started to come down hard.

It was approaching evening. Draylon was freezing cold and could barely hold the handlebars, but he was determined to make the journey - he had to, for Paul. The bike started to splutter - the fuel was almost gone. He squeezed out another mile or so and the bike stopped. He started to run. He knew he must only be several miles from Tunguska ground zero, where the alien craft crashed in 1908. He was running as fast as he could.

Snow covered the ground, and he could barely make out his footing when he tripped on a felled tree. He landed with tremendous force and shouted out loud with pain. He looked down at his left leg. His tibia had snapped, piercing his skin and tearing his trousers clean open. Blood was flowing freely. He knew he had to manipulate the bone back into place quickly before the healing process went too far. He grabbed the bone and screamed so loudly that the very heavens shook, and the sound echoed for miles, causing snow to avalanche off hills and mountains far away. He pushed the bone into place, tears coursing down his face, and then his breathing started to slow, the leg started to mend, and in minutes, it was healed and he was ready to advance.

Draylon sensed danger and turned to see a craft in the sky in the distance. It was twilight and the white lights of the saucer reflected off its shiny metal surface. Draylon panicked. He had no hope of escape now, but he started to run anyway - he wasn't going to give up. His breathing became laboured because of the sheer cold of the evening air, and he fell again on another unseen branch. All of a sudden, he heard a high-pitched noise before him. He quickly dug down with his hands. He found it; the third piece of the amulet, almost as if the pale green alien race had foretold this very moment.

Draylon placed the piece on the snow before him and pulled the other two pieces from his pocket. They shot out of his hands with immense speed and became one with the third piece. The craft was now just a hundred feet away. Draylon ripped open his top and placed the amulet around his neck. There was an awesome light emanating from the crystal at the amulet's centre and then it started to dissolve into Draylon. There was no pain. The amulet dispersed throughout his entire body, infusing every last molecule. Draylon looked up and then held his right hand out before him. There was a blast from the craft. He closed his eyes - nothing happened. He looked up. Where he had his hand up, there was a blue force field. It expelled the laser from the craft. Draylon used his ability to draw on energy from all available power sources and blasted the craft in a tremendous fury. A great beam of intense white light hit the craft and it exploded in an instant with a noise and brightness that shook the foundations of the Earth. Draylon was blown hundreds of feet from the blast and fell unconscious.

He awoke a short while later feeling as good as new. His clothes were badly burned and torn and hanging off him, but he felt no cold. He felt better than he had ever felt in his life. His limbs felt strong, as if he could shatter the Earth's surface beneath his feet. He could feel something still happening from within, as if the amulet hadn't quite finished its work yet, and then it was done. Draylon felt an odd sensation, like a weightlessness. He looked down and he was several feet from the ground. He was shocked at the revelation. "I can fly!" he said aloud.

Draylon thought of Paul. He shed his extra clothing but for his jeans and T-shirt. He bent his knees and leapt. He shot into the sky so fast, it was like he was bending the very fabric of time. He tore through the sky, leaving a storm in his wake.

In seconds he arrived at The Great Pyramid in Egypt. It was approaching midnight - nearly 48 hours since Paul's death. Draylon shot down to the subterranean chamber and manipulated matter to unseal Paul from the passageway. He gently picked up Paul and laid him down in the chamber. He closed his eyes, slowed his breathing, prayed to humanity's God and focused all of his being. Minutes went by. Draylon could feel Paul's body start to warm. He focused harder and then fell back when Paul choked back into existence. Draylon was ecstatic.

"Paul, Paul, can you hear me?"

Paul opened his eyes. "What happened? How long have I been out? I've had the strangest dream. And why are your clothes all burnt?"

Draylon laughed out loud. "It's good to have you back with us my friend."

"I have this strange feeling, like I've been out for days."

"Let's go back to the hotel, I'll tell you all about it on the way." Draylon clapped his friend on the shoulder and smiled.

On the way back to Hotel Khufu, Draylon told Paul all about what had happened. Paul was stunned by what he had heard, and couldn't believe he'd been brought back to life after two whole days. He thanked Draylon for bringing him back to being. Draylon explained that if it wasn't for Paul distracting Karlon in the pyramid, it was he who would have been dead now.

They stopped at a café that was open late and Draylon ordered a pot of tea for Paul and coffee for himself.

"What did the amulet look like then?" Paul enquired.

"You saw the two end pieces that were like two semi-circles; well the third piece, the middle piece, had a clear crystal in the middle, a silver chain attached at the top and a symbol across its entire surface. The symbol was like the letter X - it had a line joining the left and right sides of the X. That is where the two semi-circular pieces fit, and of course, the line jutting out from the main symbol that was on one of the pieces you saw."

Draylon asked the waiter in his Arabic tongue for a piece of paper and a pen. He then drew the symbol for Paul.

ιat does it mean?"

ι have no idea. Maybe I shall never know."

"Tell me about your new abilities."

"My original abilities have been amplified on a massive scale, and I can fly, which was an unbelievable experience, and I assume my amplified healing abilities have made me invulnerable, but I don't wish to test that. Do you fancy flying with me?"

"Not a chance! I am keeping my feet firmly on the ground, except for maybe a plane or two." Paul laughed to himself. "What a journey this last month has been."

"I fear that was just the beginning for me. I can only assume that the pale green aliens that created the amulet, and foretold my coming, were correct about my kin. And if that is so, then I am now a protector of humanity, for with technology evolving so quickly now on Earth, I believe it won't be long before the greys are visiting on a more regular basis. Maybe they've already started plans for annihilation, which is why they no longer felt they needed me. I did not see this coming. But I will do all in my power to prevent it."

"I find it really hard to digest this. So much has happened so quickly. I don't envy you, except for the flying thing, perhaps," Paul smiled at his friend then suggested getting back to the hotel as he was shattered.

They arrived at the hotel, went straight to their room and slept through to the latter hours of the morning. When they awoke, Paul asked Draylon if they could head back to Easter Island the next day. Draylon thought it a good idea and suggested they spend the rest of their day relaxing. Paul acquiesced. Draylon noticed that although he enjoyed resting for the night, there was absolutely no need; his body felt charged, as if he had a battery with limitless reserves, but Paul deserved a rest, so he was more than happy to lounge around for a while.

It was Wednesday 2nd February; they awoke early, washed, got dressed, and checked out of the hotel. They spent the day relaxing, drinking, chatting and enjoying the sights, and by early evening, they got a taxi to the airport and booked their flights to Easter Island. Eventually, it was time to board the plane. They got on, found their favourite seats in the safer rear part of the plane, and then the captain announced their departure. The plane took off, first stop, Madrid with a long layover, and then on to Santiago with another long layover, and eventually on to Easter Island, estimated time of arrival Saturday 5th February, just after midday.

CHAPTER EIGHT

The beginning

It was a beautiful Saturday afternoon on Easter Island. They got off the plane and Paul took the deepest breath. He felt like a changed man. It had only been a month since that night when he first saw the light in the sky, but it seemed like more. He felt relaxed now and was enjoying the fact that he had enough money to not have to work for several years if he so wished, and it was a good feeling. They went through customs and left the airport. They both decided to walk to Paul's flat and enjoy the warm day. Draylon asked if Paul would be wanting his old job back. Paul said that maybe in time he would, but not just yet. He said that he was thinking about writing a science fiction novel about their adventures and laughed. Draylon frowned at his friend and then laughed too.

Once at Paul's flat, Draylon said that he quite fancied a run. Paul said that he would see him in about an hour then; there was a tremendous rush of wind.

"I'm back!"

"That was a little quick, where did you go?"

"Just around the outskirts of the island."

"Unbelievable, you've only been gone a second."

"I know. Running isn't quite the same now, I must admit, but I'll save money on transport, I suppose."

"Maybe later we should go to the quarry, or maybe Tongariki, where you found the tablet in the Moai. I think if no one is around, we should check out your abilities and find out what you can really do, what do you think?"

"I think that's a plan. I'm going to go and see Adriana; I'll catch up with you later."

"Good luck! Say hi for me, I'll catch up with her sometime soon."

Paul went straight to his bedroom and crashed out on the bed, deep in thought. He smiled to himself. He could not believe all of the places he had been and all of the adventures. Most of all, Paul found it hard to believe that he had actually been dead, and that he played his part in Draylon's foretold destiny. One thing he did know is that he was going to enjoy his life; he was going to be more outgoing and milk every last drop out of every day. Paul put his mp3 player on, relaxed and closed his eyes.

Draylon arrived at the supermarket where Adriana worked. He walked in and saw her at the rear of the shop stacking shelves. He felt nervous. She turned to see him, her eyes lit up; they walked over to each other and embraced.

"I've missed you!" Adriana was excited; she hoped that Draylon was still going to ask her out.

"I've missed you too! How are you?" Draylon could hear his own heart beating.

"I'm good, not much has happened around here really. How is Paul? Is he coming out of his shell at last?" She smiled at the thought of Paul and how quiet he could be.

"I believe he is a changed man. He's become a good friend - my only friend, in fact."

"What about me - aren't I your friend?"

"I was hoping for that - maybe more than a friend. Would you like to go out sometime?"

"I would love to!" Adriana was ecstatic; she hadn't had anyone in her life for quite some time.

"Maybe tomorrow?" Draylon said nervously. Despite his strength, Adriana made him go weak at the knees.

"Tomorrow would be perfect." She was already wondering what to wear.

Draylon kissed her cheek. They both smiled and looked at each other nervously - they could feel the electricity between them. Draylon said that he was going to get a couple of energy drinks, changing the subject and stumbling on his words a little. He paid for his drinks. Adriana suggested he be careful with those drinks - he wouldn't want to become addicted. Draylon laughed, saying that Paul said the very same thing, but he feared it was too late for that. Draylon said that he'd see Adriana tomorrow and that he was looking forward to their date very much. He then made his way back to Paul's.

Paul was relaxing, listening to his mp3 player. Draylon startled him when he came in. Paul asked him how things went with Adriana. Draylon said that they were going out tomorrow night; he couldn't wait, but felt a little anxious. Paul congratulated him, saying that she was a lovely girl and that he hoped everything went well. Paul asked if being a hybrid would present any problems with having a relationship. Draylon smiled and replied that it was just a date, but he said that he would look into it, just in case his relationship with Adriana did ever reach the next level. He said he had no desire to start a family in the foreseeable future anyway, especially with what he now knew about his kin, the greys. With that, Draylon asked if Paul was ready to go to Tongariki. Paul said that he was very much looking forward to driving his yellow Suzuki Alto again and laughed - he missed his Mustang very much.

Paul connected his mp3 player up to his stereo, started the car, revved the engine a little, and told Draylon to hold on tight. They both laughed as the car went from 0 to 60 in over ten seconds. They were on their way to Tongariki, the place where he found the first tablet, the place where it all started. They arrived and got out of the car and stood looking at the large Moai statues; the proud faces of the Moai staring back at them. It was an awesome spectacle.

Paul said to Draylon that he loved his home on Easter Island, but very much missed their adventure. He said that he had the time of his life, literally, and hoped that they could go off on a voyage again in the not too distant future. Draylon assured him that there would be many more to come. There were no other people at the site and

Paul suggested that now would be a great time to see what Draylon could do. Draylon held up his right hand, facing the largest of the Moai. Using his amplified telekinetic powers, he easily raised the massive statue ten feet in the air. He held it for a while and then slowly lowered it down again. Paul's jaw gaped.

"That was unbelievable - how about your strength, has that improved?"

Draylon went over to Paul's car and lifted up the back end with his left hand easily. "Would you like me to lift it above my head?" Draylon grinned.

Paul felt protective of his little yellow car. "No, no. Thank you! You're strong, I get it. I know - I want you to fly to Egypt and get me a scarab necklace; I've always wanted one of those, I would have got one whilst we were there, but I was distracted."

Draylon bent his knees and leapt; he shot off at an astounding speed and vanished out of sight in a second. A couple of minutes later, he returned, landing with the grace of a gymnast in the Olympics. He gave Paul the scarab necklace.

"That is unbelievable! You're like Superman or something."

"Superman is fictional Paul." Draylon laughed, "Anything else my friend?"

With that, Draylon heard the high-pitched noise again. It was coming from the smallest Moai statue. He told Paul and they both went over to see what it was. Draylon held out his right hand and using his ability to manipulate matter, created an opening in the statue. He reached in and found another metallic rectangular tablet. He then resealed the Moai and stood in thought, Paul asked him what he was waiting for, anxious as to what information the tablet held within. Draylon held his hand over the tablet. The information within it flooded into his sub conscious at the speed of light and then the metallic object disintegrated into tiny particles.

"What is it?" Paul asked curiously.

"The tablet was obviously triggered by the amulet that is now a part of me. The message was that of the pale green alien race. It read, "'Draylon, you have completed your quest successfully, humankind are predominantly good, and we spent many years nurturing them. You now have the ability to do much good on Earth. The amulet contained within it all of our knowledge and power, and that is now yours. By now, the technologies of humans will be such that your race will see them as a threat. You know what that means. Protect them, and let our demise not have been in vain.'"

"No pressure then!" Paul remarked with a smile.

"Well one thing's for sure, it looks like you're going to get your adventure, my friend - this is the beginning!"

To be continued!

Breinigsville, PA USA
28 March 2011
258656BV00001B/22/P